James Samuel Stone

The Heart of Merrie England

James Samuel Stone

The Heart of Merrie England

ISBN/EAN: 9783744723657

Printed in Europe, USA, Canada, Australia, Japan

Cover: Foto ©Thomas Meinert / pixelio.de

More available books at **www.hansebooks.com**

THE HEART

OF

MERRIE ENGLAND

BY

JAMES S. STONE, D.D.
Author of "Readings in Church History."

ILLUSTRATED

PHILADELPHIA
HENRY T. COATES & CO.
1898

LIST OF ILLUSTRATIONS

	PAGE
WESTMINSTER ABBEY,	Frontispiece
AN ENGLISH VILLAGE,	26
"FIELD AND GORSE ARE CLOTHED IN A VESTURE OF LIVING GREEN,"	56
THE VILLAGE CHURCH,	78
"HER EYES SPARKLE WITH DELIGHT,"	100
OXFORD,	120
"THERE IS A DELIGHTFUL LOOK OF OLD TIMES IN THE NARROW WINDING STREETS,"	154
AN OLD-TIME ENGLISH INN,	174
MERCERY LANE, CANTERBURY,	224
CANTERBURY CATHEDRAL,	238
ANN HATHAWAY'S COTTAGE,	256
THE AVON AND STRATFORD CHURCH,	274
"A GENTLEMAN'S HOUSE SET WITH SHRUBBERY,"	306
"ALL IS STILL AND RESTFUL,"	324
"VILLAGE CHILDREN SINGING CAROLS,"	358
HAMPTON COURT PALACE,	382

To Her

WHOSE COMPANIONSHIP OF SYMPATHY AND AFFECTION
HAS MADE LIFE MORE THAN HAPPY.

PREFACE.

IN the following pages are brought together sketches and reminiscences of the old land which can scarcely fail to interest those who love its history, its antiquities and its rural life.

The book is intended rather as a suggestion of than as a guide to England. The writer has sought to foster tender memories and to strengthen loving ties. He has wandered from places well known to neighborhoods remote and secluded—from the cathedral of Canterbury to the cromlechs of Chipping Norton. The villages described are not richer in interest than other villages: they only illustrate how much pleasure the stranger from afar may find in the country districts of England.

The book will serve, if for no other purpose, to while away an idle hour. Nevertheless, it has a value beyond that of amusement. Every line is written in truth—not merely intentional, but actual, truth. The places spoken of are familiar to the author. The greatest care has been taken to attain accuracy, and every temptation to exaggerate in any sense has been studiously avoided. It is well to state this, as the ground gone over in this volume is almost entirely new. With the exception of London, Oxford, Stratford and Canterbury, no other writer has dealt with the subject-matter of the book—most certainly, not in the way the reader will find it dealt with here.

A few historical items in the second and third chapters were gathered from a parish magazine published some years since at Shipston. The fourth chapter, it is hoped, will be acceptable from the world-wide interest in the subject, and the fourteenth illustrates the customs and the superstitions which are not yet extinct in the regions touched upon in the volume. They who are familiar with English folk-lore and country-life will detect in almost every sentence of the "Merry Legend" some allusion to old-time manners and ideas. The outline of the story is true, the life suggested by it such as still exists; and if the workmanship of the writer please not, let its purpose be considered—its endeavor to weave into the ground-work sayings and practices, homely pictures and rude scenes, which shall illustrate the days of yore and the country far away. In no part of the book is a character given that is not sketched from life—sometimes so faintly disguised that not a few into whose hands this volume may come will easily recognize the author's model and purpose.

A residence of fourteen years on the western side of

the Atlantic and a readiness to appreciate and enter into the American life have in a measure, no doubt, unfitted the writer to speak of England from a purely English standpoint. He has done his best to show that love for his native land which none know better how to honor than the American people. They know full well that he who readily casts off old ties will as readily sever himself from the new. But without becoming more and more imbued with its spirit no one can live in a land which one has learned to love. It must give its influence to his thought. He is as the man who in the home of his bride looks back to the home of his mother: perfect loyalty to both is consonant with perfect love for both. But he is not, and cannot be, the same in the one as in the other. He has left the mother for ever, not with regret—far from that—but to fulfil the destiny and the duty ordained for him by God. They, therefore, in the old land who may chance to read these pages must not expect too much. The son going home is not as the son who has never left home.

Perhaps than at this time the two nations were never closer knit together. Old feelings have died out, and both peoples are content to let bygones be bygones. May they learn to love each other more and more as the ages roll on!

PHILADELPHIA, June 21, 1887.

CONTENTS.

CHAPTER I.
                                                              PAGE
INTRODUCTORY.................. 9

CHAPTER II.
THE VILLAGE ON THE STOUR....................... 25

CHAPTER III.
THE REGION ROUNDABOUT................... 52

CHAPTER IV.
LOVE IN YE OLDEN TIME......................... 82

CHAPTER V.
AT OXFORD.................................... 113

CHAPTER VI.
AN EVENING WALK.............................. 127

CHAPTER VII.
A TOWN IN THE CHILTERNS.... 154

CHAPTER VIII.
THAME.. 178

CONTENTS.

CHAPTER IX.
THE PILGRIMAGE TO CANTERBURY .... PAGE 216

CHAPTER X.
IN THE CATHEDRAL............................. 237

CHAPTER XI.
AT STRATFORD-ON-AVON.......................... 255

CHAPTER XII.
TO EDGEHILL.................................. 281

CHAPTER XIII.
OVER THE COUNTRY............................. 301

CHAPTER XIV.
A MERRY LEGEND............................... 329

CHAPTER XV.
LAST GLIMPSES................................ 382

THE HEART OF MERRIE ENGLAND.

CHAPTER I.

Introductory.

> "This little world,
> This precious stone set in the silver sea!"

THERE are two countries which we as Christians and men of Anglo-Saxon race must ever think of with affection—viz., Palestine, the birthplace of our Christianity, and England, the cradle of our civilization and our Church. Both of these lands have, apart from these considerations, had an important share in the world's history; both lie on the western border of their respective continents, and both are small in extent and irregular in physical formation; furthermore, both were peopled by a race foreign to the soil: the Israelites came from beyond the Euphrates, and the English from beyond the German Ocean. These races, though belonging to distinct families, had in common a religious spirit, a love of freedom, commercial rather than warlike instincts, an undying affection for home and an exalted ideal of womanhood. We admire alike the heroes of both peoples—men such as Barak and Gideon, who fought and won on the plain of Esdraelon; men such as Harold Godwin, who fought and lost on the field of Senlac. Both have had their kings and prophets and poets of great excellence, and with equal pleasure the mind recalls the names of David the shepherd-king and Alfred the fugitive prince; Moses the lawgiver and Anselm the saint; the rapturous Isaiah and the holy Herbert. Nor do we remember save with the same delight the snow-crowned Lebanon, and the steep, rugged Cumbrians; the blue waters of Tiberias, and the quiet beauty of Windermere; the Jordan rushing through a ravine deserted, and the Thames meandering through vales and plains of rich fertility; the city crowned with the cross of a grand cathedral, and the city crowned with the pinnacles of a glorious temple; the shore washed with the murmuring waves of a sunny Mediterranean, and the coast where wildly break the billows of an untamed Atlantic. Some associations would urge us to compare England and Greece, and others, again, England and Italy; but the most precious inheritance of religion, which made both Canaan and Britain holy, God-fearing lands, suggests the linking together of the land of roses and the land which floweth with milk and honey.

England in the olden time—say about the age in which Augustine and his monks sang the Alleluia of the gospel and uplifted the cross of Christ before the gates of a heathen Canterbury—was a very different country from the England of the nineteenth century. Thirteen hundred years have wrought changes vast and almost inconceivable. Then the British Isles lay on, if not outside, the confines of civilization. Beyond them was nothing but the unexplored Atlantic—the ocean which skirted the empty and illimitable space. A bold voyager was he who had seen the western coast of Ireland—a still bolder one who had tempted the gods by venturing into the waters beyond the horizon and had ridden in his frail craft upon the green-crested billows of the blue-black sea. No keel then ploughed the Mersey; rarely indeed did a vessel enter the Tyne, the Humber or the Thames. The country still lay in its primitive wildness. Dark and impenetrable forests spread over vast tracts of land; deep fens and sluggish marshes covered miles of plain. The climate was wet, dreary and inhospitable. The sparse population, whether British or English, was fierce and cruel. Communication was difficult and mostly by water, while the few towns and villages which existed were rude and rough. To compare England then and now is something like comparing a storm-wrought sky in March with the starstrewn heavens of July. The wilderness has been converted into a garden; cities have arisen where once the wild boar had his lair and the bittern her nest; the best roads in the world overspread the island; mansions nestle in picturesque beauty where once mud cottages sheltered rugged chieftains from the inclement weather; woods have been cleared and fens drained; the end of the earth has become the heart of the world; and on every sea and in every breeze, from castle-tower, fortress, mast and spire, there waves the bright red cross of good Saint George. The change is vast in every way. Not only is the physical aspect of the country different, but the political, social, numerical and religious conditions of the people are also different. Instead of a score—or it may have been a hundred—petty tribes warring one against another, we see a strong united kingdom, the centre of an empire and the mother of nations. Instead of wending our way slowly and tediously up forest-shaded rivers or cutting a path through a trackless wild, we can walk along pleasant highways or travel in swift haste over the iron road. The reeking torch or the flickering candle which served to guide our forefathers to their bed of straw or of rushes has given place to brilliant illuminations. Even the lightning, which in its furious might split the gnarled oak, rent the black clouds and struck brave Viking hearts with fear, has been taught to turn our night into day and bear our tidings round the world. The whole earth has changed, but no part more than England; and, while Palestine has become a desolation and Jerusalem a heap of stones, that other holy land has become a paradise and her cities habitations of beauty.

The land, small in territory, is confessedly great in deeds. Her race seems to retain the vitality and vigor of perennial youth. It was young when Greek ships sailed the midland waters and Roman hands built the Colosseum and made captives lay the roads which should lead from the ends of the earth to the Imperial City; it was young a thousand years ago, when Charlemagne reunited the divided empire and Egbert made the Saxon principalities one kingdom; it was young when the Norman duke fought on the seaside battlefield and was crowned with the crown of the island-realm in the minster in the marsh; it was young when in its sturdy strength and growing ambition it wrested from John the Magna Carta of freedom and strove with kings till its voice was allowed and its rights were secured; it was still young three hundred years ago, when the Reformation gave it the liberty of the gospel of Christ and it began its work of subduing the untrodden wilds of lands beyond the seas; and so through the struggles of the Commonwealth, the wars in which a Marlborough, a Nelson and a Wellington won renown for themselves and glory for their land, and the political changes of the present century, its youth seems to be like that of the sun, renewed every morning, or like that of the giant oaks, slow in growth and continually reproducing themselves in the seeds planted in the soil fertilized by their cast-off leaves. A thousand and half a thousand years ago the ships of that race went forth to conquer and to colonize from the rivers and harbors of the wild Northern sea; a thousand and half a thousand years later the ships of that race spread their sails before every breeze that stirs earth's waters and bear from land to land and from shore to shore the riches of earth's treasures. When the morning sun begins to cast its roseate beams on sky and sea, the banner of England is unfurled in the glory-stream and its blood-red tints fall on gentle wavelet and long-sweeping billow; and when it sinks to rest within the Occidental clouds, it leaves peace with the many multitudes who speak the tongue of Alfred and of Spenser and name the name of Him whom Canaan rejected, but whom Britain loves. And to-day, while the ocean owns her as its mistress and one-seventh of the solid earth calls her queen, her men of high degree and her men of low degree, her lords who sit in purple and ermine in royal halls and her laborers who till the soil and wear rough clothing, they who abide within the old land itself and they who dwell in distant parts,—all with one heart believe and with one voice proclaim that the glory of the past shall shine through the ages of the future, and that the cross of three ancient kingdoms shall be for ever the symbol and the proof of freedom, of righteousness and of law.

Where is the Heart of this Merrie England? Some have said "London;" perhaps the people of England themselves say "London," and not without reason. We think, however, that the rural districts have more right to that title, and especially that part of the island which is geographically the centre. There are twenty border counties and twenty inland counties, and in none of them is old Merry England better seen than in the fair counties of Warwick, Worcester and Oxford. Hither shall we lead our readers, only once going beyond them— into distant Kent that we may look upon the glories of England's mother-church. Untrodden ground we shall go over, with that one, and possibly a second, exception; and when we shall finish our story, we trust we shall have vindicated our title—at least to the extent of suggesting how much there is to be seen and known in the region of which we write. Alas! we can give only the fragments, only the outlines: the reader must himself allow imagination to piece together, color and picture the beautiful whole.

Nevertheless, before we begin that work, let us look somewhat at the great city itself. Everybody goes to London: a book on England without some mention of London would be like the play of *Hamlet* with the prince left out. As to the provincial people of the land, their ambition is to visit the metropolis—once in their life, at least. That immediately raises a man to a pinnacle of fame far higher than he would reach by a voyage across the Atlantic, or even to the ends of the earth. He is an authority upon extraordinary matters for ever after, seeing that London is a tangible thing, and America, Australia and China are, after all, as mysterious and questionable as the mountains of the moon or the rings of Saturn.

And a wonderful place the capital is, with its five millions of people, its thronging streets, its fine buildings, its restless life, its noble river and its long, thrilling history. It would take fifteen or sixteen of the largest towns in England to equal that vast population. There human life swarms; there all that is noble and all that is base in man are developed and manifested.

One singular thing about London is that the stranger feels at home within the first hour of his entering its streets. This arises partly from the widespread information concerning the place and everything belonging to it, partly from its admirable accommodations both for travelling about and for lodging and eating, and partly from the fact that here one is left absolutely alone. Nobody looks at you; nobody gives you a thought. Each follows out the thread of his own life and cares nothing for any one else's. No man, however ambitious or ostentatious he may be, can make an impression in London; he may live like a prince or dress like a beggar and nobody will take the least notice of him. He is a drop in the ocean of humanity—that, and nothing more.

The Abbey is the first place to be seen. Enter as the bells are chiming for morning prayer and listen to the rendering of the service in a perfect way. The voices are correct; the customs are simple. The General Confession is said after, and not with, the minister; the Psalms are not announced; the reader, when he leaves his stall for the lectern, is preceded by a verger carrying a long wand. During the lesson this official holds the clergyman's cap and at the close accompanies him back again. Owing to draughts some of the clergy wear skull-caps. Before the prayers are ended the devout worshipper will wonder if heaven itself is more impressive and beautiful than this marvellous building, with its lofty height and hallowed associations. When this duty is over, the guides are ready to take visitors around the building.

Guides are useful if they know anything. Generally speaking, they have deep sepulchral voices and depressingly melancholy manners. They go over the same story so often that their interest in it is very small. Fortunately, the means of description are not confined to them, and the intelligent visitor can, if he will, know beforehand more than they can tell him. He will look with reverence upon the tomb of Edward the Confessor and walk with awe near the grave of the good Queen Maud. This is the most sacred part of the building, and the dark arched recesses in the shrine remind one of the days when men knelt therein, pressed their foreheads against the cold stone and prayed for healing or for pardon. The dust of kings and of queens is beneath almost every part of this hallowed chapel. There lie the remains of Henry III., Edward I. and the beloved Queen Eleanor, Edward III. and Henry V., and close by is the ancient coronation-chair with the veritable stone upon which Jacob slept at Bethel and on which the kings of Scotland and of England have been crowned for many centuries. The chapel of Henry VII. is one of the most lovely Gothic buildings in the world. There is the tomb of that king, and over the grave of Edward VI. a modern communion-table of rich materials has been placed. Objects of interest await one at every turn—in the main structure and in the chapels. Earth's great ones lie on every side—poets, statesmen and warriors, as well as they who have borne the sceptre and worn the crown. The extent and massiveness of the building, as well as its rare beauty and splendor, are marvellous and grow upon one. Nor should the Chapter-House or the Dean's Yard be overlooked. A day within the sacred precincts is better than a thousand elsewhere.

The effect of St. Paul's upon the mind is different. Its vastness overpowers, but the pagan architecture cannot impress one in the same way as the Gothic. Nor has the place the history of the Abbey. The monuments are severe in tone; the pulpit is of costly material. In the dome is the Whispering Gallery, and from the Stone Gallery outside a splendid view of the city may be had on a fine day. From the ground to this point are five hundred and sixty steps. Lord Nelson and the duke of Wellington lie in the crypt—the former in the sarcophagus which Wolsey intended for himself; but he fell from favor, and it was kept unused.

Few places are more interesting than is the Tower. We were more impressed with the buildings themselves than with the crown jewels, resplendent and of untold wealth though they are. The past came back again, only the Beefeaters, with their nice clean collars and well-blacked boots, seemed somewhat out of place. The "Traitors' Gate" tells its own story. In the armories are the ancient equipments of war—battle-axes, swords, lances, etc. How the soldiers moved in such heavy encasements or wielded such long pikes is a question. Instruments of torture are also to be seen—the thumbscrews, a model of the rack and the block and axe with which some great ones were executed. Between the White Tower and the Beauchamp Tower is the spot where the prisoners condemned to die were beheaded, and in the Beauchamp Tower itself is the room where the state offenders of high rank were kept. They seem to have spent some of their time in cutting out their names or devices in the wall. There is the name of "Jane"—the poor lady remembered by all as one of the sweetest and most unfortunate of women. In St. Peter's Chapel, close by, are the monuments of many of those who suffered in the Tower. Two of Henry VIII.'s wives lie side by side near the altar; Lady Jane Grey is also there, with many another. The Beefeater told us of the honor of being put to death within the Tower: outside, a rude and thoughtless mob annoyed and maltreated the condemned prisoner, but here he died in peace. This is grim glory, and one is thankful that times have changed.

The Tower brings history home quicker than any other place in London. Its stories of woe, its legends and traditions, weird, sad, mysterious, are written in living lines. Its very ground was once trodden by mighty ones; we see the same great walls they saw, thread our way through the same dark, narrow passages and sit in the rooms where many of them spent their last hours. It is a past full of shadows—the young princes smothering in the dead of the night, Anne Boleyn suffering the cruelty of a selfish king, and many another character famous in history passing through trial for charges, sometimes, of suspicion or jealousy only. Will that gloomy fortress ever reveal the secrets in its keeping?

Up the Thames, near to the Abbey, are the Parliament Buildings, stately and large. The Victoria Tower is a work of art; under it we enter, and pass through the Queen's Robing-Room, the Royal Galleries and the Princes' Chamber into the House of Lords. The paintings, statuary, decorations and architecture are elaborate; the throne and woolsack, of interest. On the way to the House of Commons are some remarkable pictures, but in the chamber where the faithful representatives of the boroughs and shires meet splendor has given place to severe simplicity. From St. Stephen's Hall is reached the famous Westminster Hall; here the carved and wide roof attracts attention. The remembrance of the historical scenes which have taken place there subdues the mind. Within these walls were tried Charles I. and the seven bishops; within these walls the unfortunate Richard II. was deposed and Oliver Cromwell was installed as Lord Protector. It is a place for thinking mighty thoughts.

Of the Guildhall, with its picture-gallery, museum, library and great chamber, the Royal Exchange, the Bank of England, Paternoster Row and the Monument it is unnecessary to say anything. The British Museum contains some of the greatest wonders in the world. The buildings are so large and have so many curiosities that one can get only a vague bird's-eye view of the whole. There are old manuscripts and illuminated books beautifully and wonderfully executed by the men of bygone days. Printing can scarcely equal some of the monkish work: the colors are bright and fresh as ever, the penmanship—oftentimes exceedingly small—is accurate and the binding is strong and lasting. Next to Bibles, missals, psalters and *Hours of the Virgin*, the most popular manuscript books were the *Romaunt de la Rose* and *Froissart*. Some of these volumes—or, at least, the like—were handled by men and women whose ashes lie in the Abbey or at the Tower. In the Museum, however, one is taken back to ages which were ancient when England was young. In one of the Egyptian rooms are mummies two or three thousand years old. Some of the coffins are very elaborately painted in bright colors, with figures of gods and many devices. The face of the deceased is delineated on the coffin, and such designs differ enough from one another to make one pretty sure that they are correct, and not conventional representations. The wood of the coffin is very thick—in some instances, eight inches—and some bodies have two coffins. The hands of the deceased are frequently represented as crossed on the breast. There is a coffin containing the mummy of a Græco-Egyptian child—probably a girl, and about six years old—dating, according to the printed label from Thebes, about A. D. 100. On the painted cover she is represented as having a wreath upon her head and a flower in her left hand—somebody's darling sent into the dark realm from amid the sorrowings of loved ones left behind. There are also the mummies of many of the great Egyptian princes and statesmen; also of cats, snakes, ibis, geese and gazelles. "Tabby" is there, unmistakably. Figures of the deity are common; so are Egyptian hairpins with the image of Aphrodite on the top, and lamps curiously ornamented with devices of Dionysos and Ariadne, Venus, and other favorite personages. There is one lamp with a cast of a locust on an ear of corn. That children have always been children the ancient toys testify.

In the Assyrian and other departments the objects of interest are as great. The wealth of collection is enormous. One is bewildered—perhaps provoked—with the consciousness of brief time; there is the material for years of study. The place is worthy of England; to see the Reading-Room is itself deserving of a trip to London.

It is the correct thing to visit and admire the waxworks of Madame Tussaud in Marylebone. We did the one; the other was not so easy. At the best the characters presented are only imitations; there is nothing real. The "Chamber of Horrors" contains a ghastly array of celebrated murderers; morbid taste which makes it the favorite corner of the building! In the grand salon are wax figures of old men and women sitting or standing here and there, turning their heads and looking so like life that many visitors find themselves for the moment deceived.

They who love pictures will visit the Royal Academy and the National Gallery. Kew Gardens will satisfy the disciples of botany with its lovely grounds, noble vistas and extensive collection of flowers, trees and plants. The Cleopatra obelisk looks unspeakably lonely on the Thames Embankment. A day at the Zoological Gardens will not exhaust its treasures.

But we may not thus travel over London. Volumes would be needed to tell the story of its wonderful places. The people themselves are curious.

Is there a busier thoroughfare in the world than Fleet street and the Strand? A river of humanity flowing hither and thither ceaselessly! Strange in an instant to turn aside into the calm of the Temple! That is the peculiarity of London—its quiet nooks and corners close to its noisy centres. And there are streets of rare splendor where wealth displays itself in unequalled magnificence, and there are streets of rare poverty such as the world knows nothing of elsewhere. It is not very far from Rotten Row to the slums of vice and infamy, but the contrast is beyond measuring. The want and misery, the brazen-faced sin, of these back streets and lanes, are terrible. The Church is striving to grapple with the evil, but the work is appalling. Where and how do the millions live? Yet there is no confusion, no bustle; everything is orderly: the great city has too much to do to be in a hurry.

London has some great preachers. Their names are on every one's lips—Liddon, Spurgeon and Parker. They are not to be compared together; each is a master in his own way. When they preach, thousands of people go to hear them. They are the world's favorites, and each of them addresses an audience gathered from all parts of the earth. After them come others at a respectful distance—some about as far as the west is from the east. There is no doubt that the English and American ideals of preaching differ, but the standard is higher on the western side of the Atlantic, the preacher is better able to attract his hearers and the people are quicker in appreciation. England, however, more than holds its own in singing. The masses have voices and the choirs a perfection of which we can only dream. On one church door I saw a notice that on the following Sunday would be held the annual baptismal service. Whether this meant that baptism was administered only once a year I do not know, but underneath the notice was, "Baptism is a sign that God loves us all, even little children."

English is spoken in London, but among the ordinary people the aspirate suffers. One day the conductor on an omnibus cried out, "'Yde Park!" and a gentleman said to him, "You have dropped something."—"What?" he asked, in alarm, looking around.—"An H," the gentleman replied.—"That's nothing," was the answer from the much-relieved official; "I shall pick it up in Hislington."

The well-paved and orderly streets attract as much attention as does the dim, smoky atmosphere. The effect of the latter on one's linen is soon discerned; the former are as clean as a new pin. A yellow fog is the most distressing calamity, but in the summer such rarely or never occurs. Nowhere do the people seem more happy. The bootblack and the apple-woman have the sunshine of felicity upon them. "Misery" appears to be a relative term. The poor are not so miserable as their betters suppose them to be; indeed, they manage to squeeze as much pleasure out of life as they who live in palaces of cedar. Nor have the poor complained: their grievances have been made known by those in higher circumstances. Some of them love their poverty. Alas that it should be so! for poverty means degradation and dependence—in many instances, vice unnamable.

We hurry out of the smoke and bustle and seek the railway-station. Here we read of the "Daily Service of Trains;" the meaning is obvious, though the use is startling.

The railway-coaches appear tiny and quaint to one accustomed to the huge, pew-like cars of America. Some do not like the compartments, though a little use shows that they have advantages, and are, at any rate, snug and comfortable. If you wish for amusement, see how the open, honest-looking, apple-round faces of the railway servants expand under the genial influence of a tip. The chances for trying this experiment on others besides railway servants are of frequent occurrence in England, and, though the effect may be otherwise with the giver, there is no doubt of its pleasing efficacy with the receiver. Away rushes the train into the heart of merry and lovely England. The haymakers are busy in the fields; the trees and hedgerows display their sweet, fresh green; peace and beauty rest and play in the sunshine, on the soft and velvety lawns and in the shaded lanes. Cottages and mansions spring into view, and flower-gardens rich with a profusion of roses such as can grow only in this rich land. The villages through which we pass seem to sleep in the indolence of rural glory and the quietude of honored age. One has the sign on its solitary tavern of "The Old House at Home"—a happy suggestion.

When our journey ends, it is in one of the districts of England as delightful in its quiet beauty as it is precious to us for its associations of bygone days.

CHAPTER II.

The Village on the Stour.

> "And the voice of man is a voice of change,
> Mirthful and passionate, loving and strange;
> But, be the day cloudy or brief or long,
> The river will sing you the same old song."

IN a secluded and detached part of Worcestershire, ten miles to the south of Stratford-on-Avon, and surrounded by the counties of Warwick, Oxford and Gloucester, is the forgotten town of Shipston-on-Stour. The town is pre-Norman in origin and was once famous for its sheep-markets. It fell asleep some two centuries since, and so far the tumult and turmoil of the present age have failed to awaken it. A single telegraph-wire, a mail-cart passing through early in the morning and late at night and two carriers' vans connect it with the outside world, and weekly papers from Banbury, Evesham and Stratford keep the inhabitants informed on the changes of the moon and the alternations of government. The people lament their isolation. Thirty years ago they decided that a railway was necessary for their welfare and progress; they have affirmed that decision several times since, but the railway has not come. Two or three times they have started a newspaper of their own, but the enterprise speedily came to grief. Its drapers and milliners furnish the latest styles in gowns and bonnets, cloths and collars—that is to say, the latest styles of which they know anything, though in London they are spoken of as "late" in another sense. The streets are old; the houses are old; the men and women, the boys and girls, are old; everything is musty with age and quaint with peculiarity. There are fences and barns, tumble-down, patched-up, worn-out, as they were twenty or thirty years since. Some of the thatch has not been touched for half a century. The wooden pump in the middle of New street was old when the paint on the rectory fence was new—apparently in the days of William IV. Inns and their signs, cottages and their windows, the lamp-posts and the trees, look as if they had never known anything but age and rest. It is hard to realize that the streets have been mended since the day when troopers rattled over them on their way to Edgehill. In 1780, Nash, the historian of Worcestershire, wrote: "Here was a considerable manufacture of shaggs, carried on by one Mr. Hart, but, that declining, the town was left in great poverty. Many of the houses are still thatched, but, as the unemployed manufacturers die, migrate to other places or take to other businesses, the town is not so burthened with poor, and subsequently improves much in appearance." Seventy years later another visitor wrote: The place "leads one's thoughts irresistibly to the past, and to the conclusion that this is by no means a 'go-ahead' town." In 1851 the population numbered 1757 persons; in 1881, 1600.

And in this lies its charm: its very dulness attracts and pleases. It is something to go back to times when the world was different from the present. Here one can

An English Village.

without effort picture village life as it was centuries ago, and see for one's self how and where past generations lived. The restfulness is refreshing and delightful. Decay may be in all one sees; change is not.

To describe the topography of Shipston is somewhat difficult. The town is on the highway from Birmingham to Oxford—about halfway between those places, and between Stratford and Chapel House. The "Halfway House," a secluded cottage, is by the side of the road, between Tredington and the Honington tollgate. The highway enters the place at its northern end, and, bending a little to the left, goes for some distance past the church, when it divides, one branch turning to the east for Banbury, and the other, the main road, after a twist to the right and then to the left, passing through New street to Chipping Norton. This highway may be called the base of the town; it is irregularly built up, and, as the river runs along the gardens of the houses on the eastern side, there are no streets in that direction. Its principal feature is the church, of which more presently. On the western side there are other thoroughfares coming in. The first, Horn lane, is a narrow way running the full breadth of the place; a little farther is a short street called the Shambles, branching off like the arms of the letter Y, one of which branches runs parallel with Horn lane into a continuation known as Sheep street, and the other into the centre of the town. This centre is a sort of crooked square, a queer-looking triangle with a narrow base and the apex cut off—an approach to a parallelogram. Euclid has no diagram that comes near that "centre;" and if he had tried to describe it mathematically, he would never have made AB equal to CD, nor AC equal to BD, nor any other combinations or comparisons coequal. This "centre," with Sheep street at one end, and the twist of the London highway at the other, contains the principal shops, banks and one of the leading hotels of the place. At its southern end another lane joins the London road, forming the third and last street across the town. In this lane was till lately an old tavern known as the "Swan," hence its name. Between the "Swan" and the High street—that is the name of the indescribable centre—is the Back road, which runs in the same direction as New street, and finally joins it. The Swan lane changes into the road to Moreton-in-the-Marsh, and at right angles with its western end is the road passing by Sheep street and Horn lane to Darlingscote. There are few really old houses in Shipston, but one at the top of Sheep street dates from 1678, another in the same street from 1714, and the Crown Inn, in the Shambles, also from this later year.

In Sheep street is the building formerly used by the national school. It is a small old cottage with one room, in which the poor boys and girls of the town received their "education." It is now empty and deserted, the one window broken, the roof falling in and the little tin kettle of a bell rusty and bent. Possibly the house was built in the early part of the last century. A relic of departed grandeur, but nearly all the old folks in the place who can read their Bible and write their name obtained the rudiments there. If they did not learn decimal fractions, they were drilled in the Catechism; and, as all men know, it is better to understand how to live than how to get a living. Now the youth are sent to the new and commodious buildings in the Stratford road. The board school has possession of the town, and the board school is struggling to brighten the juvenile intelligence. It has its hands full. The boys, girls and infants are separated; teachers and monitors are set in each department; excellent text-books are used, and everything is done to give a fair secular education. Religion is not taught: the English people are religious by instinct, and do not need to learn anything of that kind. In days gone by, when the State appreciated the education and health of the spiritual faculties, it insisted upon every one attending church, and fined and punished those who stayed away; a great outcry was made in later years, and even now some are not tired of flinging abuse of every kind at our forefathers because of this, as its opponents called it, tyranny and bigotry; but in this age the State, in its desire to educate and enliven the mental faculties, insists upon every boy and every girl going to school, and, if the child does not, fines and punishes the parents. Nay, the people are obliged to pay in taxes for the maintenance of a school system in which many of them do not believe. Still, we must remember that arithmetic is of more consequence than are Scripture lessons, and that it is vastly more important that a boy's mind should be filled with the scraps of erudition which are chipped off the school-board curriculum than that his soul should be possessed with a sense of his duty toward God and his neighbor. Times have changed. The State, which neither endowed nor established the Church, but, on the other hand, robbed her of half her wealth at the Reformation, and is now contemplating taking away the other half, has given largely to the school and supports it with all the force of its authority. There is in England no such thing as an established Church, but there is an established school. Valiantly is the school board fighting its way. But the material! Is there anything in the lands beyond the setting sun approaching the pure blockheadedness of the English peasant-boy? He is dull, heavy, stupid, and, compared with the youth on the western shores of the Atlantic, is as the blunt edge of a rusty knife beside the fine keen edge of a good razor. The transformation of a thick-limbed dray-horse into a light, fleet racer or a nimble circus-performer presents no greater difficulty than does the uplifting and bettering of the sons and daughters of poor Hodge. In the palace of the Cæsars at Rome there is a rude sketch on the wall, done many centuries ago, of a schoolmaster wearing an ass's head and turning the handle of a conical stone mill, into which he is putting boys to grind. The point of the satire is that the boys are coming out at the bottom exactly as they went in. I do not imply that this is the case with the material of the school board; I only tell a pleasant story. But, as caste is very strongly marked, as soon as the middle class is reached a higher grade of intellectual power is manifest. For the boys of the better-to-do people in Shipston there is a large and good school under private auspices and dignified with the name of "the Academy." It is not so styled after the Académie Française, but it can give a lad a start toward the higher life. Some of its scholars have gone creditably through the university, and it is said that its earnest and accomplished master once succeeded in carrying a heavy son of a heavy farmer as far as the eleventh page of Hopkins's orthographical exercises and up to the verb "To have" in Lindley Murray. Of this latter feat I cannot speak with certainty, but at seven o'clock every summer morning the whole school was marshalled in the courtyard for an hour's drill. There was an opinion that this was necessary in order to vindicate the right of the institution to be called an "academy."

The present parish church was built on the site of an older one about the year 1853. The old church had reached a state when removal was absolutely necessary. It was remarkable not only for its slovenly and mongrel appearance, but also for the egotism and petty vanity displayed on its walls. About 1826 the building was whitewashed, and the churchwardens under whose directions this important work was done had their names inscribed in large letters at the western end. "So, likewise," said one who knew the old edifice well, "on the table of charities, whoever had presented a pulpit-cloth or furniture for the communion-table, or repaired the front of the gallery, or some other little matter, was posted up for the admiring eyes of after-generations." One of these benefactors repaired the pavement in the churchyard, it has been said, by abstracting the gravestones of his neighbors. The only thing which saved the place from the lowest kind of obituary desecration was that it had no tablet like unto one which is to be found in the porch of another Worcestershire church. It is to the memory of a man who died in 1772, and the inscription is as follows:

> "A man for polite knowledge and true taste in useful literature justly esteemed; nor in the social virtues as a sincere friend, a good neighbour, and an honest man, less regarded. At his own

particular desire he was buried beneath this stone, that his friends the poor, as they pass over his grave, might lay their hands upon their hearts, and say, 'It was his modesty, not his pride, that directed this request.'"

The following epitaphs were preserved at Shipston; the first is still at the west end of the church, but the others were in the yard, and are now undecipherable:

TO GULIELMUS HYCKES (1652).

"Here lies entomb'd more men than Greece admired,
More than Pythagoras transient soule inspir'd,
Many in one, a man accumulate,
Gentleman, Artist, Scholar, Church, World, State:
Soe wise, soe just, that spot him noe man could.
Pitty that I, with my weake prayses should.
Goe then, greate spirit, obey thy suddaine call—
Wild fruits hang long—the purer tymely fall."

"Beneath this stone three tender buds are laid,
No sooner blossom'd but alas they fade;
In silence lie, in hopes again to bloom
After the final day of mortal doom.
Oh then these buds which did so early blast,
Shall flourish whilst eternal ages last."

"Death lopt me of, and laide me here to sleepe;
My viol's tun'd to th' sound of them that weep.
Yett God, I trust, will grant my soul's desire,
To sing a part in His most heavenly quire."

Of the old church, only the tower remains. The new building has a nave and two aisles and is singularly void of ornamentation. A few texts over the arches and a colored eastern window are the only attempts at æsthetic display. The architectural proportions are good, but the pews are narrow and not made for kneeling-purposes, and the pulpit is of a shape and character to suggest its having once been a chimney-pot on an old-time mansion. A dreary building, drearier still in its reproachful emptiness. Formerly the edifice was crowded at both Sunday services; now a bare handful of worshippers in the morning and a scarcely larger company in the evening indicate either inefficiency of ministration or the dying out of church-interest. Matins and evensong are said every day; the rector is there, the pillars and pews are there, but even the bell-ringer runs off to attend to her household duties as soon as the service begins. The parish priest is conscientious in his performance of this daily office; the people are as conscientious in staying away. Were half a dozen worshippers present, the surprise and excitement would endanger the health of the rector for some time. In view of the apparent change in his parishioners and the approaching end of the world, he would apply himself with renewed vigor to the house-to-house visitation of the people. The nonconformist places of worship, however, are filled to overflowing and street-preachers are common. The glory has departed! This, which should be the centre of Church power and influence throughout the district, neither recognizes the dignity and extent of its capabilities nor puts forth a sign of interest or vitality. Perhaps the most painful thought connected with this decay of a once-prosperous parish is its suggestion of the powerlessness of the ecclesiastical organization. The diocesan authorities may see the church go to ruin, but they cannot interfere. The parishioners may watch the wasting away of their spiritual heritage, but they can do nothing. Even the bishop has no coercive jurisdiction. We manage these things better in America. There the whole force and authority of the Church would be brought to bear upon such a state of affairs as that which here exists, and either the parish would have to live and work or it would be put away to rest for ever. The rectorial income, derived from endowment, is upward of eight hundred pounds a year; the church income, derived from the pew-rents and offertory, is not sufficient to pay the small expenses of the building. The best pews contain five sittings and rent for twenty-nine shillings a year; in America the same pews would rent for upward of fifteen pounds, and in large Church centres for even twenty-five pounds. The well-to-do folk of Shipston can make two guineas cover their individual church expenses; the same class of people in the United States would not find the limit under fifty times that amount. A parish of sixteen hundred souls, without debt to satisfy, endowment to secure or clergyman to support, which is obliged to send its churchwardens around the town to collect a deficit of seventeen pounds —which personal canvass resulted an Easter or so since in gathering but ten pounds—can neither live with credit nor die with dignity. The hopelessness of its condition appears in the lack of hospitality: the stranger will find no welcome either by a visit from the rector or an offer of a seat in the church from the parishioners.

The edifice is dedicated to St. Edmund of Canterbury. He was born at Abingdon about the year 1190, and was remarkable for his scholarship, his ascetic and pure life and his bold efforts to better the times in which he lived. He inherited his mother's severe religious convictions: " She fasted much and slept little, wore a hair chemise and iron stays, and made her household so uncomfortable by her arrangements that her husband, with her consent, retired to a monastery at Eynesham, as likely to be a more enjoyable home." At Oxford, while a mere grammar student, he determined never to wed an earthly bride: "Standing alone one day in church, he plighted his troth to the Blessed Virgin, and in token thereof placed a gold ring on the finger of her image. He placed another ring, similarly inscribed with the words of the angelic salutation, on his own finger, where he wore it constantly until the day of his death." After a career of honor and usefulness he was made archbishop of Canterbury in 1234, and it has well been said that "in the long succession of primates it is not easy to find one who surpasses him in the perfections of the Christian character or in the attributes of a Christian bishop." His patriotism, resistance to Rome and efforts to reform the Church give him a lasting place in the pages of English history. There was much evil in the age, but he was as a clear and shining light in the darkness. When, owing to repeated defeat, he resigned the see of Canterbury, he retired to the Continent, and in 1240, at the priory of Soissy, he died. His remains were interred at Pontigny, and soon his fame rivalled that of his predecessor, St. Thomas. He was canonized, and miracles were performed at his shrine.

The parish was down to the year 1720 subject to and part of the jurisdiction of Tredington. An almost complete list of the rectors of the parish from the year 1282 is extant. From 1427 to 1873 there were twenty-two rectors, of whom Peter Vannes, archdeacon of Worcester, was remarkable both for his incumbency being the longest of any—fifty years—and also for his guiding the parish through the trying Reformation era, from 1541 to 1591. The continuity of the Church of England is thus exemplified. Other long rectorships were those of Walter Fitzwarin (1282–1310), Felix de Massaveria (1503–1541) and William Evans (1827–1873). The first of these was probably of Norman descent; the second was an Italian, and the third a Welshman. In Henry Sampson, who died in 1482 and has a brass to his memory in the mother-church at Tredington, we are reminded of one of Carlyle's characters; but whether he were like unto the hero of *Past and Present* we know not. A complete list of the curates of Shipston from 1596 is also in existence.

In the old registers are items of interest to the curiously inclined. It was in the twenty-ninth year of the reign of Henry VIII. (1538) the injunction was issued directing that registers on vellum should be kept in every parish in the realm. The oldest registers of this neighborhood are those of Tredington, which begin in 1541; after them come those of Halford, beginning in 1545, and Shipston, in 1572. They are written partly in Latin and partly in English, some in a good hand and some frightful to behold. During the troublous times of the Commonwealth the registers as well as the churches were in great danger of desecration. The rector of Barcheston, a village half a mile from Shipston, in 1647 wrote in his register, dating from 1559, " Digne hoc antiquum perdet quicunq registrum, filius appellatus perditionis sit" ("Whosoever destroys this ancient register will rightly be called the son of perdition"). Mixed up with the ordinary entries occur notices of parochial events of more or less importance.

At Shipston, under date of October 12, 1612, we find the record, "Peter Churchporch, fond in ye churchporch at Todnam, was baptized at Shipston, and had the name then given him, Peter Todnam, alias Churchporch." The following entry is also suggestive: "Elizabeth Thornet, widow, was buried in 1695, at ye upper end of the highway leading from ye Custard Lane, through ye piece of ground commonly called ye Horse Fair, for hanging herself ye day before; she was blind and 86 years of age." The old law directed the suicide to be buried in a cross-road with a stake driven through his body, and a finger-post to be erected to mark his grave for public scorn; this poor blind wretch, weary of life, perhaps abused and maltreated, insane, and very likely regarded as a witch, suffered the legal penalty of her crime. In 1678 the statute was passed enforcing the burial of the dead in woollen shrouds for the encouragement of the manufacturers, and, though affidavits had to be made that the law had been complied with, the registers show that it was easy enough to evade it by paying a fine. Even now the people always lay out their dead in a white shroud pure as the robe they shall wear in the kingdom of their Lord, with the face upward, in token of hope, and the feet to the east, symbolical of the resurrection; and though they bury them in a coffin, while in olden time they were commonly put simply in the grave, they have not yet learned the horrible and ghastly word "casket." Mention is frequently made of the "briefs," the circular letters spoken of in the rubric after the Nicene Creed. These briefs were issued by the bishop or government, generally in alleviation of losses by fire or flood or disease of cattle, for building of churches, the redemption of slaves, and other charitable purposes. The sympathy for the Protestants of Switzerland and France in the Reformation times, and for the latter after the revocation of the Edict of Nantes, was great in this neighborhood. An entry of April 6, 1688, states that in the town of Shipston there was gathered toward the relief of the French Protestants the sum of eighteen shillings and tenpence. Tidmington, united with Shipston under the one rector, though a separate parish a mile and a half distant, in 1692 gathered for the same purpose one pound seven shillings, and in 1699, "for the poor Protestant Vaudois, £0. 3s. 0d.," and for the redemption of captives three pounds ten shillings and nine pence. In 1723 the same register records the giving of sixpence to "three slaves which was abused by the Turks." For their souls' health certain evil people were "cited" to appear before the vicar-general and do penance; offenders at Shipston had to go to the rector of Tredington. The relief of beggars fell largely upon the churchwardens. We read of alms given "to a poor sailor," "to a lame seaman," "to a man that was drownded out," "to a man who was burnt out," "to a poor man that was robbed," "to two men and their wives and six children that were robbed agoing to New England," and "to sum seamen that ye ship was destroyed by a tempest at sea last December, of thunder and lightning." The registers also speak of the visitations and record the expenses connected therewith; thus, in 1708, at Tredington, "our dinners" cost two shillings and "extraordinaries" two shillings and fourpence. What these "extraordinaries" were can easily be surmised. In the register at Solihull are these curious items, under date of 1658: "Paid for making a cucking stoole, and for beere at the drawing it up to the Crosse, 10s. 4d.;" "A penniworth of paper for ye parishners;" "To W. Stretch to stop his mouth, 2s.;" "To Widow Bird pitifully complayning, 1s.;" "To a woman which sat in the churchyard a great while, 1s.;" and "To agoing before justice St. Nicholas with the young people which would not go to service, 1s. 2d."

In the Shipston books there is an inventory, made in 1638, of the church goods and furniture. The books enumerated are one great Bible, two Common Prayers, Jewell's *Works*, Erasmus's *Paraphrase*, *The Book of Homilies*, *The Constitutions*, Mustullus's *Works*, the register books, two paper books to write account of officers, and Edward Pittway's gift-books. The Pittways were an ancient and honorable family in the town; the first burial recorded is that of "Edward Pitway," and in 1706 John Pittway, ironmonger, bequeathed lands and tenements out of which four pounds a year was to be paid to the minister to teach six poor boys to "write a legible hand and say the Church Catechism, with the exposition thereof, without book, and to learn two or three rules in arithmetic." Besides the books, the church owned a surplice, a poor-box, a linen tablecloth, a ladder and two pewter flagons. There are entries of expenses for making the tablecloth and washing the surplice; also, in 1592, for repairing one of the bells. It would appear that the clapper of this bell had broken; the clapper had therefore to be sent to Wotton and the bell to be taken down. Items are given "for drink when the bell was taken down" and "for drink at the hanging up of the bell." "Old Herst" was paid "for going to Brayles for Tooley," and Tooley was paid "for the hanging up of the bell." Then "grease for the bells" was bought, and in the course of the work or the ensuing festivities "a jug of the goodwife Wooley was lost," which had to be paid for. In October, 1695, we read, "Memorandum, that the 5 old bells were new cast by Mr. Koon, of Woodstock. The waight was 34 cwt. 3 qrs. 10 lbs., and to have £18 for casting them, some of this money collected by subscription, and other by levy." The old bells were made up into six, and the six still ring in the same ancient tower. A curious custom has held its own both here and at Barcheston—viz., the tolling of a bell at the end of the Sunday-morning service. No satisfactory reason has been given for either the origin or the continuance of the custom. There is also a bell rung at Shipston every morning at five o'clock and every evening at eight, and at the end of the toll the day of the month is numbered. The common opinion is that many years ago a gentleman who had chanced to lose his way in the neighborhood left money for the ringing of the bell. In 1739 the item is given, "Rump of beef for ringers at Christmas, 4s.;" the great Yuletide is still rung in as in the days of yore. In 1731 "it was agreed upon that the churchwardens, overseers of the poor and the constable shall hold a vestry the first Sunday in every month after evening prayer and bring their accounts to be examined." The first year after death is still called the "dead year," and in the parish records it is termed "the dead's year, according to the custom of the manor." Thus a bequest is made to a person for his natural life and for the dead's year—that is, to his estate for a year after his death.

The holding of a vestry on Sunday seems to indicate that Puritan ideas concerning the Sabbath did not prevail at Shipston. The tendency has rather been to a more liberal observance of the day. The Puritans imitated the Jews in this respect, as in others. The rabbis were excessive in their reverence for the day. If a house were burning, one could save one's clothes only by wearing them: they could not be carried out except by successively putting them on. If a hen laid an egg on the Sabbath-day, it might not be eaten, because she had no right to break the commandment. Women were forbidden to look into the glass on the Sabbath, because they might discover a white hair and attempt to pull it out, which would be a grievous sin. One was not allowed to wear false teeth on the Sabbath, because they might fall out and their owner be tempted to pick them up and put them back or carry them. So the Puritan, partaking of the same spirit, held that to do any work on that day was as great a sin as murder or adultery. He was not allowed to smile or to kiss his wife on the Sabbath. To shave or to cut finger-nails was extreme profligacy and a sure sign of reprobation. The water which was drawn from the well on Saturday night had to last till Monday morning. Such fine distinctions are sometimes awkward, as an old story tells us. In 1260 a Jew of Tewkesbury fell into a sink on the Sabbath-day, and because of his reverence for that day he would not suffer himself to be drawn out; on Sunday the earl's reverence would not allow him to be delivered; and so between the two he died. There is no evidence that Shipston ever favored such extreme views, or that the people objected to the *Book of Sports.* They were dull, but they were not narrow.

The first mention of Shipston occurs more than a thousand years ago. It was probably so called on account of its famous and extensive sheep-markets, noted as ancient by Camden and still among the largest in the kingdom. At the present day the local pronunciation of the singular of the word "sheep" is "ship," and "ton" is the common Saxon termination for the homestead of the yeoman, simply defended by a quickset hedge, or "tun." We may picture the settlement on the Stour amid the great wilds as consisting of a few huts in which the shepherds lived guarded from the wolves of the forest and the inroads of hostile men—the Wealas, or even other tribes of their own race—by thick mounds of trees and high hedges of thorn. They fed their sheep in the rich grass-yielding "opens," sheared and washed them at the river, sent the wool and the mutton away—perhaps to Chipping Camden or Chipping Norton, or other near marts where people resorted to "ceapian," till the place grew large enough to attract traders to itself—and lived a life of primitive simplicity. Then the night-silence was broken by the howling of wild beasts in the neighboring woods and of dogs within the "tun," and from the distant marshes came the booming of the bittern and the screeching of the white owl. Day followed day with its monotonous variations incident to such pursuits as sheep-farming and to a life in such surroundings. Rudely clad, roughly housed and having little intercourse with the outside world, the shepherds were scarcely less wild than was the country around them.

In their cabins the one room served for all the purposes of the family. Around the fire in the middle of the earthen floor father, mother and children slept at night, the ground their couch and sheepskins their covering. They neither washed nor undressed, and nearly their only approach to intellectual life was in the time between the dying of the sunlight in the west and the dying of the embers on the hearth, when they sang rude melodies, sipped home-made mead and propounded such riddles as "What does a goose do when standing on one leg?" When the answer came, "Holds the other up," they no doubt laughed that full, hearty laugh which seems ever to have been characteristic of the English. They ate four meals a day and with their heads covered. Time was measured, the day by the sun and the month by the moon. Their scavengers were kites. In the Wolf-month, when the thick fogs and the chill rain-winds swept over the land and the frost hardened the ground and the river, they kept much at home; but in the bright Weyd-month the children plucked the flowers, the women repaired the house and the men were off to their summer toil. They were heathen then; later they were taught to carve the cross out of the oak from which they had shaped the spear. When Offa, "Rex Anglorum sive Merciorum potentissimus," reigned (*ante* 802), the manor of Shipston was granted by Ulhredus, duke of the Wiccians, to the priors of Worcester. The connection has never been broken; at the Reformation the rights of the priors were taken up by the dean and chapter.

The prior held his manorial court at a village some two miles off, called Blackwell, from a well whose water is darkened by some mineral admixture. It was once a considerable place, having, besides other buildings, a chapel dedicated to St. Nicholas; but at one period, history informs us, its entire population consisted of six men and one maid. From the few facts recorded we gather that the rule of the priors was very arbitrary and, owing to the many fines exacted from the unfortunate townsmen, not much enjoyed. The latter were obliged to have their corn ground at a high rate at the prior's mill, to pay a fine to every new prior, and a penny—called "hedsilver"—for every inhabitant above the age of twelve years, every year when the prior held his court at Blackwell. About the year 1268, Henry III. granted the town a charter for the holding of markets and fairs for the sale of cattle, and about 1405 the townsmen, exasperated beyond all endurance by the fines imposed on them by the priors, broke out into open revolt and rioting. They more particularly objected to the payment of heriots, a fine taken out of a dead man's estate, corresponding somewhat with our modern legacy-duty. Several of the leading inhabitants went to Worcester to intercede with the prior, and after much delay it was decided that on the death of a tenant his best animal should go to the prior and his second best to the rector of the parish. The tenants were also required to spend twenty days in each year in ploughing and sowing the prior's land; also to mow four days, to winnow four days and to carry the corn from the manor to Wethington. For every beast they sold they paid a penny—a sum equal to half a crown of present money. Beyond the fact that in the reign of King John some dispute arose between the townspeople and the rector of Tredington which was settled only by an appeal to

Innocent III., nothing of much interest is recorded, save the perennial quarrels with the prior of Worcester, till after the Reformation.

During the eighteenth century the town was several times and severely visited with small-pox. In 1731 it affected 523 persons, of whom 45 died; and in 1744, 406 persons, of whom 48 died. Under date of 1767 an eminent physician in London writes concerning Shipston: "A poor vagabond was seen in the streets with the small-pox upon him; the people, frightened, took care to have him carried to a little house situated upon a hill at some distance from the town, providing him with necessaries. In a few days the man died; they ordered him to be buried deep in the ground, and the house with his clothes to be burnt. The wind, being pretty high, blew the smoke upon the houses on one side of the town, and a few days after eight persons were slain with the small-pox." In 1772 a subscription was collected to pay for the inoculation of every poor parishioner, and for one hundred and fifty-seven persons the apothecary was paid six shillings a head. When the dread of this dire disease passed away under the benign influence of Dr. Jenner, a new fear took its place: the French became a greater terror than the variola. England looked on aghast at the great Revolution and the victories of Bonaparte, but, though the alarm was great, the country remained loyal and hopeful. The patriotic spirit reached Shipston, and, in spite of the heavy and burdensome taxation, in 1798, when Nelson destroyed the French fleet at the Nile, the townsmen made a voluntary collection of over sixty-one pounds to assist the government. Some gave five guineas, and some gave twopence. Then they formed a volunteer corps, but what became of it or what it did no one knows. In 1803 another company was formed, consisting of four officers and about one hundred and forty men. They agreed to pay certain fines for misconduct—*e. g.*, sixpence for inattention, a shilling for drunkenness and half a crown for fighting; from which we infer that the Shipston men of that day were above all anxious to suppress their weakness for pugilistic enterprises. Their colors are still preserved, and are occasionally hoisted on the church-tower. What duty this corps did history has not recorded, but the memory of the noble men who volunteered for service in the hour of their country's need is still fragrant in the minds of some.

One of the events in the year is the October fair. The picture of the old life is worthy of study. Early in the morning the streets are thronged with people from the neighboring villages, with farm and domestic servants and itinerant showmen. Everything assumes a holiday appearance: shopkeepers have their windows arrayed with the most tempting attractions; fruit-stands and toy-stalls are set about the streets; the inns are busier than usually; hawkers cry their wares; bands play, and everybody is awake to the importance of the occasion. Down in the Shambles, in front of a blacksmith's shop and the Crown Inn, a huge fireplace is built, before which an ox is roasted whole. Possibly this was originally a gift from the lords of the manor, the priors of Worcester, but it is now subscribed for by the people. Everybody tastes the ox, the slices of which are sold at a shilling apiece. In the High street —that undefinable place already mentioned—are the shows, the ubiquitous and ever-genuine Tom Thumb, the original fat woman and the real red man from the wilds of America. Here are the shooting-galleries, where the possibility of a shilling prize is offered at the low price of one penny; also the travelling portrait-taker, who will perpetuate any physiognomy for a mere trifle; also the Cheap John, ever stout and sturdy, whose disinterestedness for the good of the purchasing public is proverbial; also the dog-fancier, with his best specimens of thoroughbreds. For twopence you can get your fortune told by the old woman sitting on yonder doorstep, and, considering the outlay, you will be satisfied. This broad-faced, round-shouldered youth will live with you as ploughman, shepherd, groom, or anything else you wish, at fair wages and plenty to eat and drink. You can take your choice; the street is full of such, all wearing whipcord in their hats and all well recommended. This hiring feature of the fair gives it the name of the "mop"—or, as it was called a century and a half since, the "mapp"—and till the middle of the afternoon farmers and laborers, mistresses and maids, are making, sometimes driving, bargains. The mop was a great attraction in bygone days; an old advertisement of 1743 invites the public to come to the hiring of servants, "where all gentlemen, dealers and chapmen may depend upon good entertainment and encouragement." By sunset everybody is merry, and not a few are drunk. The taverns do a good business all day, and there are dinners at the "George," the "Bell," the "White Horse" and the smaller hostelries. Here are lads and lasses arm in arm, light and gay; here, boys on the lookout for mischief; there, men trying to walk steadily and to sing or whistle, but the goodly potions have disabled them from doing either. Yonder is the police-sergeant wheeling home one of his constables in a barrow, and followed by an admiring throng of rag-tag and bob-tail. Across the way are two young men indulging in the supreme pleasure of a prize-fight and surrounded by a cheering crowd. And the showmen shout, and the drums and gongs rattle, and the blazing paraffin-lights hiss and splutter, and children blow their penny trumpets, tin whistles and horns, and the people laugh and talk, till one forgets that this is sleepy and old-fashioned Shipston. In old times rougher sports prevailed. The following advertisement referring to this October "roast" explains itself:

"SHIPSTON-ON-STOWER.

"On Tuesday the 17th of October, 1783, will be played for at Backswords, a purse of Five Guineas, by seven or nine of a side. If no sides appear by nine o'clock in the Forenoon, Eight Shillings will be given to each man who breaks a head; Two Shillings and Sixpence to each man that has his head broken; to begin playing exactly at nine o'clock."

On this occasion the Shipston men suffered severely at the hands of combatants from Wiltshire, whom they nicknamed "Sawnees." Down to within the memory of some now living bull-baiting and pigeon-shooting took place at these fairs, and cock-fighting was common at all times.

Other festivals were kept besides this one. The Fifth of November was not forgot. Christmas was ushered in with the merry pealing of bells, the waits and carol-singers; everybody had plum-pudding, if nothing else. Some there were who thought that the cattle went down on their knees and the ghosts remained in their tombs at the midnight of the Nativity. Strange life! The narrow, irregular streets do not belong to the common, every-day world. That house in Church street with the little bow-windows was once the post-office. Up this alley is a small dissenting chapel where the remnant of Israel comfort themselves with invectives against their neighbors. This dull, odd-looking building is the Quakers' meeting-house; only a few Friends remain, but they wear drab and broad brims and are still very good folks. That spruce youth with the white hat strutting down toward the mill is a visitor —perhaps from Birmingham. He is well dressed and walks swinging his cane with an air of superiority and contempt. He looks down upon place, people and everything. The cobble sidewalks, of which the natives are justly proud—so proud, indeed, that for fear of wearing them out they walk in the middle of the street—he regards as unworthy of scorn. He is—and he knows it—a stranger to this strange world, and in days when sawmills abound laughs heartily at the sight of the old-fashioned sawyer standing on a log over a pit. But let him go, and look at the people themselves. Here is your wagoner in his smock-frock, and here your artisan in his corduroy breeches and rough-spun jacket, and here a gentleman dressed some years behind the times. The parson with his white necktie and black frock-coat is an incongruity in a place where everything suggests the cassocked priest or the cowled monk. The carpenter, across the way, with the flag basket of tools on his back, moving along as though life had no end, was once the parish clerk and the parson's right-hand man.

The blacksmith, standing by that old broken-down wagon, is the great man in the Baptist chapel, and he will tell you with some pride that his chapel is "general" and not "particular"—a distinction of great consequence. The most important people of the place are the shopkeepers—a highly-respectable and intelligent class whose dignity appears to best advantage in a gig, and whose obsequiousness exceeds that of the ordinary shopkeeper elsewhere as the humility of a grasshopper exceeds in loveliness the pride of a gnat. Society is rather select and commendably exclusive, but good manners and courtesy are not so general as one might judge from the pretensions. Two things most people do on Sunday: they go to church or chapel, and they take their dinner to the bakehouse. You may see a man on a Sabbath morning, just before the bells begin to ring for service, carrying a shallow tin pan with a bit of meat in the middle surrounded with batter-pudding or peeled potatoes. This he leaves at the baker's, and then, taking a turn around and looking as innocent and unconscious as if he had done a thing no one else did or saw him do, he starts off for church, and, though he makes little and gets still less out of the sermon, he sings his hymns and says his prayers with a devotion to duty highly commendable. Coming out, he slips off for his dinner, and carries it home smoking hot. And then—the only time in the week—one of his boys says grace, and all set to with a relish. Probably half the people in the place go through this programme every Sunday. I believe it is not considered the right thing to ask a blessing except at this meal; the others are such that it is not worth while to say anything about them. Ruddy cheeks, stalwart limbs and stout forms abound, and testify to the healthfulness of the place. The death-rate is low—about fourteen per thousand. For a picture of rugged beauty see these four girls, evidently sisters. They appear as fresh as the field-daisies in the early morning and as gay as the crickets that chirp in the kitchen. Doubtless they can both thump the piano and churn butter, play croquet and knit stockings; and, though they may at night stick a pin through the wick of the candle to judge by its remaining in or falling out if their lover will keep true, they look like sensible and quick-witted maidens.

CHAPTER III.

The Region Round About.

> The sheltered cot, the cultivated farm,
> The never-failing brook, the busy mill,
> The decent church that topt the neighboring hill,
> The hawthorn bush, with seats beneath the shade
> For talking age and whispering lovers made."

THE country around Shipston-on-Stour is beautifully undulating, its fertile hills and dales producing rich grain-harvests and affording abundant pasture for numerous flocks and herds. The little river on the western bank of which the town is built is as pretty and dainty a stream as could be found anywhere. Its name is not unique: there is a "Stour" in Dorset, Suffolk, Cambridge and Kent as well as in Warwickshire. The word is derived from the Saxon *styrian*, to "stir" or "move," and probably alludes to its rapid course— "the swift river." It rises in Oxfordshire, and from the Traitor's Ford, where it enters the county of Warwick, to Milcote, below Stratford, where it joins the Avon, is, owing to its winding course, about thirty miles long, though the distance as the crow flies is not more than fifteen. Busily it turns the millwheel at Burmington, flows deeply and quietly past Tidmington and Willington, turns the wheel again at Barcheston, gathers its strength for the mill at Shipston, and then runs laughingly off in its childish glee till it broadens itself as it flows by Honington, and afterward, as though half ashamed of its attempt at stateliness, modestly narrows for its duty again at Tredington and Harford. Bright green meadows and banks where wild flowers grow in rich profusion border it on either side; willows cast their shadows upon its sparkling waters; here and there in a deep bend are tall flags and nodding rushes and broad-leafed lilies, and many are the quiet nooks where the pike and the perch have their haunt. In this brook the angler finds his patience and skill rewarded, the oarsman discovers water deep and steady enough for his skiff, and the schoolboy enjoys his swim and catches his minnows unmolested—a merry, light-hearted stream in summer, but when swollen by the floods of autumn and spring angry and turbulent. Then the yellow, foaming waters rush fiercely through the valley, sweeping across the fields with impetuous haste and passionate violence, carrying away gates, hurdles, fences, bridges, and whatever else may stand in the way, and exciting astonishment in every breast. The roads near the brook are impassable at such times, and the villagers have perforce to stay at home. Traditions of hairbreath escapes and of extraordinary floods, as well as of damages and deaths from that cause, are as common as are stories of immense beasts fattened in the meadow and of heavy fish caught in the brook. The dimensions of eels which have been found in Fletcher's Pool and the weight of cows which have been fed at Wolford are proofs of the fertility of both country and river and of the salubrity of air and water.

There are fishermen hereabouts—few in number, but

expert in their art. Most villages near the river have their Izaak Walton—an individual, as a rule, more qualified to quaff ale or cider than to write the *Lives* of divines or such a book as the *Compleat Angler*. He is frequently a decayed tradesman whose love for sport has injured his business. Here is such a one on his way over the mill-bridge. He is accompanied by a boy who carries his can of bait and looks as if he had reached the acme of honor. Their path lies across the meadows. Let us follow them. The birds and butterflies flit hither and thither; the trees and flowers and green sod are fresh and bright. Now and then they surprise a squirrel or a rabbit in the long wayside grass, but quicker than the boy can run it disappears in the blackberry- or hazel-bushes or in the deep burrows. The contented murmur of the heavily-laden bee as she speeds her way home from the honey-sweetened blossoms of the pimpernel, the agrimony or the wood-betony; the quiet, and yet striking, whistle of the chiff-chaff; the cries of the shepherds and the anxious bleating of the sheep borne on the gentle breeze from far up the river, where the annual washing and shearing is being performed; the singing and prattle of village children rambling in the fields or by the hedgerows in search of flowers or fledglings,— these are among the many sounds which fall upon their ears. An hour's walk, and they are on the banks of the brook. The high trees cast their shadows almost to the other side of the bright, translucent waters, and in the quiet deep corner the fisherman prepares to cast his line. In silence he makes ready his fishing-tackle, fastening a well-scoured worm on the hook, and in a few minutes the white-and-green-striped float is bobbing on the tiny wavelets. The boy pulls up what he calls butter reeds and eats the soft end. There is no bite; only once in the first quarter of an hour is there the sign of one, and then it is only a gudgeon nibbling, and as he turns away he passes down the capacious gullet of a monstrous luce at that moment looking around for his supper. "Never waste a good bait on a poor fish," the angler remarks; and a volume could scarcely impart more wisdom. The line is drawn out, fresh tackle is prepared, a frog is put on the hook even as though he loved him, and the baited barb is dropped silently into the stream. How still is everything in that riverside corner! Even the sobbing brook is quiet and the sighing wind is hushed. Beneath the thick overhanging boughs of the willows are clouds of swarming gnats and flies; once in a while a brilliantly-colored dragon-fly whizzes past; now a rat starts to swim across the brook, but disappears in midstream, no doubt seized and swallowed by some monster of the deep; yonder a bright-hued kingfisher skims the surface of the water; and the silence is only made more intense by the sound of falling water in the distance and the occasional tapping of the woodpecker in the thicket. How intently both man and boy watch at their shadows' length from the brink! They speak only in whispers. They grow pale and nervous with excitement. At last! Hush! There is a bite, a tug, and the line is whirling and rattling over the reel, and across the water the thin, gleaming foam is cast up as the captured fish rushes to its lair. By and by the line is drawn in, and soon on the green sward lies a splendid jack, his sides glittering in the sunshine and his eyes darting angry glances. Pike thirty-two inches in length and weighing eight and nine pounds have of late years been pulled out of the Stour. When the man returns to town, he will sell his fish and have a pint or two of extra stout on his luck.

The scenery around Shipston, though not romantic, is picturesque and pleasing. There are low swelling hills and broad smiling plains where in the spring meadow, field and copse are clothed in vesture of living green, and in the autumn in robes of red and gray and brown. Standing on one of the many rising grounds, the spectator beholds the country rolling in waves of quiet, happy beauty. Farms and hamlets nestling among the trees; roads running hither and thither, now across open fields, and now between high hedges where grow the crab and the may, here through the greenwood, and there winding up the hillside; church-towers and spires rising from the heart of some rural Eden—perhaps in a valley-depth of charming grace, perhaps on an elevation of commanding loveliness; quaint, restful, homelike mansions peeping out of sylvan retreats and surrounded by wide parks within whose glades and beneath whose broad-spreading oaks feed the antlered deer and the striped Alderney cattle,—such are among the objects which attract his attention and excite his admiration. The views from Brailes Hill and from Tredington Hill are for gentle, suggestive beauty and exquisite natural charm all that can be desired, while from Edgehill, a little out of sight of Shipston, is a landscape which is unrivalled in England and unexcelled in the world.

Travel in the olden time was a very different affair from travel in the nineteenth century. Not only was the railway not invented, but the roads were neither good nor safe and the conveyances were unwieldy and

uncomfortable. In rainy weather no vehicle could be dragged through the deep mud; even on horseback the journey was not easy, while on foot it was tiring and difficult. Deep rivers had bridges over them, but shallow streams were forded except in time of flood, when the passage was impossible. Every manor or parish was obliged to keep its own roads in repair, but no one saw that the work was done, and parsimonious squires and vestries therefore did as little as possible. In the Middle Ages people left money for the repairing and making of highways, and they who did so—even later by the Reformers themselves—were esteemed to have done much to ensure their salvation. But mud, slush and swollen streams in rainy weather and unimaginable depths of sand and dust in dry weather were not the only inconveniences. The danger from highwaymen was ever present, and centuries passed before such robbery was suppressed. In one age it was the retainers and servants of the baron through whose estate the road ran that sought to lighten the burden of the stranger: perchance the baron himself helped in the work; then outlaws and professional bandits did the same thing; and thus from time immemorial till near our own day the Jack Sheppards and Dick Turpins levied mail of the passers-by. In this way the men of Sherwood, whom romance has made virtuous, got their wealth and made merry, and, though we are told that the brave Robin spared the poor and lay in wait only for rich abbots and wealthy merchants, there is too strong a suspicion of business about this discrimination to suffer one to think much of his great-heartedness. Down in secluded hollows in the forest or the glen or by the stream was done the deed which made even strong men dread travelling and made women shiver with fear. Occasionally the robbery was committed in gentler and more legal form. Heavy toll was exacted for crossing a bridge or passing through a town or by a castle, or a still heavier fine for having incurred the suspicion of being a spy or a foe. As a man cannot help other people's suspicions, and as there was no available appeal from the bench of country justice, the traveller was lucky if he escaped with half his goods and less than a day in the stocks. Dangers such as these made it necessary for travellers to unite in companies large enough for self-defence, and every wise man before he left his own roof-tree for a distance paid his debts, bade farewell to his friends and disposed of his family and property with far more care than is displayed in these degenerate days by many who are on the eve of taking their journey to that bourne from whence no traveller returns. As an illustration of the perils of the road the following from a newspaper presumably of about the year 1770 is interesting: "On Thursday night about eight o'clock Mr. Thomas Pratt, farmer and corn-dealer, of Shipston, was stopped between Newbold and Tredington, on his return from Stratford, by a footpad, who rushed from the roadside and knocked him off his horse by striking him several times with a hedge-stake or heavy bludgeon. The villain then knelt on Mr. Pratt's breast and took from him a pocket-book containing Stratford bank-bills to the amount of £99. Mr. Pratt was found lying on the ground about a quarter of an hour afterward very much cut and bruised about the head, two of his teeth having been knocked out by the blows. The robber was a stout, lusty man." There is no record of his capture.

Travel a long way back was done mostly on horseback or on foot, though there were wagons and carts used for the purpose. The first coach seen in England was about the year 1553, and another hundred and twenty years passed before stage-coaches began to run; they were not received with much favor. In 1673 a treatise was published in London by "A Lover of his Country, and Well-wisher to the Prosperity both of the King and Kingdoms," in which were used many elaborate arguments and violent tirades against them. "These coaches and caravans," said the writer, "are one of the greatest mischiefs that hath happened of late years to the kingdom, mischievous to the publick, destructive to trade, and prejudicial to lands." He laments the decay of good horsemanship which would follow if everybody rode to London in a coach. He calculates that a stage-coach from York, Chester or Exeter would have forty horses on the journey to the capital and carry eighteen passengers a week. In the whole year it would carry about eighteen hundred and seventy-two. Supposing they were returning passengers, there would be nine hundred and thirty-six, and for these forty horses would be sufficient; but if people travelled in the good old-fashioned way, then at least five hundred horses would be required for this work. The use of so many horses would give employment to many who were by the stage-coach thrown out of work, such as cloth-workers, drapers, tailors, saddlers, tanners, curriers, shoemakers, spurriers, lorimers and fellmakers. The inns also suffer, for the stage-coach stops at only a few; but when gentlemen travelled on horseback, accompanied, as they usually were, by three or four servants, they stopped at any and as often as they liked, and thus encouraged trade. Farmers will be ruined, he says, by the stage-coach; for how can they dispose of their hay, straw and horse-corn? Moreover, the influence on health would be bad: men called out of their beds before daylight, hurried from place to place till far on into the night, in the summer stifled with heat and choked with dust, in the winter starving and freezing with cold or choked with filthy fog, obliged to ride all day with strangers and with sick, ancient and diseased persons and young children crying, poisoned with fetid breaths and crippled by the crowd of boxes and bundles. Besides all these troubles, there were the accidents arising from rotten coaches and foul roads. In short, the writer is fully convinced that if stage-coach travelling becomes popular the country will go to ruin. Had he lived to see the railway, he would have been bereft of his senses. Had he lived to see the day when gallows should not be erected by the highway, nor suicides buried in the cross-roads, nor ghosts haunt the uncanny corners, he would have given up his spirit in despair.

The roads around Shipston are interesting. The Fossway, an ancient Roman thoroughfare running in an almost straight line across the country from Lincoln to Bath, passes the town to the north-west at a distance of two or three miles. It is a well-kept though rather unfrequented road. Once in a while the pedestrian meets a gig or a wagon, but one might go from the cross-roads between Tredington and Newbold to Stretton and see no one. In the hedges dog-roses grow in early summer and large luscious blackberries in the autumn. Birds and ploughboys here as elsewhere whistle and sing with varying sweetness and strength; the "Tally-ho!" of the huntsman, the baying of the hounds and the sharp crack of the whip are sometimes heard, as are also the lowing of cattle, the bleating of flocks and the cries and shouts of laborers; but the impression one has in traversing the Fossway—so far, at least, as man is concerned—is that of loneliness and lifelessness. It was a busy road when Roman legions moved through the country; now it is the retreat of the health-seeker, the lover and the antiquary.

There is a characteristic lane running from Tysoe by Tredington, Honington and Barcheston to Willington. Such roads are peculiarly English. In places the grass grows from hedge to hedge. A little beyond Honington it threads its way through a long avenue of tall, stately elms. Near Barcheston it crosses an open field on a rising ground from which a good view of Shipston may be had—the still place with its square church-tower snug down in the hollow. At Barcheston one can turn aside to the village, consisting of an ancient church, the parsonage, a mill, a farmhouse, and possibly two cottages, and take a footpath across the fields to Willington—a walk almost as pleasant as the one from Tredington to Blackwell by the high hedge.

The turnpike-roads are, of course, somewhat busier, but scarcely less attractive. There are footpaths by the side of the way, hedges and trees for shade and here and there a rustic seat where the tired traveller may sit and rest. The ride from Shipston to Stratford is delightful, and, indeed, one could walk the ten miles without noticing the distance, so velvety the turf, so firm the path, so charming the country. That to Banbury is almost as pleasant; the one to Moreton-in-the-Marsh, wilder and more secluded; and that to Chipping Norton, more romantic. This last-named road leads by the new cemetery, the ancient Tidmington and the once-famous but now deserted hostelry at Chapel-House, some ten miles from Shipston.

The district is dotted with villages and hamlets, many of them small and secluded, but all ancient and interesting. A few minutes' walk over the mill-bridge and across the meadows brings one to Barcheston—or Barson, as it was anciently, and is still locally, pronounced. In *Henry IV.*, Part II., Act V., Scene 3, we read of "Goodman Puff of Barson," which some have thought was a corruption of Barton, the village on the Heath, but which others—perhaps more correctly—have identified with this place. It is of great antiquity, and was once of sufficient importance to give its name to the hundred to which it belonged. In Doomsday the place is called Berricestone. In the reign of Henry VII. a wealthy merchant, William Willington by name, pulled down the few houses which the village then contained and built a spacious mansion, turning over five hundred acres of the land into a park. He died in 1563, and in a small chapel of the parish church he and his wife lie in effigy on an altar-tomb. The monument has been much mutilated. The little church, dedicated to St. Martin, was built in 1281. It is of Early English style and contains some brasses, an ancient font, an old black-lettered copy of Erasmus's Paraphrases—which was formerly chained to the bench—and in the tower a priest's chamber. This is said to be a good specimen of the *domus inclusi.* Towers were once frequently used for residence. What a weird sort of home! Jackdaws chattering among the bells, ghosts lurking in the dark corners, the loneliness calling up legends and creating fancies of soul-subduing and mind-bewildering power, and the wind, as it swept against the buttressed walls and through the narrow loopholes, now sobbing and sighing like poor souls in agony and now roaring and raging, furious as the storm-waves of the sea or the shrieks of despairing demons! Dismal, dull, melancholy! There are three bells, which are popularly supposed to ring this melody as they chime for service:

> "' Long-tailed sow,
>   Where be'st going?'
> ' To th' bean-mow.'
> ' May I go wi' thee?'
> ' No; not now.'"

The tower leans perceptibly. On the south side of the church is a curious spout—two arms extended holding a bucket or tub to catch the water. The building has accommodation for about a hundred and fifty people, and a whisper can be heard in it from one end to the other. Here survives the time-honored parish clerk, a worthy man who for many years has rung the bells, dusted the pews, waited upon the parson and led the choir. Some of his honors have been taken away: there was once a time when the parish clerk read the first lesson and gave out the psalm.

The greater part of the congregation live at a hamlet about a mile across the fields from the church. The intervening ground was in the park, long since broken up, and to the place where the villagers were removed William Willington gave his own name. A simple place is that Willington, without either a public-house or a dissenter. A few cottages scattered along the irregularly-laid-out lanes, in which shepherds, carters and farm-laborers live, a little shop where a few necessaries, such as needles and thread, sugar and soap, can be bought, a farmhouse,—that is all. The place is healthful: there is no excitement to injure the inhabitants. The geese eating the grass by the roadside in front of the houses take their time and scarcely notice the passers-by. The pigs and the dogs grow fat and indolent in no time. The old folks take snuff and drink small beer and sit for hours in solemn vacuity of thought. When the annual wake is held, the people dress in their gayest and best, a fiddler from Shipston scrapes music for the dancers and everybody makes merry. At Christmas most of the natives have a bit of roast beef and a bouncing plum-pudding of approved weight and color; at Easter, a chine of bacon—perhaps a survival of the old custom of eating pork at that season to show contempt for the Jews. Long ago the villagers went to the bull-baitings and cock-fights at Shipston, and some of the ancients will justify the former sport on the ground that baiting made the bull's flesh wholesome. An old pastime in this county was the "grinning-match." In a newspaper of 1711 it is said that the Warwickshire men were as famous for their grins as the Kentish men were for their tails. Grinning is better than crying, and at these matches a substantial prize was given to the best competing grinner. Whistling in unison was also practised, but the tendency to laugh at a row of screwed-up mouths was so great that a good bout was seldom secured.

A little farther up the river is Tidelmington—or, as it is now called, Tidmington—a church, a mansion, a farmhouse and a few cottages. The last parish clerk here served for thirty-one years—an old-fashioned type

> "Who thought no song was like a psalm,
> No music like a bell."

Not long since, he was carried to his grave by four of his grandchildren, and his office is now declared obsolete. This parish borders on that of Todenham. There the ancient custom of "beating the bounds" is still kept up. This in days gone by was generally observed throughout the country, and consisted of an annual procession or ambulation around the bourns or boundaries of the parish by the rector, churchwardens, prominent parishioners, meresmen and young people. The leading metes and points having been ascertained, they were severally indicated to the village boys and impressed upon their memories by such means as throwing one of them into the water, giving another a sound thrashing or bumping a third against a wall, tree, post, or any other hard substance near at hand. This was supposed to fasten the fact of the parish limits upon the juvenile intelligence, and took the place of the ordnance map. At Todenham, if a stranger happens to be going along the road while the procession is passing, the people leave off beating the bounds and cudgel him instead. Beyond Tidmington is Burmington, and beyond that again is Little Wolford, an ancient hamlet lying off the highway and containing an interesting mansion, partly of thirteenth-century date, of which the dining-hall, buttery-hatch and minstrels' gallery have been preserved. Cherrington, Stourton and Sutton are not far distant. In this same direction, seven or eight miles from Shipston, a little off the highway to Chapel-House, is an ancient stone circle similar to that at Stonehenge, known as the Rollendrych, Rowldrich or, more commonly, Rollright Stones. There are about sixty stones, some buried beneath the turf, others less than and some about four feet above the ground, and one over seven feet high, arranged in a ring thirty-five yards in diameter, in the middle of which is a clump of firs. Outside of the circle is the King Stone, eight feet high, and in another direction till lately were the Whispering Knights, five stones leaning against one another, the highest of which was nearly eleven feet. Local tradition has for centuries held that the stones are the transformed bodies of an army. A certain king of the neighboring part of the country, the story says, desiring to be ruler of all England, marched with his men across the country, and when on this spot exclaimed,

> "If Long Compton I can see,
> King of England I shall be."

Three or four steps farther he would have seen the village he desired, but at that moment a wise woman cried,

> "Move no more! Stand fast, Stone!
> King of England thou shalt be none!"

and he and his knights and soldiers were instantly turned into stone. Superstition kept the place from being meddled with. A farmer once carried away one of the Whispering Knights to make a stepping-stone over his brook, but his rest was so disturbed by tormenting spirits that he returned it to its place. Five horses were needed to cart it away; one sufficed to bring it back again. The nature of the stones proves that they were originally brought from a long distance, thus suggesting anew the mooted question of mechanical arts among the ancients. Camden thinks the stones commemorate a Danish victory; Plot, that they mark the place where kings were elected and crowned; but most authorities regard them as sepulchral. Some have held that the circle is part of the outer boundary of a Celtic barrow and is at least two thousand years old. Two hundred yards east of the King Stone is a bank running north and south, where the exposed soil is of a darker color than the surrounding earth and covers the remains of men and horses. Various relics have been found close by, and everything seems to support the conclusion that here the people long ago buried their dead, and that the stones remaining formed the temple used for ancestor-worship. The Whispering Knights are possibly the remains of an altar, though the upper slab has been removed, and the King Stone may have served either as a pedestal for an idol or as a mark to guide worshippers from the opposite hills and the valley beneath to the temple. Within the circle itself no remains of bodies have been found, and we may reasonably conjecture that this was the sanctuary, the place where the worship—whether of the sun or of other forces of nature, or of ancestors—was offered up, around which, as in our modern churchyards, the dead were interred. The weird grandeur and the impressive silence speak of the mutability of human affairs and the transitoriness of human life. Not a name abides; priests and people, mourners and mourned, have passed away. The sacrificial fires are unkindled, the hymns to the gods unsung. Nothing remains of the temple so lone and grand in the wilderness, open to the winds and rains of heaven, but the gray and lichen-stained stones and an entrancing and strange mystery. How modern the oldest church in the land seems beside those rude and ancient relics!

About five miles from the Long Compton which the traditionary king desired to see is Compton Wingate, also called Compton-in-the-Hole because seated in a deep valley. Close by is Hook Norton, a picturesque village once held by a countess of Salisbury by the tenure of "carving before the king, and to have the knife with which she carved." Camden, writing in the reign of James I., says that the inhabitants of this place were formerly such clowns that "to be born at Hook Norton became a proverb to denote rudeness and ill-breeding." In his day, as at the present time, the people of the neighborhood commonly called it "Hog's Norton, where the pigs play upon organs," alluding, it is said, to a native who aspired to be a musician.

On the opposite side of Shipston, two miles toward Stratford-on-Avon, is Tredington, once the great ecclesiastical centre of the district. No less than ten chapelries in the largest and richest parish in the diocese of Worcester owed allegiance to the great church of St. Gregory. The church is of magnificent proportions and noble architecture. Norman pillars supporting pointed arches and the clerestory separate the nave from the aisles; the rood-screen between the nave and the chancel remains; the seats and the pulpit are of carved Perpendicular work, and at the west end is a long low gallery running the whole breadth of the church. The roof is flat and open, the wall timbers resting on grotesque heads, chiefly of animals resembling bears. In the aisle is a trefoliated piscina; near to it is an old lectern, to which is chained a copy of Jewel's *Apology*, and in the floor, close by, is a large stone on which may be discerned the carved outlines of a chalice and a book. It is probably the monument of a priest, but no inscription remains. In the north aisle is an aumbry, square, with a wooden shelf. The chancel has among other tablets and slabs two fine brasses of the fifteenth century. The walls were once covered with painted scenes from Scripture and legend, but in 1841 they were scraped away; nor did the authorities follow the example of the Reformers and place texts from the Bible in their stead. The noble tower contains a good peal of bells, mostly of seventeenth-century make. On some of them are inscriptions, such as "Drawe neare to God" and "Gloria Deo in excelsis; Jesu be our speed." The view from the parapet is very fine. Thirty years ago the choir was accompanied by a flute, clarionet, fiddle, base-violin and other musical instruments. There was singing in those days—part-singing of an elaborate nature. How the tuning of the instruments just before the chant or the hymn was begun used to echo through the dark nave and aisles! and when all was ready, how lustily and heartily the sacred minstrelsy poured out its melody and song! In the churchyard—so full of graves that it is much higher than the floor of the church and the outside roadway—is an elegant cross of fourteenth-century work, nearly thirteen feet high. Among the many quaint inscriptions on the tombstones are the following:

> MARY HALL (1682).
>
> "Here lyes that duste which did enthrone
> A sovle soe piovs soe divine,
> That not a daye to her was given .
> But shee advanced a step towrds heaven;
> Whither shee now is fled to bee
> Partaker of a blest eternity."

> LAWRANDS SMITH (1680).
>
> "All heads like mine must surely come
> With natur's pasport to the tomb;
> Like vagabonds on earth they must
> Returne vnto their native duste."

The equivocal character of this latter one is matched by another, which, referring to the departed, speaks of

> "His spirit *sinking* to its rest."

The district was once celebrated for its parish clerks. A noble specimen held office here till within some twenty years. He succeeded his father—indeed, I believe the position was in the family for three generations and upward of a century. He knew the services by heart and as a psalm-singer was unrivalled. For a crinclepouch—that is to say, for a sixpence—he would show the church to visitors and tell the unked stories of its nooks and corners. What he did not know about ghosts was not worth knowing—not, as he used to say, that he had ever seen one himself or anybody else that ever had, but he had heard people who knew people that had heard of others who had, and surely that was evidence enough. When in his desk below the rector's, during the service he kept one eye on the book and the other on the congregation, as much to look out for strangers and mark new hats and coats as to preserve order and decorum. Prayers ended and sermon begun, he would take out his red silk handkerchief—used only on Sundays and at Christmas and Easter—and throw it over his head (the church had draughts) and compose himself contentedly with a done-my-duty sort of air in a corner of his box-like desk to listen to the discourse. That he did not sleep was evident from the fact that he could tell what the sermon was about; which was more than most of the congregation could do. He was a good old fellow, faithful, loyal and earnest, and at the annual tithe-dinner —always held at the White Lion—he sang his song, cracked his jokes and drank his ale with a good courage. Both parson and farmers liked him, but then those were wicked old times when people loved their beer and thought they would go to heaven.

Across the road is the rectory, a new building replacing one of great age. On the opposite side of the churchyard are the stocks and the whipping-post, long since disused, but in good preservation. The village consists of small, irregularly-built stone houses, many of them of considerable antiquity. Its life has departed; a highway inn and a wheelwright's shop are the only signs of trade. There are no dissenters, but not many years since the churchwardens were asked to weigh a woman against the Bible to prove to her neighbors that she had not a familiar spirit. In the old register we read of payments being made to parishioners for killing ob noxious animals; thus, adders were valued at twopence each, urchins at fourpence and foxes at a shilling. Of late years sparrows' heads were paid for by the church-wardens at the rate of three farthings a dozen. In 1714 a man was paid half a crown for "whipping ye dogs out of ye church." Curious customs prevailed here, as elsewhere in the neighborhood. Two or three evenings every week during Advent the bells were rung to herald in with joyous peals the merry Christmastide. The "passing-bell," formerly tolled at the dying of a parishioner to warn his friends and neighbors of their own mortality and to urge them to pray that he might find mercy with God, now rings immediately after the death —two strokes for a woman, twice repeated, and three strokes for a man, thrice repeated, followed by a long toll; and as the solemn tones are wafted over the village and fields the housewife will stay her hand and the ploughman will lift his hat and utter a prayer that God will keep them in the dark hour. At some places in the diocese a muffled peal was rung on Innocents' Day in token of sorrow for the babes of Bethlehem, and an unmuffled peal as a thanksgiving for the escape of the infant Saviour. Among the payments made the rector were Easter offerings, three or four pence for each communicant. Householders also paid the smoke-penny and the garden-penny, and the tribute of "saddle-silver" was made to the prior of Worcester for the privilege of riding on horseback through the ecclesiastical estate. In Saxon times the place belonged to Eanberht, duke of the Wiccians, and at the Conquest it passed into the possession of the bishop of Worcester. In the fourteenth century Robert Walden, of Warwick, founded a chantry in the parish church. Until the Reformation the manor remained mostly in ecclesiastical hands; it was then confiscated and given to the earl of Warwick. Darlingscote and Blackwell, two tiny hamlets, still belong to the parish; Armscott, formerly Edmundscote, and Newbold were cut off about fifty years since. In the latter village, three miles and a half from Shipston, on the highway to Stratford, is a neat little church dedicated to St. David, and containing in the chancel two painted lancets less in size than, but superior in delicacy of coloring and beauty of design to, even the well-executed eastern window containing the scene of the Last Judgment. On the Foss road, to the east of the highway between Tredington and Newbold, about a mile from either place, is Halford, noted for the beauty of its bowling-green. Here, in 1608, the rector of Tredington, then recently appointed, was "married openlie in the church." Throughout the reign of Elizabeth clerical marriages, though permitted, were discountenanced, and were performed in secret. In the reign of Edward I. part of the manor was made over by Henry de Halford to a man named Bregge on condition of his supplying thirty-six people on Christmas Day with a loaf of bread, a herring and a flagon of beer. The place shared with Stratford the honor of a poet. There are poets of various sorts. William Shakespeare, the actor, was of one kind; George Grainger, the parson of Halford, was of another. He was presented to the living in 1659, and commemorates his predecessor as follows:

"Here lyes a modell of the Pastour pure,
Described by Paul, who undertook the cure

> Of congregation all, and gave example
> From Timothy and Titus large and ample;
> He was no fighter, drunkard, nor yong scholar,
> Not avaricious nor o'ercome with choller."

To his own ministry, just beginning, he thus refers:

> "Oh, that this Pastour and this people too
>   In apostolique rules would dwell;
> Whatever Sodom and Gomorrah doo,
>   Our little Zoar shall fare well."

In this church there is a squint in the wall behind the reading-desk, so that formerly the people in the south aisle could see the priest at the altar; Chipping Norton also has one. In many ancient chancels there is a low side-window commonly called a leper-window, through which lepers or sick persons during the time of plague might witness the mass and receive communion without contaminating the congregation. Some, however, think these windows were lychnoscopes, and that their object was to allow the light of the lamp burning in the sanctuary to fall on the graves in the churchyard. There was such a window in Tredington church, but it is now stopped up.

We may not wander farther through this pleasing neighborhood. Places as interesting as any we have spoken of abound. Ilmington, Ebrington and Blockley have each a story which we may not in this place tell.

The peculiarities of dialect are many, and, though there is a decided approach to the general English tongue, many of the common people still retain the lingual idiosyncrasies of their fathers. One of the leading features of the dialect is the lengthening of the vowels. This is done so as to give them a double quantity, and frequently to cause them to be repeated as in a diæresis. For instance, the following are common examples: "don't" is pronounced "doōn't;" "won't," "woōn't;" "like," "liīke;" "time," "tiīme." "Come" runs "coom," like the word "coo;" and "there" becomes "theer," like "thee" with an *r*.

Another leading characteristic is the general drawl. The words are long drawn out, fairly enunciated, but uttered very slowly. The pitch of voice is high and the tone loud; both painfully so. The sentence is more or less inflected, at times running into a disagreeable sort of rhythm. The aspirate is, of course, utterly neglected. Occasionally it is prefixed to a word to which it does not belong, but not often, for that would need effort; and the prolonged drawl precludes anything like effort. There appears to be no difficulty in the way of their clearly understanding one another, even in words where the *spiritus asper* seems to an educated ear absolutely necessary. They neither notice its presence nor miss its absence. The liquids are still clear, making a remarkable contrast to the London speech. On the whole, there is a harshness, a barbarism, which makes the tongue the reverse of attractive.

The grammatical blunders are many. The nominative and objective cases are freely transposed. "Hur güved hit to I" is the common style. Instead of "are," the use of "be" is general; *e. g.*, "You beean't ah gooin;" "I bee gooōd;" "Him bee ah stunner." The number of verbs is woefully disregarded; *e. g.*, "I cooms," "we is" or "us is," and "him up and hit he." This last example we heard given "'Im hup and 'it 'ee."

There are not many words peculiar to the dialect. They use "gammy" for "bad," "ship" for the singular of "sheep," "scrimmut" for a piece of anything, and "lissom" for "lithesome" or nimble. A fence is called a "mound;" a heap or rick of hay, a "mow;" and a master, a "gaffer." The Transatlantic "ain't" is supplied by the equally unpleasant "ahn't or "han't." Most people use the word "Protestant" as descriptive only of the Church of England; what they do in parishes where the parson repudiates that honored title we do not know.

The vocabulary in the use of country-people is small, their power to grasp ideas very slight, and hence the difficulty in communicating thought. The clergy, who as a class are by no means apt in the pulpit, have their troubles increased on this account. They cannot come down to the rude and narrow colloquial speech of their rustic parishioners. The dissenting preacher, being taken from a lower class and having an inferior education, can. To imagine an Oxford don placed in charge of a remote country parish preaching according to the barbarous dialect of his people is to imagine that which is absurd and unreasonable. An eagle and a crow or a nightingale and a sparrow could as well hold communication. Thus the very scholarship of the English clergy sometimes becomes a hindrance to the Church, though with the spread of education this difficulty will disappear.

The position and the influence of the country clergy are, on the whole, unique in Christendom. Nowhere are they more respected; nowhere are they better provided for. If there is a nicer house set in prettier grounds than any other in the village, that is the rector's. The love which his people will have for him will depend largely upon the manner in which he fulfils his sacred functions. If careless, worldly, unsympathetic or indifferent, they will speak against him without qualification; if, on the other hand, he is faithful and loving, they will yield him an obedience and an affection knowing no restraints. Clergymen differ. We heard one pastor—who probably had had some dispute with his congregation—preach upon the Israelites asking Samuel for a king. It was not wrong, he said, for them to desire a king, since a king was a necessity to every well-constituted nation: "Honor the king" was the apostolic injunction. No; the wrong was committed in their wishing to set aside their good old clergyman, Samuel. The pathos passed into vigor when he concluded, " My friends, never oppose your clergyman." The sermon was prosy and soporific, the season was that of making the hay, and, even if his hearers had the presumption to understand, it is probable that the exhortation fell upon hard hearts. People seldom repent when ministers scold, and a scolding minister indicates an unsatisfactory parish and shortcomings on both sides.

It was our good fortune to have come into contact with one clergyman who brought vividly to mind Chaucer's and Cowper's description of a good pastor. His influence upon his parish and neighborhood was as that of the sun in its quiet, steady round of work. The people loved him; all men admired him. There were in him the gentleness and holiness, the churchliness and poetry, of a George Herbert, and the forty years of his ministry in the one parish had made it as a garden of the Lord. One summer evening we drove to his church and attended service—a plain little church, but at this time filled with worshippers. Before the evensong began a woman was churched at the altar-rails; the office was read distinctly, and the congregation joined in the responses. A choir of girls in white led the people in singing; and lusty singing it was, such as made one's heart glad. In the fields around the church the red-brown wheat rustling in the evening breeze and softly lightened up by the sinking sun made a picture never to be forgotten. After the third collect a young preacher went up into the pulpit and delivered a sermon upon the first verse of the Nunc Dimittis. Before he had finished, the twilight darkened, so that the unlighted church was filled with gloom. After the sermon, in the night-shadows, the aged rector read the Litany most impressively. The twinkling taper at his stall was the only light in the church. Then the people rose and sang the hymn, "Sun of my soul." They knew it by heart and needed no book, while the ever-deepening shadows added emphasis to the line, "It is not night if thou be near."

It is the work of such men as this worthy rector which makes the Church dear to the hearts of the people. We heard something of disestablishment, but always as a remote possibility. Some country-people asked us who would support the clergyman in such an event taking place. "We could not," they added, "and the result would be that we should soon become heathen." As the Church does not receive one penny from

The Village Church.

the State from one year's end to the other, and as she was never established by the State, being, indeed, some centuries older, it is difficult to understand what is meant by disestablishment, unless it be confiscation. Such a robbery is possible, but it is only likely when Socialism has so prevailed as to take away all rights of personal property. The tithes and the endowments are not the gifts of the nation at large, but the bequests of the faithful of past ages. They belong to the individual parish, even as buildings and trusts do in America; if taken away, then schools, colleges, hospitals and all endowed institutions are likewise liable.

Oftentimes in this district of which we are writing the people have real humor—not the wit of the Irish, but the rarer and higher gift of a merry, lightsome disposition. Here and there a delightful stupidity is shown. The story is told of two men disputing over the purchase of pigs. One believed in buying large ones; the other, in buying small ones. The question turned upon the quantity which the latter would eat. It seemed that the one who opposed their purchase had once bought one, intending to fatten it, but, though it ate a bucketful of meal at a time, it would not grow. One morning the man carried out a bucketful of food, and after the little pig had swallowed it all he picked it up and put it into the same bucket, and the little wretch did not fill it half full!

Some years ago a man and his wife belonging to a village close by Shipston resolved to go to America; but when at Liverpool they saw the great sea, the good fellow exclaimed, "Let's go back, Betty, till the flood's gone down." This was the contrary of the impression which was made upon another man when he took his sweetheart to spend a day at the seaside, and arrived just in time for the ebb tide: "Wy, Ann, danged if they bain't a-lettin t' watter off!" One of the sayings in the country is, "If you only wait, you may carry water in a sieve."—"How long?" you ask.—"Till it freezes," is the triumphant reply. Some one told us of a woman who had six children, the eldest only seven years old. She was very careful about the Saturday-night scrub, in accordance with the custom of this neighborhood, and we asked if she put them all in a big tub together. "Oh no," was the reply; "she washes them as she can catch them." The picture of a mother running after her little ones in that fashion struck us as highly amusing.

A talkative old fellow was speaking of his wife in terms of lavish praise. She was the best this and the best that the world had ever known. She had a conscience, was industrious, thrifty and tidy, and, in short, to use his expression, was an uncommonly good woman. Above all, she was ever ready to help her neighbors. As he paused for breath another garrulous individual abruptly injected the observation, possibly to confirm the story of her many virtues, "Yes; and if there is any sore throat around, she is bound to take it."

In old time the dry humor of the people was frequently expressed in the sculptured faces in the churches. In one porch we saw a figure in which the hands were drawn over the stomach and the face had the woebegone expression which follows a nauseous dose of medicine or indicates an active stage of seasickness. As one looked at the grim-cut and blackened countenance it seemed to say, "That's the sort of stuff you get in this place." At Badsey was a home for the sick monks of the abbey of Evesham; the sculptured heads in the church represent men in the pains of illness—toothache, colic, etc. This sort of humor is now expressed in obituary poetry—unconsciously, of course, as in the following lines taken from a stone in a Birmingham graveyard:

> "O cruel death! How could you be so unkind
> As to take him before and leave me behind?
> You should have taken both, if either,
> Which would have been more pleasant to the survivor."

This at Naunton Beauchamp upon a Captain Wambey is too good to be omitted:

> "Here lies, retired from worldly deeds,
> An old officer of the Invalids,
> Who in the army was born and bred,
> But now lies quarter'd with the dead.
> Stripp'd of all his warlike show,
> And laid in box of oak below,
> Confin'd in earth, in narrow borders,
> *He rises not till further orders!*"

CHAPTER IV.

Love in ye Olden Time.

"Say that she frown; I'll say she looks as clear
As morning roses newly washed with dew."

THE title will suggest the nature of the chapter, and they who are not interested in either the "sweet story" or how it was told in these remote districts of England in bygone days may omit the next twenty pages without injury to themselves and without interfering with the thread of the book. But you, gentle reader—and I call you "gentle" the more heartily because you are willing to follow me along—will find herein something that will please your heart even if it does not tell you anything new. How can the first story of Eden be told again with freshness? But who does not like to listen to its undying echoes, and to recall the days, so full of romance and poetry and pretty dreams, when innocence and beauty adorned the present with their gentle grace, and over the future happiness and truth and faith hung like soft clouds of the morning dyed with the splendor and the glory of the rising sun? Then love was trustful, all-absorbing, devoted—pure and passionate, perhaps, as in Juliet; silent and patient, as in Viola; thoughtful, inexperienced and sad, as in Ophelia; mirthful, witty, sprightly, as in Rosalind; refined, exquisite, heavenly, as in

Miranda. Then life had not subdued the soul nor hardened the heart, and the spirit lived as in a fairyland with the pretty elves and happy imps that dance and sing and romp and play in the merry greenwood or amid the woodbine and the roses.

The rural people of England are in no sense poetical and refined: they are of sterner stuff than Italian or French, more practical and matter of fact; yet as we look back upon the customs which once prevailed largely, and in some places still linger more or less, we see much that is as pleasing as the song of gay troubadours or the romance of Southern bards.

There was then the same anxiety and care displayed in the matter of love as now. All sorts of charms were tried, first to ensnare some unwary one of the opposite sex, and then to prove if he or she were true. Lovesick maidens—*i. e.*, maidens who were sick, not with love, but with the lack of it—looked for their lovers in the grounds of their teacups, tied strings nine times round the bedpost for their future lord to untie, sowed hempseed in the back yard that he might mow it, and watched the Midsummer-night out in the church porch that they might catch a glimpse of him. As young ladies nowadays place a piece of their newly-married friend's wedding-cake under their pillow that they may dream of their own future, so two hundred years ago young men used to hang their shoes out of the window and hide daisy-roots under their pillow for the same purpose. A charm which one would hope was not very general was first to boil an egg hard and after taking out the contents fill the shell with salt, and then, on going to bed at night, eat shell and salt without either speaking or drinking after it: a happy vision would reveal the one to be beloved. There was once sold a most efficacious love-powder that could not fail to produce the most desirable affection in any upon whom it was sprinkled. Whether it had the effect that the juice of Oberon's little Western flower had, of making "the man or woman madly dote upon the next live creature that it sees," I do not know. One thing is certain—that by some means or other many a poor laddie's heart was stolen away and in many a sweet maiden's eyes tears hung like beauteous pearls. Beatrice and Benedick may both resolve never to marry, but some day Beatrice will tame her wild heart to his loving hand, and Benedick will exclaim in all the repentance of love, "When I said I would die a bachelor, I did not think I should live till I were married." Should the lover have any desire to know if his lady were true, he could resort to some of the many charms then in vogue among the curious of both sexes. A favorite plan was to take a leaf of yarrow and tickle the inside of the nostril, at the same time repeating these lines:

> "Green 'arrow, green 'arrow, you bear a white blow:
> If my love love me, my nose will bleed now;
> If my love don't love me, it 'ont bleed a drop;
> If my love do love me, 'twill bleed every drop."

And thus love's sweet flower took root in each heart, and all that could be done was done to make it grow. He wore her favors—her glove or scarf or kerchief—in his hat or on his breast, wrote verses in her praise, carved her name on tree or post or fence, sang songs to her in the quiet eventide, conned pretty sayings that should please her ear and touch her heart, fought for her against all rivals and detractors, sent her choice presents—ribbons and laces, sugar and cakes, cloves and cinnamon, perhaps his best and bravest hawk or his own true, trusted greyhound; she talked and dreamed of him; waited, watched and wept for him, wore her prettiest gown and finest headdress, bathed her face in May-dew and scented herself with lavender and musk, prayed that he might be her Valentine and she his dear May-queen, and when he stood before her blushed with a beauty and a loveliness that shamed the roses of the garden, the ruby-tinted morning sky itself.

But suppose all the charms and plots failed to touch the angel of the opposite sex; what then? Well, then, as Sir Roger de Coverley hath it, "there is a good deal to be said on both sides." Some would pine and sorrow; some, look farther afield. Viola would

> "let concealment, like a worm i' the bud,
> Feed on her damask cheek,"

and Ophelia would drown herself in the willow-shaded brook; but Philarete would most likely meditate upon the inevitable after this fashion:

> "Shall I, wasting in despaire,
> Dye, because a woman's fair?
> Or make pale my cheeks with care
> 'Cause another's Rosie are?
>   Be she fairer than the Day
>   Or the flow'ry Meads in May,
>   If she thinke not well of me
>   What care I *how* faire she be?
>
> "Shall my seely heart be pin'd
> 'Cause I see a woman kind?

>   Or a well-disposèd Nature
>   Joynèd with a lovely feature?
>   Be she Meeker, Kinder than
>   *Turtle-dove* or *Pellican*,
>   If she be not so to me,
>   What care I how kind she be?
>
> "Great or Good or Kind or Faire,
> I will ne'er the more despaire:
> If she love me (this beleeve),
> I will Die ere she shall grieve.
>   If she slight me when I woe,
>   I can scorne and let her goe;
>   For if she be not for me,
>   What care I for whom she be?"

The good old ballad is not far from wrong, though the song says:

> "A poore soule sat sighing under a sicamore tree;
>   O willow, willow, willow!
> With his hand on his bosom, his head on his knee;
>   O willow, willow, willow!
>   O willow, willow, willow!
> Sing, O the greene willow shall be my garlànd."

A youth so far gone as that would be likely to have neither the garland of a bachelor at his funeral nor sweet-william and rosemary on his grave, for, on the principle that an overdose of poison defeats its purpose, he would recover. As Rosalind said, "Men have died from time to time, and worms have eaten them, but not for love." Only remember,

> "A man his mynd should never set
> Upon a thing he cannot get."

There is one question always asked concerning lovers:
"What did he see in her?" or "What did she see in
him?" It is, I presume, a natural inquiry, though
slightly touched with a mild spitefulness and envy.
But here, if anywhere, there is no accounting for
tastes. There is such a wide and happy diversity
that, no matter if a world cannot see anything to admire in a youth of either sex, some one individual will
be likely to discover a charm that will lead him or her
captive. It has been asked, "Who ever loved that loved
not at first sight?" and we further ask, "What did Love
see at first sight? What sends the arrow speeding to
its mark?" Perhaps, as far as he is concerned—and I
would not venture to say aught of a woman's inclina-
tions—it may be a dimple in her cheek, a playful
twitching of her lips, a pretty frown upon her forehead, a sparkling glance in her eye. It may be the
color of her eyes—black, brown, blue, green or gray.
In Chaucer's time a gray eye was considered the
height of perfection, Dante knew no prettier than the
green eyes of his Beatrice; and with the latter Cer-
vantes and Cicero both agree. It may be the color of
her hair—anything from the white flaxen to the raven
black. Spenser was evidently partial to yellow hair.
His Florimell, Belphœbe, Alma, Una, Britomart, and
others of his creations, have all hair like the Virgin
Queen herself, of the bright golden hue. Or it may
be her nose—a straight nose or a crooked nose, a wee
little thing or a miniature elephantine model, a pug or
a turn-up or a sharp point. Possibly it is her eyebrows
—arched, full, dark, expressive; or her eyelashes—
long, short, even, tear-bedewed or fringe-like. Perhaps

it is her complexion—white as the pale lily or bright as the red rose; or her hands—fat and plump, or long and lean; or her general carriage—stately and grand or sprightly and gay. Perhaps your wise young man remembers that

"The fairest rose in shortest time decays,"

and so he is attracted by accomplishments rather than by charms. Nobody knows what men may fall in love with. It may be something better than any other qualification whatsoever, a noble, loving, devoted soul—a soul that reveals itself to none but the one it loves, a soul that remains ever constant and faithful, ever gentle and kind, and gives to the body its sweetest grace, its truest life, its most winning charm. Happy is the man who is won by such an attraction as this. It matters little whether his lady-love be as beautiful as Herrick's Sappho, whose pure paleness the white roses tried to outrival and blushed for very failure, or as plain and homely as the plainest and homeliest damsel you can find: she will be true when all else is false, precious when all else is worthless, lovely when all else has lost its charm, and young when all else is old.

There is extant an interesting letter written by an Eton boy in the year 1479 to his brother, describing how he had met at a wedding the younger daughter of a widow, a gentlewoman eighteen or nineteen years old, and how he had fallen desperately in love with her. He wished his brother to go and see her. She would have something when she married, and more at her mother's death; "and," adds he, "as for hyr bewte, juge you that when ye see hyr, yf so be that ye take the laubore, and specialy beolde hyr handys." Like many another schoolboy's love, so earnest and sincere for the time, William Paston's came to nothing.

And this brings us to the famous lines,

> "For aught that ever I could read,
> Could ever hear by tale or history,
> The course of true love never did run smooth."

The proof is to be found in the times when the unmarried possessor or inheritor of wealth was a marketable commodity and was sold very much as a horse or a cow was sold. From the days of William Rufus down to the times of the Commonwealth an heir or an heiress was the ward—I should say the property—of the Crown, and could get married only with the consent of the king and by payment of a heavy fee. Frequently the match was made by the sovereign or the council, and the parties concerned were forced to accept the arrangement and make the best of it. The same practice ran through all society. If not the king or the feudal lord, then the parents or other relatives, decided the question. Thus in those happy ages a maiden's heart was rarely her own to give. If she ventured to love when she should not or failed to love when she should, it was not unusual to lock her up, beat her, starve her, and ill-treat her generally, until her affections were brought into proper subjection. Of a girl of twenty who refused to marry a disfigured widower of fifty we are told in a letter written in the year 1449 to her brother, "She hath since Easter the most part been beaten once in the week or twice, and sometimes twice in one day, and her head broken in two or three places." This was in high life and under her own mother's roof, but the girl was disobedient and plucky, nor did she have the widower. She was an exception to the rule. A dutiful child did not think of falling in love or of selecting a partner in matrimony. The utmost freedom existed between young people of the opposite sexes. Young ladies and young gentlemen kissed each other freely whenever they met, in the streets or in the houses. As Erasmus tells us, "there were kisses when you came, and kisses when you went away—delicate, fragrant kisses that would assuredly tempt a poet from abroad to stay in England all his days." But there was no thought of marriage. That was a thing others would arrange; and if once in a while the rule were broken and the liberty of loving without permission indulged in, then, most assuredly, the course of true love did not run smoothly. As a rule, however, the young people of the Middle Ages had a most excellent control over their affections. They generally loved when told to do so, and generally kept their hearts whole when their friends thought it desirable.

We have an interesting illustration of all this in a Norfolkshire family in the reign of Henry IV. John Paston, a younger and needy brother of a man of considerable position and wealth in that county, was a free, jovial, good-natured fellow with only one thing wanting to complete his happiness—viz., a rich wife. He did not care much about the woman, so that she had money: she was only a necessary inconvenience attached to an estate. The elder brother did his best for him. On John's behalf he wooed every likely spinster and widow he could find. It was nothing to have two or three strings to his bow at the same time. He tried—or, at least, was told by John to try—to get a pretty daughter of a London draper, also a young "thing," as he significantly and business-like calls her, in the same city, and also "some old thrifty draff-wife" in the same city. All these attempts, and others like them, failed, but at last a suitable damsel was found, sweet Margery Brews, a bright, spry girl, who when once she learned that John's heart was touched and that he was negotiating with her mother gave the latter no rest till the affair was satisfactorily settled. She was head over heels in love—wildly, madly in love; but her father was not willing to pay down with her quite so much as John desired, and for a time things looked doubtful. Her mother promised to give the young couple three years' board if they would only marry. "I shall give you," she further says, writing to John, "a greater treasure—that is, a witty gentlewoman, and, if I say it, both good and virtuous; for if I should take money for her, I would not give her for a thousand pounds." And dear Margery herself wrote to him some of the sweetest love-letters any girl could write, in which she begs him not to give her up for the sake of the money. She had him; they were married and lived happily.

Two hundred years later, and we find our old friend Mr. Samuel Pepys doing the same sort of thing. He and Sir John Paston, the elder brother of the John just mentioned, were two of the most energetic and accomplished of matchmakers. Samuel had a sister, Paulina, who was, he says, proud and idle, not over-friendly to his wife, "so cruel an hypocrite that she can cry when she pleases," and so ill-natured that he could not love her. Moreover, he adds, "she grows old and ugly."

Everything that he could do to "dispose of her" he did. He got his wife to speak to a clerk on Miss Pepys's behalf, and he received the advice "with mighty acknowledgements," but "had no intention to alter his condition." A young parson was tried, but in vain. Time rolled by, and no husband for Paulina. At last "a plain young man, handsome enough for Pall, one of no education nor discourse," was found, and for a comfortable consideration he took her; and so, says Pepys, "that work is, I hope, well over." He was engaged in more serious matchmaking than this, but really it was mean of him after going to church one Christmas day to write, "Saw a wedding in the church, which I have not seen for many a day; and the young people so merry one with another! and strange to see what delight we married people have to see these poor fools decoyed into our condition, every man and woman gazing and smiling at them."

Not always did such matches turn out well. There was in the year 1294 in a little Norfolk village a widow named Sara Felix. Her husband had left her considerable property and three daughters, the eldest of whom was not more than eight or nine years old when her father died. This daughter, whose name was Alice, we may imagine was, from the fact of her mother's wealth, if not for her own beauty, a lovable object in the eyes of young men far and near. At any rate, when she was about fifteen, she was wooed and won by an eligible youth named John of Thyrsford. In all probability, I should say, her mother was wooed and her fortune was won, the girl being thrown in as an unimportant, though necessary, part of the matrimonial bargain. I fancy there was very little of the sunshine and poetry that lovers nowadays contrive to get into their courtship. The marriage was an unhappy one. John had not been married more than a year or two when he began to devise means to regain his freedom.

Divorces were difficult to obtain in those days, and, except by payment of heavy costs, there was but one way by which it was possible to get one. This one way was both easy and cheap, and that way John tried. Could a man but get a bishop to admit him to orders —the minor orders would do—he became at once, if a serf, free from villeinage; if a husband, free from matrimony. Clerics could not be slaves either to a lord or to a wife: they were sons of liberty. So John got ordained, and thus got divorced from poor little Alice. The worst of it was that the girl could not marry again, and, as she had no child, she was doomed to a lonely life.

Easy would it be to draw a sketch of the child-wife in her deserted youth. We might picture her sighing and sobbing in the eventide, weeping under the lonely willows, ministering to loving cats and tricksy dogs. We might picture her wearing the weeds of widowhood, singing mournful ditties as she picked apples in the orchard or turnips in the field, going to church twice a day by way of desperation and attending executions and ordeals by way of amusement. But such pictures would be purely imaginary. We are not told whether the roses faded in her cheeks or the lustre died in her eyes; in fact, though we may reasonably suppose she had cheeks and eyes, we have no evidence that she had either roses or lustre. We do not know if she lamented her loss to her friends, if she learned to hate mankind in general or John of Thyrsford in particular: these are points fancy, and not history, can deal with. Perhaps she was as glad to get rid of him as he was to get rid of her: the wedding had turned out badly. Any way, she managed to live on as the lady of the village for nearly fifty years after her divorce. Her husband became vicar of the same village—perhaps the divorce did not mean so much, after all, though the story is provokingly silent on that point—and vicar he remained for some forty years. He died ten years before Alice. When old age came upon her, and the tresses of youth were gray, if not gone, and the dimples of maidenhood had changed into the wrinkles of senility, she gave up her property, went into a nunnery, and there died.

This is the true and faithful history of Alice the wife of John of Thyrsford and the daughter of Thomas the Lucky of Rougham, and they who wish to verify it can go to the writings of an erudite divine of Norwich, Dr. Jessop by name.

It is pleasing to know that there were other motives than those we have mentioned—happy exceptions to the rule—which moved parents to give their daughters in marriage. About the year 1559, Sir William Hewet, the lord mayor, lived on London Bridge, and one day, when the nurse was playing with his little daughter Anne at one of the broad lattice-windows overlooking the Thames, the child fell into the water. A young apprentice named Osborne, seeing the accident, leaped into the fierce current below the arches and saved the infant. The story is told and an illustration of the leap given in Cassell's *Old and New London*. "Years after, many great courtiers, including the earl of Shrewsbury, came courting fair Mistress Anne, the rich citizen's heiress. Sir William, her father, said to one and all, 'No; Osborne saved her, and Osborne shall have her.' And so Osborne did, and became a rich citizen, and lord mayor in 1583."

Assuming that the friends and the law were satisfied, and that the affection of the parties most concerned was as warm and true as it should be, the thing had to be made public and an open betrothal to be performed. It was from the friends and acquaintances the awkwardness would chiefly arise. The would-be bridegroom, and the would-be bride scarcely less so, would have to endure many a queer joke, coarse jest and broad laugh—good-natured enough, no doubt, but none the less hard to suffer. They would be watched in church and in the street, mimicked and rhymed, asked all sorts of awkward questions and played all sorts of tricks, serenaded, toasted, gossiped over, sneered at, praised, disparaged, encouraged, caricatured, till life would not have been worth living had it not had love to sustain it. But, like all other nine-day wonders, this would die out and the match come to be looked upon as a matter of fact.

And some evening there would be a grand party at the house of the maiden's father. All the relatives and friends far and near, including his reverence the parson and his scarcely less reverence the clerk, would be invited to witness the betrothal or engagement of Corydon and Philida. Fresh green rushes would be strewn over the floor, the tables and settees scrubbed clean and white, the candlesticks, snuffers, flagons, tankards and cups polished to look as bright as new, and the larder filled with good things—perhaps a piece of fresh beef, a rare article in olden time, perhaps a choice turkey, goose or fowl from the barnyard. In the cellar would be a bountiful supply of strong, heady ale and mead—maybe a cask or two of good wine from beyond the seas or home made—and the best minstrel or fiddler in the neighborhood would be engaged for the occasion. What a free, happy, boisterous time! The old house would ring with the merry song and the loud chorus. A silver—perhaps a gold—coin would be broken in two between the lovers; they would kiss each other, join hands and exchange rings, and vow to keep the faith now given. And the great silver cup was filled with the frothy, foaming ale and emptied by each guest to the honor and health of the young couple, and the men kissed the pretty, blushing girl and the women kissed the awkward, gawkish and supremely happy lad, and the fiddler exercised his art, and up the hall and down the hall the gay, light-hearted folks danced as we can never dance and shouted as we can never shout. Oh, they were merry!

Even the aged people forgot themselves. The old grandfather laughed and sang till the tears ran down his withered cheeks, and the ancient dame his wife rested not till she had had her hop and jump—it could scarcely be called a dance, for she used crutches and was nearly double—with the brightest and liveliest of the crowd. Away they go!

"If music be the food of love, play on!"

Hither and thither, in and out, off and back again, till, exhausted, they sit down around the festive board.

There are, of course, love-letters—private, confidential,

eloquent. Many have survived the wasting of time; of which, take the following, written by the pretty Margery already mentioned to her lover, John Paston. It is dated February, 1477, and, while illustrating the universal spirit of such effusions, will by reprinting do no possible harm to people who have so long passed away:

"*Unto my ryght welebelovyd Voluntyn, John Paston, Squyer, be this bill delyvered, etc.*

"Ryght reverent and wurschypfull, and my ryght welebeloved Voluntyne, I recomande me unto yowe, ffull hertely desyring to here of yowr welefare, whech I beseche Almyghty God long for to preserve un to Hys plesur, and yowr herts desyre. And yf it please yowe to here of my welefar, I am not in good heele of body, nor of herte, nor schall be tyll I her ffrom yowe;

> For there wottys no creature what peyn that I endure,
> And for to be deede, I dare it not dyscure.

And my lady my moder hath labored the mater to my ffader full delygently, but sche can no mor gete then ye knowe of, for the whech God knowyth I am full sory. But yf that ye loffe me, as I tryste verely that ye do, ye will not leffe me therefor; for if that ye hade not halfe the lyvelode that ye hafe, for to do the grettest labur that any woman on lyve myght, I wold not forsake yowe.

> And yf ye commande me to kepe me true wherever I go,
> I wyse I will do all my myght yowe to love and never no mo,
> And yf my freends say, that I do amys,
>   Thei schal not me let so for to do,

> Myne herte me bydds ever more to love yowe
> Truly over all erthely thing,
> And yf thei be never so wroth,
> I tryst it schall be better in tyme commyng.

"No more to yowe at this tyme, but the Holy Trinitie hafe yowe in kepyng. And I besech yowe that this bill be not seyn of none erthely creatur safe only your selffe, etc.

"And thys letter was indyte at Topcroft, with full hevy herte, etc.,

"By your own,

"MARGERY BREWS."

Poor Margery! and when her lover's elder brother, Sir John, had "consyderyd hyr persone, hyr yowthe, and the stok that she is comyn offe, the love on bothe sydes, the tendre ffavor that she is in with hyr ffader and mooder, the kyndenesse off hyr ffadr and moodr to hyr in departyng with hyr, the ffavor also, and goode concéyte that they have in my brother, the worshypfull and vertuous dysposicion off hyr ffadr and moodr, whyche pronostikyth that, of lyklihod, the mayde sholde be vertuous and goode," he was agreeable to the match!

Here is another, of the seventeenth century, the original of which is in the British Museum:

"Deare Hearte, I am heartilie sorry that some occasions have hindered me from coming to see you all this while; I desire you to impute my absence not to want of love, but of leisure; and I beseech you to bee assured that there lives not a more constant, faithfull, and affectionate lover uppon the face of the whole earth than I am, of your most worthie SELFE, whose

VERTUE & BEAVTY is such that I haue ueric good cause to belejue there lives not a second to be parallell'd wth you. I haue here sent you a small token, whch I desire you to accept of; I haue allso sent you a copy of uerses made by him who is the admirer & adorer of your divjne beautje; HENRJE OXJNDEN. Barham: Feb: 26: 1641. *An*^{o} *Œtat: tuæ*, 17."

What becomes of these interesting epistles? That is more than we can say. They are written in abundance —thousands, I suppose, every day—but they are scarce as roses in Greenland. Perhaps they are burnt as soon as read—or, at least, as soon as the affair of which they treat is happily terminated. And yet, when a breach-of-promise case comes before the court, there are the letters! One young lady who collected hers made a pillow of them. She slept on that sweet bundle till one day, about four months after her wedding, she had a difference with her husband, and the pillow found its way into the fire. Another lady had hers bound in a volume, and every morning after she had read her chapter in the Bible she read one of the letters and then said her prayers. She maintained that it was her duty to keep alive the remembrances of the past and to nourish the sacred emotion. A third had hers reduced to a pulp and then made up into an antique Japanese casket for jewelry. These, however, are only a few among the myriads; where do the rest go?

Love-letters are sweet and pleasant, but the happy hours the young folks spend together are still sweeter and pleasanter. To see young Colin getting ready to go and court his lassie was a sight that would tickle and please any heart. His mother says he was never so clean and tidy and exact before in his life. There must not be a speck of dust or dirt on his clothes; his shoes must shine like a looking-glass and his handkerchief be redolent with bergamot. His sister Mary brushes him, and pins in his coat the best carnation and rosebud she can find in the garden, and sends him off with a good sisterly kiss and with kindred feelings; for she expects Tim, old Farmer Berry's son, that very evening. And Colin trudges across the fields and through the shaded lane whistling as happily and loudly as any bird in the world. He begins to think himself somebody: he intends to join the militia or the rifle volunteers—or, as they would call it many years since, the train-band; and oh how glad he will be when Lucy is his wife! As he goes by he looks in at the little cottage which his father intends to give him as the first home for his bride, and thoughts of the future fill him with joy. And when he reaches Lucy's house, how pleased she is to see him! Her eyes sparkle with delight, and no kiss was ever so sweet as that which she shyly and modestly gives him. And when she gets her hat and they go off for an hour's ramble down to the meadow or through the woods or by the side of the brook, he thinks never was girl so dear as she, and she thinks him to be the only one worth having among all the swains of the country-side. Happy dreams! Life is full of flowers and sunshine. The world is nothing to them: they are each other's world; and without a thought other than that of supremest joy they pluck the violets, the oxslips and the sweet-brier, and sing their merry lays with glad, free hearts and trilling voices, and talk of the days and the blessings that shall be

"HER EYES SPARKLE WITH DELIGHT."

theirs in the not-far-distant by and by. When they get home, they find that mother has got the tea ready; the kettle is singing on the hob, and on the table, covered with a snow-white cloth, are new-made bread, fresh butter, clotted cream and bright-green watercresses. The blackbird in the wicker cage pours forth his best and richest melody; even the cat purrs and hums as if her heart also were full of love and joy. And the old gentleman comes in and gives Colin a hearty welcome, for Colin is a good boy and already owns three cows and a dozen sheep, and is about as likely a fellow as Lucy could get. They are all happy now together. Mother pours out the tea, but Lucy puts in the sugar; and Colin is sure he never drank such tea in his life before. His appetite is not very good, and he blushes scarlet when his future father-in-law slyly asks, "Eh, Colin my lad, has thee no fancy for a bit of Lucy's home-made bread?" And the poor fellow gulps it down because she made it. There are shrimps and onions, and Colin and Lucy are both fond of them, but neither touches them. "Don't be afraid," says the tormenting father; "they won't hurt you."—" Help yourselves," says mother; "if both take some, it will be all the same." And Lucy consents and Colin agrees, and shrimps and onions begin to depart. The conversation runs along, now about the weather, now the crops, now Mary Lemon's lame cow, now about old Crumleigh's wonderful litter of pigs. "Never heard of such a thing before in my life," says Lucy's father, and Colin says he doesn't think he has, either. Then the talk turns to making butter, rearing ducks, snubbing the parson, the jockey-races, the new steward, the comet, the turkey-gobbler, the host putting in the refrain every now and then, "Shrimps and onions are nice, eh, Colin? Thought you would like them, and what's the difference, as mother says, when you both have them?" And by and by the old folks leave the lovers alone—the good souls remember the days when they were young—and another sweet hour passes away nobody knows how fast. Colin cannot believe it is time for him to go home, and Lucy wishes he was not obliged to go. The old folks wonder what they have had to talk about for so long, but, dear hearts! there is no subject so suggestive as love, and lovers could talk and talk till morning and never get tired. But they part at last; a few warm kisses, a fond embrace, and Colin is on his way home, and Lucy is helping her mother clear up the house or is putting her best gown and scarf away in the lavender-scented clothes-press till next Sunday or to the next time Colin comes. This is a sketch that will apply to any age with but little alteration, from the days long since forgotten to the present year of grace. The happiness is beyond expression; the innocence, purity and love are as perfect as in the Eden of old or in the Paradise above.

Not always, however, are things so smooth and pleasant as this. Sometimes there are misunderstandings and quarrellings. This to the point: Strephon and Celia were lovers. He was gentle and good; she was lovely as the morning star set in the dark sky. Nothing had ever arisen to mar the sweetness or to disturb the joy of their love. All who knew them said they were born for each other. If he saw a pout upon her lips, he kissed it away; if she saw a frown upon his brow, she looked upon him with her bright, sunny eyes till the cloud faded into a smile. But one day the quarrel came. It was over a trifle not worth speaking of, but the words that followed were sharp as lightning and the looks dark as the thunder-clouds. And bitter thoughts ran through their hearts—thoughts that threatened death to their love and woe to their future. Never would he speak to her again; nevermore would she look him in the face. They parted for ever. She stood on the sedgy bank of the brook in the dying sunlight. Not a breath of wind ruffled the water or stirred the rushes or the willows. The lilies in the stream were folding up their white flowers for the night, and here and there a lone bird was seeking its nest. He had left her; why should she live longer? Perhaps if she drowned herself in that silent river he would shed a tear upon her grave, perhaps plant a flower at her feet. They said that brook ran like a watery way to the sea: perhaps she might make it a path to a better and truer world. Anyway, life was not worth having without Strephon, and better die now than live with a broken heart. Hush, sad thought! The sun has gone to rest and the night-wind begins its weird moaning among the willows. There is the hooting of the owl, and from afar comes the voice of howling dog. The stream flows on its dismal course, murmuring as though it sang a death-song. Oh night of gloom! Oh thought of woe! Hush! what a shriek and plunge! And all is still save the moaning wind and the sobbing water. It was only the cry of the nighthawk and the splash of a great fish. Celia is on her way home, and to-morrow morning she will take from Strephon's hand a bunch of sweet violets and give him a kiss far more sweet and fragrant than they. Such are the storms that try love's happy life.

It is, I suppose, when reviewing all the changes and chances of sweethearting and the fortunes and accidents of matrimony that some men make up their minds never to marry. Whether they deserve praise or pity is a question not easily answered. Probably a bachelor desires neither, but the world is ever disposed to be generous in its commendation or its sympathy to those who have been fortunate or unfortunate enough to remain in single life. On the whole, the world, if forced to judge, is rather censorious than otherwise. It thinks that it is not good for man to live alone, but seeing that every man was a bachelor once, and would have remained one had he not married, it is well he should hesitate in expressing an opinion either way. But when legislation utters its voice, it is generally against the bachelor. Perhaps this is so because governing bodies are nearly always composed of married men. None other could sit in the Jewish Sanhedrin or in the Roman Senate or in the councils of Athens and Sparta. The ancients had no mercy on them. During the winter, in Sparta, they were compelled to march round the market-place singing a song composed against themselves and expressing the justice of their punishment. In Rome heavy taxes were laid upon them, and in England they were once obliged to pay a fine for their privilege. Even in the present day every remark made concerning bachelordom is not complimentary. There is a conception in the popular mind that a bachelor is the personification of a great deal that is not desirable. He is supposed to be mean, cross, grumpy, unattractive, ugly in soul if not in body, selfish, affectionless, quarrelsome, irreligious, conceited, irreconcilable, without either wit or humor and with more than his rightful share of human wickedness. The marriage service reminds him that matrimony is honorable among all men, and therefore his state is the reverse. How in the name of all that is lovable he became confirmed in his singularity no one knows. Various answers will be given—some sagacious, some spiteful, some safe, some sympathetic, some sarcastic, some satirical, and none, perhaps, true. His example, at any rate, is bad; for suppose Adam had declined Eve, what would have happened? The women look shyly upon one who has so persistently resisted the charms of their sex, and the Benedicts, being themselves in the freedom or the bondage, whichever way you take it, of wedlock, think of him as one who has evaded his duty. And he thinks it is hard a man cannot please himself in a matter of this kind. Who has any business to dictate to him what he shall do? Who has a right to reproach him for having been luckier than the most of men? If flies choose to run into spiders' webs, and fish to seize the baited hook, and men to put their heads into a noose, is he obliged to do the same? And as to women, adds he, it all depends how you look at them. Painters and poets see all the perfections, but the reality and the imagination do not always agree.

Alack, poor bachelor!

One loves to dream of the merry maidens one has known. Beneath the greenwood tree in such a sylvan nook as that in which the mischievous and witty Rosalind cured her Orlando of his sickness, or in the quiet of such a moonlight eventide as that in which Lorenzo and sweet Jessica told anew their love, or in a rural spot where flowers in all their sweetness and their grace abound, like unto that in which the pretty Perdita and the noble Florizel found their souls knit in one, or beside a stream like that in which the love-deceived Ophelia drowned herself,—these are the scenes of fancy's revels, the scenes where memory and imagination walk hand in hand together. In the early morning, when the dawn with rosy fingers unbars the gates of light; or, better still, in the evening, when Venus blushingly lays herself down upon her bed of glory in the west, so softly white, so sweetly tinted; or in the stilly night, when upon the mountains, with their pinnacles of snowy splendor and depths of sombre gloom, falls the stars' soft light,—comes the happy dream-time when mind and heart are one. Wandering and dreaming through the woodland groves, one can see the milk-white palfrey of fair Florimell breaking through the thick brush, the golden hair of the beautiful maiden flowing in long streams as she seeks to escape from the false Archimago. On she speeds till lost to sight in the winding lanes of the forest, and ere long comes that true knight Prince Arthur to save the maid of his friend Marinell. And fancy follows her to the cottage built of sticks and reeds in a gloomy glen where she hoped to receive shelter and found witchcraft. Fear gave her strength and speed, and soon we see her tossed on ocean-wave, ere long to fall into the deep dungeon of the sea-monster Proteus. Never was grief so terrible as that of Cymoent over the body of Marinell or of Satyrane over the loss of Florimell. But in that fairyland strange things are brought about: Marinell is restored to life, Florimell is rescued from her watery prison, and in the fair sunshine their faith is rewarded and they are given to each other. As in the dreamy drama this chaste and lovely lady fades into the fleeting moments' mists others no less beautiful and fair appear. There are the twin daughters of Chrysogone, the brave Belphœbe and the sweet Amoretta, and, like stars of early eve, Britomart, Columbell, Hellenore, Alma and Una. There is Sabrina, who, fleeing from her angry step-dame, Gwendolen, plunged into the Severn flood, where the water-nymphs bore her to the aged Nereus's hall. Here was she made goddess of the river, and now the shepherds sing of her maiden gentleness, tell how she visits the herds in the twilight meadows, and as a votive offering to her throw their garland wreaths of pansies, pinks and gaudy daffodils into the stream. And who can forget Herrick's Julia, with her dainty cherry lips and silken drapery; or Keats's Madeline as in the wintry moonlight, pure and free, she prays for Heaven's grace; or Coleridge's Christabel as she rescues the high-born Geraldine; or Fielding's Sophia, the spirit of truth in an atmosphere of ill; or Boccaccio's Griselda, so constant in her love and obedient in her life; or Scott's Lucy Ashton, the beautiful and ill-fated bride of Lammermoor? These are among the maids and matrons one has known. They flit like fairies before the mind. They are as real as though they were true flesh and blood. And one wonders which of them all one loves the best. We like Jessica, the sweet Christian pagan, better than the intellectual and yellow-haired Portia; we like Juliet, the passionate, whole-souled girl of the South, better than Isabella, Helena or Beatrice, though we prefer Perdita and Miranda to the romantic bride of Romeo. Viola appears as queen of queens. Florimell is the first of Spenser's creations, but we do not like her half so much as sweet Anne Page or the tender, steadfast Imogen or the pure Marina—perhaps because they have a more distinct personality. As to those of less position, we are not sure whether we like Agnes Wickfield better than Sophia Western, or Lorna Doone better than either. Lydia Languish, Emilia Gauntlet, Lydia Melford, Narcissa Topehall and Fanny Andrews are very well in their way, but their way is a long way from the fair dames who live in Shakespeare's pages. Molière has nothing for us; his Lucille, Dorimene, Lucinde, Mélicerte and Daphne are not to be thought of with, say, Ben Jonson's Charis, Lodge's Rosalynd or Chaucer's Dorigen. As we cease our dreaming there comes upon the scene an endless procession of merry maidens whom we have known— the fair Emmeline, free Dowsabell, Maid Marion, peerless Rosamond, Bessee of Bednall-Green, and the Nut-brown Maid, whose praises abide in minstrel's song; but we turn away and ask, " How can a man remain a bachelor in the presence of such beauty?"

Alack, poor bachelor!

And now I haste to the end of the subject—to the day and the ceremony that concluded and crowned the vision of love in the olden time. In spite of the fact that there are old bachelors and old maids, it is said that married life is the mystery into which all who are not in seek to enter and all who are in seek to leave. This, if true, proves not only the desirability and the painfulness of matrimony, but also the weakness of human nature; for neither advice nor experience avails in the matter. St.

Jerome mentions a widow that married her twenty-second husband, who in his turn had been married to twenty wives; a gentleman died at Bordeaux in 1772 who had been married sixteen times; so that the wise saw, "A burnt child dreads the fire," does not apply to matrimony. Nor should it, according to our doctrine and to the consensus of mankind.

June was the favorite month for weddings, and Sunday the favorite day; May and Friday were ever thought unlucky. The old Jews, as a rule, married maidens on a Wednesday and widows on a Thursday. A bright, clear morning was deemed propitious, for happy is the bride that the sun shines on. The church-bells rang their merry peals and the whole village prepared to keep holiday, for such an event occurred only once in a while. Long before the sun arose the preparations were going on. The girls were off to the woods and the meadows at daybreak to gather flowers and rushes to strew in the pathway of the bridal-party, and while the older people were getting the house ready for the feast the young men were preparing for the sports and the pastimes on the village green. The bride was arrayed in her gay garments—generally white, in token of purity—and upon her head was placed a garland of flowers as a sign of her queenly station. Our garland consists of orange-blossoms, but in the olden time it was made of myrtle or roses or wheat-ears. In some lands it was even made of prickles, to signify to the husband that he had tied himself to a thorny pleasure. Everybody had posies of maiden-blushes, primroses, violets, pansies, rosemary or bay. Sometimes festoons and arches of evergreen were made, in which laurel, denoting triumph, was conspicuous. The bridegroom was taken to the church porch by the bridesmaids, and the bride by the groomsmen. The ceremony did not take place in the church, but at the door, till after the Reformation. There the happy couple stood before the village parson, and there the plighted troth was redeemed and the sentence spoken that made them man and wife—in words that have been used in the Church of England for more than a thousand years. Oh how wildly, cheerily, gladly, the bells pealed out in the church-tower! And the minstrels played, and the neighbors cheered, and showers of roses or of wheat were poured upon the bridal pair, just as we cast rice, in token of prosperity. All were happy. The bride looked upon her wedding-ring, made of pure gold, to tell her that her lord's love was pure and true and endless as the ring was endless. Friends told her that as the ring wore out so her cares would wear away: I am not sure they told the truth. She gave her favors—gloves, ribbons, scarfs and garters—to the young men and maidens. She cut the wedding-cake—an institution of unknown antiquity—and the maid that was lucky enough to receive the first piece would be the next bride. The bridal ale was drunk, and in the afternoon there were dancing and sporting till evensong. If there were an elder unmarried sister, she would have to dance barefooted lest she should die an old maid; the others all danced and played in green stockings. There were fun and merry-making—perhaps more and of another character than we should approve of, but our forefathers were blunt, plain folk overflowing with good-humor and animal spirits. When the bridegroom blundered and blushed, as bridegrooms sometimes will, they cheered and laughed with a freedom and a heartiness that to him must have been anything but pleasant. The bride was encouraged in like manner till she was as red as a rose and glad to hide her face under the care-cloth.

Ah, well! this was the end of romance, and now began real life. Shall I say that in that life there were charms and graces that the romance knew nothing of? Yes, indeed; for, beautiful as it is to see a lad and a lassie love as only lads and lassies can love, there is a more beautiful picture still—to behold an aged couple who have lived and loved through long years, whose love has withstood the test of time and been purified and made more precious in the fires of life's trials. They see in their own children the return of days long, long gone by; and when they close their eyes upon this world, it is to enter into the renewed and eternal love and life of a brighter and a better world.

And here we leave " Love in ye Olden Time," and in doing so I can only say of every newly-wedded pair,

> May life to them be like a summer river
>   Where laughing ripples kissed by sunbeams dance,
> And reeds and rushes moved by soft winds quiver,
>   Till Nature falls into a dreamy trance!
>
> May life to them be like the clouds of even
>   Lighted with all the splendor of the setting sun,
> When o'er the earth there comes the peace of heaven—
>   The blessed rest that crowns a work well done!
>
> May life to them be like a song of glory
>   Such as the joyous lark sings at heaven's gate,
> Or victors tell in their glad thrilling story
>   Of triumphs won upon the fields of fate!

And when that life shall reach the deep sea's flowing,
    And earth's bright day shall make its shadows long,
May they rejoice in love's warm, earnest glowing,
    While murmuring wavelets chant the evensong.

CHAPTER V.

At Oxford.

"He that hath Oxford seen, for beauty, grace,
And healthiness, ne'er saw a better place."

To Oxford!

Train from Moreton-in-the-Marsh at eleven in the forenoon; seven miles from Shipston to the railway-station.

Shall we walk or drive?

Who could resist the temptation of walking in the gentle morning through a country pleasant to the eye, and with one who knew and loved every step of the way and was both lively in conversation and keen in observation? So, passing up the Swan lane, we began our early journey. A lovely day, the sun veiled now and then with fleecy clouds, birds singing in the hedges and trees by the wayside, the grass by the road fresh and springy to the tread, and everything such as to make the heart beat with delight and the mind dwell upon pleasant reminiscences and mirthful suggestions.

The road runs about three miles till it crosses the famous Fossway, the great Roman street already spoken of in these pages. The traveller to Moreton turns by the Porto Bello and walks where the imperial legions once rode. A little distance on is an inn, the Golden

Cross, down in a hollow by the old tramway-track from Moreton to Stratford. Once it was a busy place; now the sign is undecipherable and an ass eats the weeds which grow about the front door. The steep bit of hill leading down by it is somewhat awkward for drivers of heavy wagons; even lighter vehicles have to be guided carefully. In Egyptian darkness a trap laden with three happy-hearted fellows was once dragging its way up. They were laughing and joking, when suddenly one of them cried out, "Where is the horse?" Some part of the harness had broken, and the horse was quietly walking out of the shafts; another step, and the riders would have been thrown out, and perhaps killed. It is a place where necks have been broken. There is, indeed, an uncanny suspicion that some who have died there come back again; any way, most people who go by, especially in the evening, find it necessary to refresh their spirits at the Golden Cross. Another high hill lies before them, on the right side of which is the village of Stretton. Pluck a handful of wild flowers by the way and watch the honey-bee settling on them utterly regardless of your presence. In the little brook crossing the road have been found trout; indeed, in days gone by boys used to tickle them there. The operation is simple. Watch a fish lying in the mingling light and shade near the bank or under the bridge; lie down noiselessly on the earth and slip the bared arm into the water under the fish; tickle him: he seems to enjoy the operation, and gradually rises to the surface; then, when near enough, strike the hand hard and fling him out on the bank. Neither Dame Juliana Berners nor Izaak Walton has anything to say upon this pastime; notwithstanding, the trout is "a right deyntous fyssh," and tickling is second only to angling.

But we must move on.

This is Moreton-in-the-Marsh—a small town consisting of one wide street half a mile long and containing a church, a manufactory and a railway-station. We may not tarry; here comes the train.

Away across the quiet Oxfordshire country; pleasant, if not romantic. Once we catch a glimpse of Blenheim, the seat of the duke of Marlborough. We have been there. The grounds are exquisite, gardens and park perfect; the house is heavy and ugly. Close by is Woodstock, the town of cheerful memories, where kings dwelt and once Fair Rosamond was concealed in a maze. Here Henry III. was nearly murdered by a false priest; the wretch was caught, and torn to pieces by wild horses. Here Edward the Black Prince was born and the princess Elizabeth imprisoned by her sister Mary. The Puritans were troubled by the tricks of the "merrie devil," who turned out to have more of earth about him than ghosts generally have. Not one stone of the royal palace now remains; only the name and the memories abide. Chaucer would not know his old home were he to go back again; Alfred the Great and Henry II. would be lost.

The words of Camden concerning Oxford have the same force and truth now as they had when written in the reign of James I.: "A delicate and most beautiful city, whether we respect the neatness of private buildings, or the stateliness of publick structures, or the healthy and pleasant situation. For the plain on which it stands is walled in, as it were, with hills of wood, which, keeping out on one side the pestilential south wind, on the other the tempestuous west, admit only the purifying east, and the north, that disperses all unwholsome vapors."

The city and the university are of considerable antiquity, but both have been shorn of much of their reputed age. Tradition says that the city was founded about a thousand years before the birth of Christ by Memphric, king of the ancient Britons, and was named Caer-Memphric. Other legends connect it with Brute the Trojan and the Druids, but these stories are utterly without foundation. In like manner the university has been ascribed to Alfred the Great, and some have claimed that the place was a seat of learning in pre-Roman times; these stories are also inventions.

It was in or before the ninth century that a religious house was established some few miles from the then ancient Dorchester, the see-town of the great Mercian diocese, near to the shallow channels close by the confluence of the Cherwell and the Isis. The house was dedicated to St. Frideswyde, and around it grew a village. A school for youth also sprang up in connection with the priory. In the latter part of the ninth century it is probable a mint was established there, for coins have been discovered of that date with the legend "Oksnaforda." The earliest undoubted mention of the town is in the English Chronicle, under the year 912. From that time Oxford speedily rises in importance. The kings were frequent visitors; Edward the Elder died there in 924 and Edmund Ironsides in 1017, which gave rise to the idea that it was an ill thing for a king to enter Oxford. The place was besieged and burnt by the Danes in 1010, and in 1013 submitted to Sweyn. Here, in 1018, the great Canute held a Witanagemot in which the laws of Edgar were adopted, and in 1036 here Harold I. was crowned. During the reign of Edward the Confessor the town continued to flourish, and in 1067 made a bold, though unsuccessful, resistance to William the Conquerer. When taken by him, he gave it to Robert d'Oily, who about 1071 built a castle. In 1086 the town contained seven hundred and twenty-one houses, of which four hundred and seventy-eight had been so damaged by the siege nineteen years earlier as to be untaxable, and of the mansions one hundred and ninety-two were habitable and one hundred and six waste. The population was then about seventeen hundred. But under the strong government of D'Oily the place recovered itself, and from that time on occupied a high position in the history of England. The seat of the Mercian bishopric had long since been removed to Lincoln, and it was not till the Reformation that the diocese of Oxford was founded. Of the part the city took in the great struggles of the reigns of Stephen and Charles I. it is unnecessary to speak. Loyalty and conservatism have ever been the distinguishing features of Oxford.

It is probable that the school connected with St. Frideswyde's house continued and increased. It was, like all monastic schools, simple in its aim and small in its scope. The scholars were largely boys. However, it is not till the reign of Henry I. that we have certain information of the existence and popularity of the schools at Oxford. Why teachers and scholars gathered there we do not know, nor does the community come into prominence before the reign of John. In 1238 the schools are spoken of as the University of Oxford, though it is not known that there was any charter of incorporation. Up to 1268 the university had no buildings of its own; then the colleges began to come into being, and Oxford was recognized as the second university of Christendom. Indeed, the time came when it outshone its rival of Paris.

Notwithstanding the comparatively recent origin of the city and the university, one of their first attractions is that of age. There is that subtile charm in the very atmosphere which only a noble history and a delightful romance can give. One becomes conscious that this place is the glory of England, enwoven in all that is great and soul-quickening in her life, the home and source of her intellectual and social power, the shrine of exalted and excellent scholarship, and the abode of that beneficent spirit which, while ever pressing onward into the new, lovingly and gently cherishes and seeks to preserve all that is good and true in the old.

A pity it is that the visitor enters the city by the railway, for, though the Great Western station stands on the site of the ancient abbey of Osney, neither it nor the way into the town has any attraction. On the contrary, an unfavorable impression is apt to be made, and, instead of a quiet, studious-looking place, one is disappointed with the bustle and noise of a modern one. Drive along the Cowley road and over Magdalen bridge, and nothing can exceed the satisfaction which Oxford can give. Stand on the old bridge, quaint with its balusters, and look upon the still, shaded waters of the Cherwell—a narrow stream peaceful beneath the summer sunshine, its smooth surface gently rippled by a punt or boat occasionally passing up or down, and its onward flow suggesting its course from the hills of Warwickshire to the royal river, by ancient Banbury and the Confessor's birthplace, Islip, into Oxford itself. The building on the right side of the street is Magdalen College, the first of many noble structures, and the most beautiful of them all. It was built by Bishop Waynflete of Winchester about 1480, the society having been formally chartered by him some years earlier, and was dedicated as " Seinte Marie Maugdalene College to the honor and praise of Christ crucified, the Blessed Virgin his Mother, St. Mary Maugdalene and the various apostles and martyrs, the chief of whom are patrons of the cathedral of Winchester." Among its scholars have been many bishops and statesmen, not the least of whom was the great Wolsey. Its position in the university is supported by its renown and its wealth—an annual income from endowments of over forty-one thousand pounds and the presentation to forty-two benefices. Its most distinguishing architectural feature is the stately tower. Here on the morning of Mayday an ancient and pleasing ceremony is performed. On the summit of the tower assemble singers in surplices and members of the university. " As the last stroke of five dies upon the breeze all heads are reverently uncovered, and the singers, amid deep silence, pour forth the solemn old Latin hymn in honor of the Holy Trinity, 'Te Deum patrem colimus;'" after which, the pealing bells welcome in the spring.

It is not possible in the few pages which can be given to Oxford to mention, much less speak of, its many stately buildings, its halls, colleges and churches and their many historical and architectural features. There is not a corner in the older part of the city which is not full of interest. Beyond Magdalen, High street opens in all its dignity and beauty. On the right in rapid succession come St. Edmund's Hall, Queen's College, All Souls' College, St. Mary's church and All Saints' church, while at the back of these, like choice jewels hid away in careful seclusion, are such places as New College, Hartford College, the Radcliffe and Bodleian Libraries, the theatre, Brasenose, Lincoln, Jesus and Exeter Colleges. The other side of High street has the schools, University College and St. Mary's Hall, with Merton, Corpus Christi and Oriel Colleges beyond. High street is crossed at right angles with Cornmarket and St. Aldate's streets, St. Martin's church standing at the intersection. Some distance to the north from this cross, known as Carfax, are Baliol, Trinity and St. John's Colleges, the street widening out into the noble tree-lined thoroughfare of St. Giles. Hereabouts is the "Martyrs' Memorial," a Gothic structure after the fashion of one of the Eleanor crosses, in memory of Latimer, Ridley and Cranmer. The three martyrs are represented by statues placed in the niches. On the north side is the following inscription:

> "To the Glory of God, and in grateful commemoration of His servants, Thomas Cranmer, Nicholas Ridley, Hugh Latimer, Prelates of the Church of England, who, near this spot, yielded their bodies to be burned, bearing witness to the Sacred Truths which they had affirmed and maintained against the errors of the Church of Rome, and rejoicing that to them it was given not only to believe on Christ, but also to suffer for his sake, this monument was erected by public subscription, in the year of our Lord God, 1841."

OXFORD.

Since the memorial was built, while the honesty of Latimer and the piety of Ridley have remained undenied, the character of Cranmer has been severely and to his discredit examined, and the cause for which they died widely questioned. There is no little irony in the whole thing when seen in the light of facts. Oxford has not been altogether faithful to the spirit which dictated the inscription and raised the monument. The martyrdom is supposed to have taken place some short distance from the cross, near the corner of Broad street. Latimer and Ridley were burnt on October 16, 1555. From the tower of St. Michael's church, close by, Cranmer saw them perish; he did not hear what the world has never forgotten since—the words of good old Latimer: "Be of good comfort, Master Ridley, and play the man. We shall this day light such a candle by God's grace in England as I trust shall never be put out."

It took three loads of wood-fagots and one of furze to burn these men; the total cost of the execution was twenty-five shillings. Before the year was out, Dr. Palmer, one of the most zealous of their persecutors, became a Protestant, and in the following July he suffered the same penalty. On the 21st of March, 1556, a dull, rainy day, Archbishop Cranmer was burnt on the same spot, the same stake, chain and staple being used, and the cost amounting to twelve shillings. The bailiffs of the city charged the government sixty-three pounds, but the zeal which was vigorous enough to send men to the stake was not so ready to pay the charges thereof. Lord Williams of Thame made himself conspicuous by drowning the archbishop's words with his shouts of "Make short! make short!" It was not long before the reactionary party discovered their mistake in laying hands upon so high a dignitary as Cranmer. They erred fatally: from the time the blood of the primate of England was shed the return of England to the Roman obedience became impossible. Rome stung many a noble soul in those days, but she lost her sting when she hurried to death the man who, worthy or unworthy, was undoubtedly at the head and front of the English Reformation.

Times were rude and rough, and we must admit the fact that Protestants persecuted Romanists as readily as their opponents persecuted them: these very men who were burnt on the street at Oxford had helped and sanctioned the martyrdom of others. Both sides regarded heresy as the most dangerous of all sins; stealing meant the loss of property, and murder the loss of life, but false doctrines involved the ruin of the immortal soul. They believed what they professed: what more laudable work, then, could there be than the silencing for ever of men who were leading people to everlasting perdition? We shiver at the recital of the extreme deeds done; we could not believe them in any way excusable did we not know that even in this our day the most amiable feelings and the most friendly intercourse possible do not exist between those who follow Rome and those who follow Geneva. Which hates and dreads the other most it is not easy to say.

In St. Giles's street is held every September "the holiday of the season," a large business and pleasure fair— a veritable relic of other times. The good saint was an anchorite in the forest of Languedoc in the seventh century. There he was supported by a hind which came daily to give him its milk; in a similar manner ravens fed Elijah at Cherith, and one of the supporters to the arms of the city of Edinburgh is the figure of St. Giles's hind. He was the patron-saint of cripples and was held in great veneration, many churches being dedicated to his memory. A good citizen of the Scotch capital once bought at a great price an arm-bone of St. Giles. All about the hermit himself has long since been forgotten by the people who frequent this famous fair, if, indeed, they ever knew of him. As of everything else of bygone days, the cry is, "The fair is not what it was." The glory has not wholly departed, but it is only the old, gray-haired folk who can tell the story of its lost splendor—of the times when from all parts of the country came the carriers' wains laden with men and women, and rustic music livened the place, and stalls and shows were many and well frequented, and the ale ran like water.

We turn back to Carfax, and, passing down St. Aldate's street, enter the noble quadrangle of Christ Church. This is the largest college in Oxford and was founded by Cardinal Wolsey. Everything about it bears witness to the magnificence of the founder—a man as renowned for his tastes in art and architecture and for his liberality in the founding of schools as for his ability and integrity as a statesman. The massive tower contains, on the outside, niches, in one of which is a statue of the cardinal, and inside a remarkable staircase leading up into the glorious dining-hall. This hall is second only to those of Westminster and Hampton Court Palace. Its roof is lofty and open; upon the walls hang portraits of Christ-Church men—a host such as not only a college, but a nation also, may well be proud of. Henry VIII., Queen Elizabeth and Cardinal Wolsey are there; Bishop Fell of rhythmic memory, and old Schoolmaster Busby, who would not take off his hat before the king in the presence of the boys lest they should imagine there was a greater man in the realm than he, and so discipline come to naught; the three divines who read the Liturgy in the time of its prohibition under Cromwell; and many others famous in the pages of history.

A few steps from the hall is the cathedral, an old building partly founded upon the site of St. Frideswyde's chapel. In its tower are "the bonny Christ-Church bells." Outside are the noble and exquisite walks, one along the banks of the river, another leading to the water, and another—one of the loveliest avenues in England—called the Broad Walk. Many are the attractions of Christ Church; some will admire "Great Tom," the famous bell, and others will love the quiet, studious air of the place.

Oxford has a history as strange as it is interesting, but farther into that we may not venture. Even as we walk through its quaint streets, so fragrant with the aroma of olden time, we have to content ourselves with picturing it when in its mediæval glory—a glory not greater than that it has now, only more romantic. But there is Godstow, two miles away, in the nunnery of which the fair and frail Rosamond spent her last days. There is Cumnor Hall, three miles away, where Amy Robsart died—murdered, some said, by her unworthy husband, the earl of Leicester. And there are other spots, each with its own story inwoven in the greater thread of England's life. Oxford has had a noble past; its present is of rarest splendor, and its future, edged with the radiance flowing down the centuries, will have a magnificence unequalled.

Among the people who in years gone by were known at Oxford was one who, though a plain, simple country shopkeeper, had no small share of ready wit and keen, sharp thought. He lived in a town some twelve or more miles away, and to his shop he added the work of carrier. Twice a week, on Wednesdays and Saturdays, he drove to Oxford and transacted such business as was entrusted to him. In the city he put up at the "Crown," an old hostel with which Shakespeare was somehow or other mixed up. He was a little man, stout, ruddy, with small blue eyes, and wore a broad-brimmed beaver, a velveteen coat and knee-breeches. His humor was great; such a fact as that which happened in the elections of this summer, in which two Irish members, Mr. O'Hea and Mr. O'Shea, failed to get re-elected, would have furnished him with fun for hours. In the early days of the Oxford movement, he, being a man of extraordinary common sense, proclaimed himself in fullest sympathy with the leaders of the party, and many a battle he fought behind his counter, in his wagon and over his ale concerning a celibate clergy, fasts and services on week-days and candles in the sunshine. But he was confounded when his rector refused a white model of a horse such as veterinary surgeons have in their offices, which he in the enthusiasm of his soul gave to the church. Why doves, eagles and lambs should be allowed in the church, and not horses, was a puzzle to him—equal in mystery to the fact that ministers in their sermons speak of roses, lilies and stars, but never of onions or potatoes. Some of the stories he told jogging along the country road from Oxford are too good to be forgotten. There was the squire whose keeper caught a poacher fishing in his waters. The man had a fish in his possession, and the squire sent him to the lockup for the night and had the fish stuffed and baked for his own breakfast. The same squire's wife grew thin under her husband's economy; her dresses were being continually taken in by the dressmaker, and the dressmaker was being continually taken in by the squire. We remember the old story-teller as he passed along the streets on market-days, touching his hat to a collegian, spying out ancient friends and meditating upon or making a bargain. He knew the corners of the city. A merry soul, dead and gone now.

And this is the sad thing about Oxford, perhaps more than elsewhere, the breaking up of old ties and the constant change of faces. The streets and the buildings remain so much the same that one feels the people should remain also; a short acquaintance, and they change. Some men become fixtures—the heads of the colleges, the hosts of the inns, the carriers from the neighborhood and the shopkeepers. Memories gather around them; and when they go, they are more missed than one can tell.

The visitor will find Oxford in every sense satisfying —a noble city, an atmosphere of scholarship, splendid in buildings,

"Majestic in the moss of time,"

and in every way worthy of the praise which it has received.

CHAPTER VI.

An Evening Walk.

> "There are sunset glories to crown the view
> On the far hill-ranges showered;
> There are splendors of nearer warmth and hue
> On the homestead tree-embowered."

THERE is a direct road to Watlington from Oxford, fifteen miles long, pleasant, hilly and traversed twice a week by carriers' vans. It passes by the field of Chalgrove, where John Hampden received his death-wounds, and on which is a monument commemorating that event and stating that he fought in defence of the free monarch and ancient liberties of England. There are also the villages of Chiselhampton and Stadhampton, with a long and narrow bridge between them spanning the river Thame. This bridge is remarkable for its stout angular buttresses set against the current and as the scene of a prolonged resistance against Prince Rupert on the morning of Chalgrove battle. The name of the former village is locally shortened into Chiseleton; in the time of Henry III. it was Chevacheeshull Hampton. Our choice and purpose, however, led us to take the railway to Thame, and from there, in the cool evening, to walk to the town of the Watlings. The distance is about nine miles; the road, good and running across a fertile and well-wooded country.

It so chanced that the day was that on which the election of members for South Oxfordshire in the Eleventh Parliament of Her Majesty Queen Victoria was held, and, as we were greatly interested in one of the parties—it is immaterial which—we did not fail to take notice of the life and activity which such an occasion everywhere brings forth. The usually quiet road was lively with carts, wagons and carriages laden with voters returning from the polls. Boisterous songs and loud hurrahs disturbed the peace of one of the loveliest of England's lovely summer eventides. The contrast was great between the noisy, half-drunken patriots and the still, golden sunlight which streamed through the high hedges and the tree-tops—so gentle, calm and restful, lighting birds and squirrels home to their nests and bidding the deer in the park seek shelter beneath the oaks for the night. It is a fact that in England beer and patriotism go together—a fact curious, but not unique: it is said to occur elsewhere. Possibly the vote is more honest when the voter is far enough gone in his cups not to know how to mark his ballot-paper—when he forgets whether the cross opposite the candidate's name means "For" or "Against." At such a time he is not open to argument or to bribery—though, so far as we could learn, no party was guilty of offering either. He becomes tremendously and unshakably loyal to the Crown and the Constitution; his voice and his influence go for things as they are, Church and State, queen and royal family, the Union and the House of Lords; hence the Liberals strive to make him sober, for they have no chance with him when he is drunk, and the Conservatives try to make him drunk, for they can do nothing with him when he is sober. John Bull may be, in common with most men, an animal, but he is at least a grateful one: he never forgets the considerate body who gives him a juicy mutton-chop or an overflowing muggin of stout.

The Conservative *modus operandi* is more praiseworthy than at first sight may appear. Autolycus sang, "A quart of ale is a dish for a king;" and Armorer Horner's neighbor touched that worthy aright when he exclaimed, " Here's a pot of good double beer, neighbor; drink, and fear not your man." Nor is the spirit of malt stayed at simulating royalty or creating valiancy: Camden tells us that the secret of the longevity of the English is their ancient, peculiar and very wholesome barley-wine, and in a rare tract of the seventeenth century it is said that beer well brewed, of a low, pure amber color, clear and sparkling, is necessary not only for the poor, who commonly eat such things as afford little or bad nourishment, but is also most powerful to expel poisonous infections. Through mediæval and into post-Reformation times the wardens—who were oftentimes women—brewed and supplied the ale consumed by the people in the church nave or yard on Sundays and holy days, and down to Queen Anne's reign, and in some places much later, while the parson and the squire had their twice-baked bread and their thirst-slaking potion between the antecommunion and the sermon, nonconformists, both ministers and deacons, accepted the necessity of similar cereal refreshment before and after their services. Even at funerals it was found efficacious in inducing an appropriate and becoming sorrow or in staying an inordinate and troublesome grief. There were some—as did they who made a certain return to King Edward VI.—who spoke against "the wicked weed called hops," but, on the whole, so convinced were our forefathers of the usefulness of ale that in the year 1577, about which time inns, taverns and alehouses were an acknowledged social nuisance and the population of England did not exceed four millions, there were over sixteen thousand of them in the kingdom. Nay, in a remote antiquity, the fathers of Valhalla taught by example these virtues and mysteries; for the Alvismal says of this old British Kwrw, this Spicigenam Bromon of Julian the Apostate, "it is called ale among men, and among the gods beer." Now add to all this the political power of the beverage, and who shall say the Conservatives are at fault? If beer helps to make men grateful, kinglike, brave, healthy, religious, decorous, hilarious, followers of the gods, and, above all, to deprive them of the skill to plot and to plan against the powers that be, is it not both kind and wise to give them of it plentifully? It is true, besides these things, it will enable some to see the snakes come out of the bones of those who lie in tombs, for serpents grow of human marrow, according to P. Ovidius Naso; but Chuang Tzu, a philosopher of the Flowery Land, four hundred years before our era, observed that the mental equilibrium of a drunken man is undisturbed, the ordinary ideas of life, death and fear find no place in his breast, and were he to fall out of a cart, though he might suffer, yet he would not die. Unconscious of riding in the cart, he is equally unconscious of falling out of it. Tell me, which would you rather have on your doorstep or in your cellar, a man with a can of beer or a man with a can of dynamite? Well, one set of politicians uses the one, and another set the other, to carry out their measures for the good of society; the one, admittedly, is apt to deface the most glorious work of God's hands, but the other is likely to destroy the most glorious works of man's hands, and you into the bargain. I imagine that all dabblers in the art of government are divided into two classes, even as Hamlet divided the question of existence, To-be and Not-to-be. Beer helps the one, and dynamite the other—only in the extremes, to be sure, but then it is the extremes who do the work. The one would leave the country very much as they found it; the other would make it such as no State has ever been either in heaven above or in the earth beneath or in the wa— Stop! I am not so sure about the third place. Milton and Dante have had something to say concerning those regions, and a good man once told me that Satan was a radical, a disturber and a restless mischief-maker. He may use explosives in his domain; he certainly does not use malt beverages. Among the To-be's the opposite prevails. They employ strong, wholesome ale which makes one incapable of such gross and violent wickedness. The evidences which we saw that quiet evening in the road from Thame to Watlington showed beyond a doubt that the Conservatives had done their best to save the country. Events proved their wisdom and strength: the Union was preserved and Mr. Gladstone retired to Hawarden.

Now, what I mean, if you will allow me to talk about such things as we walk along this still road, so gloriously arched and shaded with the noblest of trees, is this: In the English elections beer wins. Speaking algebraically, beer is the x, the unknown quantity and the all-prevailing factor; whichever party uses it the most freely will succeed. The Liberals may be well-meaning enough, but they cannot approach the Conservatives in this respect—that is to say, when the Conservatives get desperate. Neither can give the voter anything before the election, but afterward the humor of the thing twinkles in his eye as he looks upon the nine-gallon keg of beer in his cellar. The innkeeper can also in a good-natured, off-hand sort of way refrain from taking payment for his supplies to the free and independent man, and later on present his little bill to the steward of the candidate. Nobody, surely, can object to a rich man paying his poor neighbor's debts. Moreover, another item comes in. Suppose a wealthy land-owner—and I am speaking exclusively of the country—desires to get his eldest son into Parliament: it is evident that the tenant-farmers will be anxious to please and propitiate their landlord, and the laborers their master, by loyalty at the polls. There is such a thing as raising the rent or refusing improvements, of lowering wages or discharging men, when things do not go as they in superior position would have them go. Not that I would imply that there is a peer or a squire—from Land's End to the house of the judicious Dutchman who in the reign of James IV. settled the question of precedency among his nine sons by having nine doors made to his cottage, one for each son, and a round table for them all—who would trouble himself whether his tenants went one way or the other; but as on board ship the mate is more to the men than is the captain, so on an estate the landlord's great man is greater to the tenants than is the landlord himself. And the landlord's great man can make things very comfortable or very uncomfortable pretty much at his own sweet will, and as surely as two and two make four he looks out for the way the people vote. It is human nature; perhaps in another world two and two may make five, and then things will be different.

Nor are the farm-laborers of England the most intelligent of mortals. I have said something illustrative of this elsewhere; now I only need add that the legend of "Three Acres and a Cow" of the previous election was not wholly without foundation. It will be remembered that some Radical candidate, speaking of the golden age when the principles he was advocating shall have triumphed, illustrated his description of the workingman's plenty by promising him three acres and a cow. I suppose he had figured up how far the land and the cattle would go, and made this out to be each man's share. It was a bit of rhetoric, possibly true enough as such things go, but it was interpreted to mean that each voter should have so munificent a gift provided the candidate got into Parliament. Crafty election agents worked to some advantage on this misinterpretation. At not a few places—for instance, in the Evesham division—a black cow was drawn around in a wagon to show the laborers the prize they would have. Cans of milk reputed to be the produce of such cow were freely distributed. Inquiries were made as to where or when the voters would like their three acres, and every man was led to believe that he would soon have a share in the parson's tithe and the squire's wealth. So the Radical candidate got into Parliament, but Ireland remained unsatisfied: the golden age did not appear, and the constituents went without their promised reward. They remembered that fact at this time; and as Israel thought of the fleshpots and the onions of Egypt, so they called to mind the flavor and the potency of old-time Conservative ale. As to the principles at stake or the consequences involved in the election they knew little and cared less. The Irish were to them naught but disturbers of the peace, enemies of the queen, benighted potato-eaters in a rainy and whiskey-loving island. Mr. Gladstone encouraged them in their rebellion; so the parson said and so the squire said; and the squire ought to know the facts and the parson to speak the truth.

Perhaps if the "Invincibles"—whoever they are—would give the English people information of the wrongs and the wishes of the Emerald Isle instead of giving them nitroglycerine, the aspect of affairs would be materially changed. As it is, the country-folk of the Midlands know no more of Tipperary than of Kwang-tung, nor of Mr. Parnell than of Abdul Hamid II. Not that the Irish are by any means silent elsewhere. Their voices are heard in all lands, and three hundred years ago there was an old opinion among them that the man who in the clamor and outcry which was made at the beginning of a battle did not shout and scream as loudly as the rest was suddenly snatched from the ground and carried flying to the lonely valleys of Kerry, there to eat grass and to lap water, with no sense of misery or of happiness, speechless, forsaken, till caught by the hunters and brought back to his own home. For some generations there is no record of any Hibernian passing through this penance—certainly not during the present century. They who believe in the Anglo-Israel theory put down the Irish as the Canaanites, but though, according to William Camden, there was once a great West-Meath chieftain who declared he would not learn English lest it should set his mouth awry, they speak the language with a sweeter brogue and a more charming vivacity than do even the people of the hill-country of the West Riding. It is well to remember that Ireland owes her connection with England largely to the good pope who handed her over to the Angevin king. Was the Holy Father acting *ex cathedrâ* that time? Speak not evil of dignities; undoubtedly the English are the better papists of the two: they recognize what the supreme pontiff did in the matter. Of all this, however, the agricultural folk were, and still are, ignorant; all they know is that Irish laborers come into English harvest-fields, and that Ireland is a wicked and rebellious land. Hence their solid vote.

Feelings one way or the other run high everywhere. A story is told—I am not responsible for its truth—of a Wesleyan brother who prayed fervently for his beloved and ideal statesman: " O Lord, grant that in these troublous times our talented Mr. Gladstone and his followers may hang together."—" Amen !" said an equally fervid Conservative brother in the congregation; " amen ! God grant they may hang together." The preacher thought he had made a mistake somehow; so he went on: " I mean, Lord, that they may hang together in accord and concord;" to which the other responded, " I don't care what cord it is, but, Lord, let them hang together."

Well, the elections did not hang them, merely suspended them.

Some ask, "Are the farm-laborers fit for the franchise?" I do not think it is so much a question of fitness as of power: Can they freely exercise it? Social conditions are against them, money is against them, and the tyranny of money is worse than was ever the tyranny of a feudal lord. He at least had some kind of a conscience, but gold has none—nor commercial corporations, nor political caucuses. I do not believe the country masses have ever been really heard, or that they will be for long years to come. They cannot speak; would things be better if such as they did speak? It is a curious fact that the town artisan looks down upon the village hind with even greater contempt and scorn than that with which the noble regards the merchant. The man who nails the shoe on the horse's feet thinks himself altogether better than the man who follows the horse along the furrow. There are gradations fine and subtile, class upon class, but they are all-powerful. The wheelwright and the wagoner or the carpenter and the shepherd will not associate together more than is necessary. Hence the wide gulf between the breaker of stones by the roadside and the dweller within the stone walls of the mansion is bridged over by innumerable sorts and conditions of men, each a step higher than the other—perhaps an almost imperceptible step, but making it next to impossible that the one should do without the other or the one should war against the other.

But it is little short of sin to waste a lovely evening along such a road as we are walking by discussing such dry and threadbare subjects. On our left is Thame

Park, once and for a long time the home of Lady Wenman. Here was formerly an abbey, founded—or, rather, translated—by Alexander, the magnificent bishop of Lincoln and lord of the manor of Thame, in 1138, to atone for his extravagance in castle-building. As this and other like "works of satisfaction" came out of the revenues of the Church, the merit was not all that it might have been. He took an important part in the troubles of the reign of Stephen, and, though said to be kindly in heart and cheerful in countenance, was as notorious for his worldliness as for his statesmanship and energy. His rapacity was almost boundless; his pomp, more secular and military than ecclesiastical, was the marvel of the age. He was present at that momentous visit to the pope in 1125 when the archbishop of Canterbury, in order to secure the supremacy of his see, accepted legatine authority and thus placed the Church of England under vassalage to the court of Rome. One of his successors, Henry Lexington, in the reign of Henry III. brought the great road, which before lay on one side of Thame, through the middle of it, and thus gave prosperity to the town. The abbey was colonized from the first Cistercian house in England, at Waverley, in Surrey, being, as the saying then went, one of the four daughters of that establishment and the mother of another house at Bindon, in Dorset. At the time of the dissolution it had a yearly revenue of two hundred and fifty-six pounds. The Cistercians were great farmers, frugal, taciturn and in some ways more austere than other branches of the great Benedictine family. They were of Burgundian origin; their houses were all of independent and equal rank, dedicated to St. Mary; and when a new site was to be occupied, an abbot and twelve brethren were sent forth for that purpose. Within the century in which Alexander built this house the order became all-powerful and embraced eight hundred of the richest abbeys of Europe. The white-robed fathers no longer walk the cloisters or the glades as of old, but some vestiges of their buildings remain. Part of the present house was built in the fifteenth century, and the drawing-room by Robert, the last abbot and the first bishop of Oxford. There is a chapel where for a long time the services have been well rendered by a surpliced choir. Lady Wenman was both fond and proud of her singers and paid them well. The congregation consisted of her own people, and a quarter of a century since strangers thought it a privilege and a pleasure to be allowed to worship once in a while in a place where art and decorum united to make devotion beautiful and attractive.

A walk through the park presents many pleasing views, and they who love well-laid-out grounds, wide stretches of sward set with clumps of broad oaks, deep copses where the pheasant roosts and the rabbit burrows, and the many charms which surround the stately homes of England's gentry, will meet with their heart's delight here. The high hedges and the closed gates at the lodge remind one that the place is private, but, as the people hereabouts are able to distinguish fairly well between a poacher and a tourist, it is possible to obtain admittance. A few hundred yards from the lodge gate, farther along the road, a young man met his death. It was on a summer day, about the year 1857. A thunderstorm came on; the rain fell in torrents and the lightning flashed fiercely. He sought shelter under a wayside tree—this opposite to us is likely the very one—and when the next traveller came by, he saw a huge limb rent off the tall oak and on the burnt grass a charred and lifeless corpse. There was great excitement in Thame, where the unfortunate youth belonged, and for a long time, when a thunderstorm occurred, people were more assiduous than ever in turning their mirrors to the wall and covering their knives and their scissors. Probably few events affected the town more than this since the year of grace 970, when Oskytel, archbishop of York, died there.

In the ditches there are stinging-nettles and on the high ground there are windmills; both are supposed to be indicative of fertility and prosperity. The land that can produce the one and needs the other is not a desert. A man in search of a farm would be guided somewhat by them, and certainly hereabouts the country abounds in rich soil and in the time of harvest the fields stand thick with corn. In bygone days country-people made use of the nettle. Its tops they used as a vegetable like spinach, its leaves in sickness to blister the skin and its fibre to make string or rope. Nevertheless, it is a nuisance, in secluded spots growing six feet high and with jungle-like density. Touch it softly and it wounds; seize it firmly and it is harmless. The sheep carry its seeds in their fleeces; hence it grows luxuriantly in churchyards, where they are often put to graze. It seems to love loneliness, like the windmill. Of all the weird, melancholy solitudes man can find, the dreariest, the most monotonous and brain-bewildering, is the neighborhood of a windmill. The roar and rush of the storm, the sob and moan of the breeze, have an unearthly sound, at times like unto the shrieking of demons, at times like the wail of pain, the deep sigh of the saddened, hopeless grief of lost souls. · In the dusky twilight the huge thing stands against the sky like a black spectre; in the busy day, when the wind sweeps briskly along, its great gaunt arms turn over and over with that supreme indifference to all things else, that constant, laborious regularity, which irritates the calmest nerve. No wonder the valorous Don Quixote was stirred to the depths of his chivalrous soul when he saw the outrageous giants in the plain. One asks if the men who live there are not among the strange fellows Nature has framed in her time.

See the sun-glory on yonder hills! How the golden light flows across the greenwood and the grassy and furze-spotted clearings! Here the road runs into the great London highway, and as we enter it we leave behind us a small post-village which in its ancient name of Tetsworth suggests a British origin and the Celtic worship of Teutates. A little way on is the hamlet of Postcomb—only a few cottages and a roadside inn which has long since passed its usefulness, and kind Time, it is hoped, will speedily relieve the place of the unsightly encumbrance. A trap stands before the door; a thin, starved-looking cur is prowling around the open space in front; the windows are without decent shades, some with a yellow-stained sheet pinned up to hide the nakedness within, and some with a broken pane or two stuffed with rags; the doorsteps are displaced, mossy and dirty, and through the open passage comes the gabble of men at their cups. There is no romance about the dingy, tumble-down, frowsty place. It is a relief to get into the footpath across the fields to Lewknor. The air fresh from the waving corn brightens one's soul and makes one rejoice in the goodness of Nature. The wheat is just turning from its fresh green into its rich russet, and the gnats play in swarms near the hedgerows and under the trees. Here the path runs beside one of the watercress streams for which Lewknor is known, and a little farther it passes through the churchyard into the highway.

The church at Lewknor is built of flint with quoins of ashlar and has a Decorated chancel, a brass of the fourteenth century and a Norman font. The place gives its name to the hundred in which it is situate, and the name may have come from the ancient family of Lewkenors. It differs little from the quiet and secluded villages around, but it has two features which attract attention—viz., a great watercress-bed close by the turnpike, and a lich-gate leading into the graveyard. They who have eaten of the cress and they who have seen the gate will not forget either. Under the latter, as in the days of old and as its name indicates, the bearers set the corpse until the priest meets it, according to the office for burial. A short distance beyond Lewknor is the road leading down to Shirbourne. Had we time, and were not the evening so far gone, we might turn aside to that little village and see therein an ancient moated castle. The present structure dates from 1377, but an earlier one was built in the reign of William I. by Robert d'Oily, to whom the Conqueror had granted Shirbourne. After the reign of Edward III. it passed successively into various families—among them, that of the Quartermains, a noble house having both power and position throughout this district, but becoming extinct in the time of Henry VIII. The last of the Quartermains, dying childless, gave his Shirbourne estate to the child of his steward, who sold it to the Chamberlains, an ancient family which so named themselves from the office their ancestors held to the dukes of Normandy. A lady of this family defended the castle against the Parliamentary forces during the Carolingian troubles. Later on, in the beginning of the last century, it was bought by Thomas Parker, a member of a junior line of a family dating from the reign of Richard II. He was a successful lawyer, a Hanoverian, and was made lord chancellor and earl of Macclesfield by George I. for his loyalty and ability. His leaning to astronomical and mathematical research led him to establish an observatory, which, though it may not have done much for the advancement of science, certainly advanced two poor men to fame and to honor. Phelps the stable-boy and Bartlett the shepherd are not unknown in the bead-roll of English astronomers. The castle is chiefly Perpendicular in style, crenellated, nearly square, with round towers at the corners, is defended by a drawbridge and portcullis, and differs little from its appearance in the fourteenth century. Upon the wide moat swans swim in all their stateliness. Inside, the building has an armory, two libraries, many valuable books and manuscripts and some very fine portraits. Among the latter are those of Erasmus, Archbishop Laud and Queen Katherine Parr. Under the portrait of the last named is a lock of hair cut from the head of the queen when her coffin was opened at Sudley Castle in the year 1799. In the year

1294, Brunetto Latini, the tutor of Dante, slept in the castle of Shirbourne on his way from London to Oxford; at that time, he says, the rough hills were infested with robbers. Six hundred years have made a great change in the social order of England, and yet standing before that old castle it is easy to recall the days when men-at-arms guarded the bridge, and archers manned the battlements, and at the bidding of the baron mailed knights wielded battle-axe and lance. The glory of a Warwick or of a Kenilworth is not here: everything is less magnificent, less entrancing; but a building such as this, five hundred years old, is not without interest and history. It, indeed, reminds us of days of splendor and romance, when imagination had not been shorn of its wings or stripped of its glories, and men strove for unsullied honor and pure truth rather in chivalric enterprise than in the paths of trade and commerce. Force mildly tempered with guile then; guile mildly tempered with force now. It also reminds us of days when the weak were helpless against the strong, when the villain was the serf of his lord and the slave of his soil, when king and barons struggled for supremacy and men did largely what was right in their own eyes, when the mighty met on thirsty battlefields and the rich left of their wealth for priests to say masses for their stained and suffering souls. In the days, for instance, of Stephen, when Shirbourne had its share in the troubles, the castles were at once the oppressors and the protectors of the people: the hand of their lord was against every man, but he suffered no man to touch his dependants. In their mud cottages they clustered around his stronghold, the old folks glad to labor if they might but save for their sustenance a portion of their crops, the young men proud to serve as retainers in the bands of their chief. Life was probably less severe and irksome than we imagine; there was an interdependence binding all into one. When Wat was among the crossbowmen, or little Robin helped to clean the armor, or Cis to serve in the lady's bower or to work in the laundry, there was a direct link between the castle and the cabin; the one depended upon the other. The castle needed men and food; the cabin, protection. In all likelihood the villagers were as proud and as desirous of the success of their lord as subjects are now for the honor of their king. Not that the life within the baronial halls was the purest and the gentlest: purity and gentleness must be sought for in the monastery, and not in the castle; but it was hearty, free and jovial. People were rude and rough, yet they were closer in their interests to one another than we are in our day. They recognized the principle that all men are unequal; we think them equal, and absolve ourselves and all others from those responsibilities which the high and the lowly observed under the old system. Possibly we shall make a better world of it than our fathers did; whether a happier is another question. Any way, Shirbourne Castle is now a quiet, harmless residence;' personal loyalty is no longer asked for nor given; the earl is liberal to his tenants and kind to his poor: the one pay their rent to his steward, the other buy their rabbits from his gamekeeper. The neighborhood is as rich and diversified in scenery as the castle is stern and imposing in structure. Chaunt a lay of the olden time, recall a scene of Froissart or a page of Chaucer, and you may see merry and mediæval England alike in the swelling, beech-clad hills of Chiltern and in the towers and the turrets of Shirbourne.

As the twilight darkens, the moon floods the country with her silvery beams. Beyond this long wall is the road leading to Pyrton, a small village with an Elizabethan mansion where Hampden's father-in-law lived. Another field and a close, and Watlington begins. Asleep, is it? It is scarcely more awake when the sun is shining. While we eat our supper and take our ease in the hotel, and to-morrow ramble about the place, I will tell you something of it. The chicken and the ale evidently belong to an uncertain age—a good quality in the latter, even if not in the former—but the cold mutton with Worcestershire sauce is all that a good appetite can desire. Mine host is busy, and the next sun will shine upon some aching heads and empty pockets. Any way, there will be no such wild riot here as that student in good-fellowship hight Philip Foulface of Alefoord described in his black-letter quarto entituled *Bacchus Bountie*. Then the thirsty sinners, prepared beforehand with such mouth-seasoning as red herring, broiled bacon and hot-spiced pudding, passed on from merriment to riot, and from riot to wrestling and war, till, exhausted, both wounded and drunken, they lay in heaps on the floor. Nothing of that will happen now. The landlord values his reputation and the constable moves about as nimbly as a dog's tail. There is a house with a yard not far from this—we passed it as we entered the town— which was many years since occupied by a wheelwright. A jovial, happy-go-lucky sort of fellow was he, a workman of the first rank, well-to-do, employing several men and apprentices and holding some respect and position in the neighborhood. He made most of the wagons and the carts used hereabouts, and once a year, after a season of good work, he gave a supper to his friends and workmen, his best customers also being invited. Instead of the smoking hoop of the wheel, the boys saw the vaporous offrisings of the big boiler into which every Monday throughout the year was put the washed linen of the household, but which now contained hams, legs of mutton and rounds of beef, carrots, potatoes and cabbage. It also served for brewing-purposes. The huge plum-puddings had been prepared for several days; and when the table in the great parlor was set, the good and solid things thereon made the round eyes of the guests glisten and their fat faces broaden with delight. What eating and drinking, to be sure! The stout little gentleman of the hub and the spoke wielded his great carving-knife and fork at the head of the table as dexterously as he was wont to swing the hammer at the anvil or the axe at the block. The beaded moisture of warmth and effort combined with the glowing beams of satisfaction to make his countenance ruddy and radiant. His hospitality was boundless, nor did he reach the acme of his joy till he knew that every one around his board was stuffed to the full, and that even the rubicund and ale-soaked farmers were so far gone as to need somebody to see them safely home. For one or two of his neighbors a wheelbarrow stood in the yard, and about midnight the good-natured apprentices would bowl them off to their domiciles with right hearty glee. Sir Walter Raleigh in a letter to William Shakespeare affirms that a kinsman made the new herb from the Chesapeake into tea; but had he seen this worthy wheelwright going through the soothing grimaces of puffing and drawing at a pipe filled and yet unlighted, and according to his own solemn affirmation, often reiterated, with satisfaction equal to that of those who applied the glowing coal or the blazing chip, he would have foreseen the ruin of the plantations of the West. There was merriment, you may be sure—an echo of the harvest-home and of the good times when hospitality and kindly feeling prevailed throughout the merry land. Songs were sung—two or three harmless ones before the women left, and then such as "The Bashful Lover" and one in "Praise of Claret," of which it need only be said that after a popularity of several generations the modesty and the purity of our age banished them from among men. Stories were also told—stories, for the most part, with more than a point in them, and which may not be repeated in days when no one cares to hear such things. That was the time to see the real side: we have passed by it all; and no one thought any the worse of the good souls who mingled merriment with religion and sang in the bar-room on Saturday and in the organ-loft on Sunday. Later on everybody went to bed—that is to say, everybody except the apprentices, whose couch in the attic being occupied by visitors from over Chinnor way obliged them to sleep on the floor with the dogs before the kitchen fire.

Among the guests there was for some years one who enjoyed the sobriquet of Tippling John. He was a decent, sleek-looking old boy of about forty-five, and did not get his nickname from his turning up his little finger, but from his skill in rendering an old melody upon the charms of drinking. He had travelled a little and read much.

He wore corduroy breeches with home-knit blue-worsted stockings and buckled shoes; his waistcoat was of crimson plush and his frock of dark-brown velvet. A great turnip-watch and a good-sized snuff-box gave him some influence among his fellows. His ability as a story-teller was good, and he claimed to have known something of the dowager countess of Macclesfield, who maintained the state and the dignity which became a lady of rank in the days of yore in a lodge on a spur of the hills within sight of Shirbourne Castle. It is probable that he was rather confused in his recollections, but as he affirmed that she was a good lady, fond of whist, wine and the diverting story of *Pamela*, but nevertheless a good lady, none of his stories of the lodge affected her reputation. She had a weakness for mushrooms and poachers—at any rate, she loved the one and hated the other—and kept the gamekeepers busy searching for them. But Tippling John's best story did not concern her in the remotest degree, and fortunately, for everybody had a suspicion that he knew nothing at all about the earl's family. This he only told when fairly on his way to maudlin exhilaration, and it had the effect of sobering him and subduing his exuberant spirits. The story ran something like this (draw up to the fire and take another pipe; the nights are chilly, though it is July, and, the pipe and story over, then to bed):

One dark stormy night many years ago—long before you and I, Joe Wiggins, began to play nine men's morris—Parson Jones was on his way home from an oyster-feast. Clergymen in those days were very partial to oysters, and with good reason, for the British oyster was famous in the days of the apostles, and large quantities of the exquisite delicacy were then sent to Rome. Parson Jones did not know this, nor even of the grand oyster-suppers his predecessors indulged in before the Reformation began, and he went jogging along on his old sorrel, thinking only of where he had been and where he was going. It was easier to decide the former than it was the latter; for when he approached the river which lay between him and his home, he found that the water had risen high up the road and was rushing and roaring over the fields and the bridge at a terrific speed. The mare stood on the brink of the flood, and Parson Jones forgot all about the oysters. Then he determined to ride on, knowing that the bridge had fairly high walls and horses were by instinct good swimmers; so into the water he went, splashing along as fast as the mare would go. But the flood was higher than he thought for, and before he reached the bridge the water rose over the stirrups; in a few minutes the mare was swimming —where, he could not tell, for the night was pitchy dark, and, to add to his confusion, the rain began to fall in driving torrents. The water surged around him, but he rode smoothly on.

"Bother the oysters!" he said to himself. "No more oysters for me in this world. Where's the confounded bridge?—Gently, Betty my girl; strike bottom.—Is it across the stream, or is it down the stream?"

At the thought of this he began to shiver, for you must know he was but a young fellow, and, though he had no wife, he had a very good living. His boots were filled with water and his clothes wringing wet. He tried to mutter a prayer, but could think of nothing except "My godfathers and my godmothers in my baptism," and that kept coming up again and again—why, he could not tell. He was certain he was drifting down the stream, and that he was lost sure enough.

"My godfathers and my godmothers in my baptism—" he kept on saying, without thinking. "There! the mare is only floating now. My godfathers and my godmothers in my baptism— I shall be drowned; I am getting weaker all the time. My godfathers and my godmothers in my baptism— Confound oysters and oyster-feasts! My legs are freezing. There goes my hat! Oh, my godfathers and my godmothers in my baptism—"

And thus he went on, his heart in his boots, as the saying is, and afraid every moment he would slip off the mare or she would sink and take him down.

But Providence looks after good men such as he, and it was decreed that Parson Jones should escape. He had drifted on for three-quarters of an hour, when in mid-stream, right before him, he saw a light. It was almost level with the water, and he remembered there was a mill a long way below the bridge. He shouted with all his might, but no answer. He pulled the bridle, and the sorrel began to swim again. Then he saw that the light shone through a window, and in a minute or two he was floating beside it.

"Let me in!" he cried, rattling the panes; and some one lifted the sash.

A leap: he was on the sill, and the mare was gone. It was no easy task lifting himself up through the narrow space; a desperate effort landed him safely inside. By the candlelight he saw a young woman standing beside some bags of flour. Her face was white.

"Where am I?" Parson Jones asked.

"In Redford mill, and I am glad somebody has come, for I am all alone and the water is rising. Father and the man went to Beckett's farm this morning, and now they cannot get back. The water is over the second floor. Who are you?"

"I am John Jones, the rector, and I have been carried down here from the bridge."

"Mr. Jones, the minister, that is. Then I am not going to be afraid any more."

But the water rose fast. It entered the story where they were.

"Is there anything higher than this?" asked the parson.

"Only the garret, and there are rats there."

"Never mind; we must try it."

They went up into the garret; it was small and stifling. In the candlelight they saw the place covered with rats. They stood on the landing, not venturing among the nibblers, though the poor things were terrified to helplessness. The candle burnt low; the river steadily rose.

"Is there a skylight?" asked Parson Jones.

"Just behind you."

"Then we must get out on the roof; that is our last chance. My godfathers and my— Bother the thing! Let me help you up, and then I can clamber through."

So he lifted the girl up, and by dint of great exertion he followed. They sat in the pelting rain by the chimney on the roof-ridge. The great flood surged and sobbed on every side—a weird sound.

"I suppose in Noah's flood people had to do as we are doing," said Madge, after a long silence.

"Oh, my godfa— Confound that! Yes, my child, I suppose they had. Only they all got drowned; and when Noah looked out of the ark, he saw them floating like reeds on the water. My godfathers and—"

"And there was no one to bury them?"

"No; they were not Christians."

Another silence.

"Madge!" whispered the parson.

There was no answer.

"Madge!"

Still no answer.

"Is she dead?"

Parson Jones touched her cold, wet face. He felt it would soon be all over with him, but he determined to hold her body as long as he could. Perhaps he might be saved, and poor Madge should have Christian burial.

But as the hours passed by the parson grew numb, and before he could arouse himself from his stupor the body slipped down the roof into the stream. He remembered nothing more after that. When he opened his eyes next, he was afraid he was in heaven. Yet that could not be, for the sun was shining brightly, the room was warm, people were moving about, and he was in bed. Weak as he was, he knew that no poet had said anything about beds in paradise. He was, then, alive. A woman's face bent over him, and the sympathetic voice of a woman greeted him:

"Hush! Mr. Jones, the Lord's name be praised!"

"My godfa—"

"No, no! You must keep still yet a while."

When he was stronger, they told him how he was

taken off the roof by the miller and by some men in a boat. They had gone for Madge.

"Poor Madge!" said the parson; "I remember. She died and slipped into the water."

"She slipped into the water, but the boat was close by then and picked her up. Here she is;" and sitting in a great arm-chair by the fire was Madge, very white, but living.

Parson Jones rubbed his eyes:

"I thought she was dead."

"Very nearly. Woefully exhausted, but the doctor brought her round, praise the Lord!"

No one in that part of the country ever forgot the great flood, the parson and Madge least of all. Many people lost everything, and much damage was done. Some time after, the parson and Madge were married; for the parson said it was only fitting that they who were spared from dying together should for the rest of their days live together. In his ninetieth year they ate an oyster-supper with their grandchildren, and he told anew the story of that night. Verily, neighbors all, there are strange things in this world!

Thus far Tippling John. And now good-night!

CHAPTER VII.

A Town in the Chilterns.

"He plucks the wild rose in the woods
And gathers eglantine,
And holds the golden buttercups
Beneath his sister's chin."

A QUAINT and ancient town is this Watlington. Its very name carries one back to British times when the Dobuni fenced their villages with trees cut down and laid across one another. The Saxons called this mode of fortification *watclar;* hence the place was "the town of the wattles" or "hurdles." A picture of primitive life: a rude clearing in the great beech-forest, which then extended from Kent to a point far beyond this, a few sheds or huts for a simple people and their cattle, and the strange manners and trying privations which were involved in a crude civilization and an almost complete isolation. There are neither Roman nor Saxon remains about the place, so far as I know, but there is a delightful look of old times both in the narrow, winding streets and in some of the houses. In the High street is a tavern styled the "Barley-Mow," whose blackened timbers in the wall indicate considerable age. The town-hall, the delight of artists and the resort of hucksters, was built in 1664 by Thomas Stonor, a member of a family which from the twelfth century has lived in the

"There is a Delightful Look of Old Times in the Narrow Winding Streets."

place near by bearing the same name. Its gray mullions, high-pointed gables, dark arches, antique clock, nail-headed door and general appearance furnish a perfect and pleasing specimen of the architecture of the age when England was rejoicing in the restoration of its king and the passing away of Puritan gloom and rigor.

From the market-hall southward is a street called Couching—to which I will return by and by—and this ends in the road leading from Henley, the oldest place in the county, to Oxford, the most celebrated. A pleasant road it is, too, running in one direction over the hills to Nettlebed, the highest point of the Chilterns, on which a windmill spreads its sails to the breezes and thick furze-bushes dot the unenclosed common. In the other direction the road passes near the parish church. A rivulet, tiny and clear, flows playfully by the side of the way, and on a calm Sunday morning the melody of the church-bells and the music of the brook blend together in sweet, suggestive harmony. There are tall hollyhocks in the gardens and bright faces in the cottage doorways, and as one walks on one would think this was amongst the purest and the brightest spots in all England. So it may be, but a certain bishop of Oxford, Samuel Wilberforce of famous memory, declared the town to be one of the worst and darkest in his whole diocese. We may not dispute His Lordship's judgment, though his opportunities for personal observation were limited to a visit of three or four hours once in every third year, and even in his day the old church used to be well filled and the people sang lustily and with a good courage.

The place belonged to the abbey of St. Mary's at Osney. This great house on the Ey, near the Ousenford, was founded in the reign of Henry I. by Robert d'Oily, a nephew of the knight of the same name who came over with the Conqueror, acquired large possessions in this county, became governor of Oxford, and among other things built Shirbourne Castle. His wife, Eadgyth, once a mistress of the king, was much troubled with the constant chattering of magpies in the garden of the castle at Oxford. She referred the subject to her confessor, who, knowing the language of birds, told her that the pies were none other than souls in purgatory beseeching her for prayers to release them from their bitter pains. Thus the abbey was founded and endowed with much land, Watlington being also in the gift, and in time it became magnificent for its appointments, "the envy of all other religious houses in England and beyond the seas." The influence in it was rather English than Norman; at any rate, the second prior and the first abbot had the name, and probably belonged to the family, of Wiggod of Wallingford, an old Saxon noble who contrived to hold his own under William. It had a church containing many chapels and twice as many altars as there were months in the year. Further estates were bestowed upon it, kings and nobles often graced it with their presence, and when dissolved its revenue was between six and seven hundred pounds. The mercy which led to its establishment was not always exhibited within its walls. In the year 1222 there was a singular imposture at Oxford. A man proclaimed himself as the Messiah, and exhibited the stigmata in his body as proofs of his assertion. Another man aided him, and two women declared themselves to be the Marys. Such a story in our day would be treated with indifference, but the thirteenth century was more serious and severe. The four impostors were brought to trial in Osney Abbey; the men were sent, one to crucifixion, the other to fire, and the women were condemned to be built up alive in the walls of the abbey. The sentence of living entombment was carried into effect. We must not judge the people of bygone ages as we would judge ourselves, only it is curious that consideration for the souls in purgatory does not seem to have induced consideration for the souls in heresy, except that material fire is easier to bear than spiritual, and may, indeed, preclude it.

The good fathers of Osney, however, must not be condemned upon an event which happened incidentally in the course of their four centuries of history, and which was, indeed, brought about by a tribunal presided over by one of the greatest and best of the primates, Stephen Langton, and composed of members mostly outside of their society. They did much for the upbuilding of the people around them. In common with other monasteries, the ecclesiastical livings which were appropriated to them, and of which they became rectors, were fairly well cared for by them and served by their vicar. They received the great or rectorial tithes, and the priest who did the duty, but was not responsible for the temporalities, was supported out of them, or by what were known as "the small tithes." When the abbey was broken up, instead of restoring the rectory to the clergyman of the parish, it, with the lands of the Church belonging to the religious house, was granted to some courtier whose interest it was to blacken the character of the monks beyond all possible recognition, and whose inheritors still retain, and unrighteously retain, that which does not belong to them. The wrong was wrought throughout the realm, and on the ruins of the monastic houses grew up a society new without nobility and powerful without rightness. Hence there are lay rectors who fill the place of the old monks, and the spiritual functions of the office are performed by a clergyman who is called, and actually is, the vicar, the substitute and deputy of the rector. Whether lay rectors are better than monastic rectors is not for me to say, nor is it possible until the problem is satisfactorily solved whether man as a squire or man as a monk is the better fitted to be the guardian of the people's spiritual rights. Any way, the Austin çanons of the abbey in the Meadow Island built the church at Watlington, and some of their work remains in the present edifice.

It is not much of a building. It was not much before its restoration, ten years since; it is still less now. The high red-tile roof of the restored portion does not correspond with the flat lead roof of the part not touched, and there is striking incongruity inside between the new and the old. Formerly the chapel on the south side was secluded and separate. There were tombs in there, and an iron railing divided them from the body of the church. I remember, when the "forty years long" in the Venite was reached, I used to look toward that dark corner and wonder if they who rested there were of the generation that grieved the Almighty. I did not know who were buried within the sacred precincts, but there were hatchments, dingy and dusty, hanging high up on the chancel-walls, and brasses four hundred years old. There was no chapel or transept on the north side, but the chancel was long and filled with pews arranged in the usual choir or college fashion. The pulpit was a mighty structure, standing at the east entrance of the nave, and had the appearance of being halfway down the church. A flight of steps led up into the great square reading-pew, and from that another flight led up into the pulpit, which stood upon one post, was round and had a sounding-board and a great red cushion. There was something of the highest dignity in the way the venerable vicar in silken gown and white bands smoothed his sermon on this cushion and cleared his throat preparatory to his fifty-minute delivery. The new school of divines cannot approach the old clergy in official gracefulness; they have lost their dignity in short surplices and thin essays. Opposite the pulpit, immediately across the passage, was the little desk for the parish clerk, a precise, prompt, rotund and ruddy individual, short in stature and a carpenter by trade, who used to strut up and down the chancel before the parson, open the door of the reading-pew or pulpit, shut him in, and when it was time let him out again with a gravity and primness which astonished strangers and delighted the parishioners. He used also to make the responses in a loud tone, the only soul in the church that presumed to do so, and he announced the hymns in a sonorous voice, absolutely inimitable, prefaced with the invariable "Let us sing to the praise and the glory of God." Perhaps the custom of the clerk instead of the parson giving out the hymn arose from the fact that once upon a time he was probably choirmaster, if not choir, and would therefore be best able to judge of what came within the compass of his powers. Sometimes it fell to his duty to trip down the church and up into the loft or gallery at the west end, where the singers and the poor-school children sat, and rebuke the bad boy who would not observe order during the service. Occasionally he would bring the said bad boy back with him and stand him on the pulpit steps, at once a punishment to the offender and an admonition to the offending. The restoration of the church has swept out that noble and worthy functionary; he is no more, either in office or in person, and somehow or other, dear as he was in the eyes and the ears of the faithful, things go on without him.

Time has also removed another individual, a trim, correct bachelor who for years sat in the great square pew under the pulpit. Wet or fine this gentleman was always in his place, and wet or fine he had always a stiff high collar and a big white cravat. He was the admired of all admirers, and every unmarried lady of middle or uncertain age in the church used to wonder when the eventful day of his life would arrive and if she could possibly do up his collars. When the sermon became unusually dry, people relieved the monotony by watching the flies on the bare round place at the back of his head enjoying themselves in ways congenial to their nature. He rarely interfered with them; when he did, he lifted his hand gently, slowly, aimfully, and then at the proper moment brought it down with a smart slap upon the caputial vacancy, only to find that the offending diptera had left the infinitesimal part of a moment before. No matter how serious the sermon, this slightly upset the spectators. They neither said anything nor laughed aloud, but they turned very red and bent over, as if for private prayer. It was rumored that he was in love with a venerable maiden-lady some fifteen years his senior, a sweet and gentle creature who, though she was suspected of wearing a wig and of having lost some teeth in the conflict with time, considered it best to wait a little longer before she threw herself away, even upon a highly-respectable bachelor. She sat some distance from him inside the chancel, and, like him, was always in her place and always devout. Both are now sleeping in the graveyard outside.

The old tower remains, partly covered with ivy. On its highest ledge, on the north side, a good-sized bush has been growing for some years; probably the seed was carried up by a bird and dropped into the mortar. At the south-west corner of the tower is a yew tree, the trunk of which four feet from the ground measures ten feet eight inches in circumference. It is most likely three or four centuries old. The ancients planted the yew to protect the church from evil spirits, also to supply wood for their bows. The torches of the Furies were made of yew, and on the Sunday next before Easter its boughs were used instead of palm or olive. It had a symbolism which spoke to all—the dark color of the mortality of man, the seemingly unfailing trunk of immortality, and hence, perhaps, its name, *ewig*, "everlasting." Gilbert White thinks the more respectable parishioners were buried under this tree, and that it was also designed as a shelter to the congregation assembling before the church doors were opened. Some have supposed it further served to shield the sacred edifice from the storm. Its leaves are poison and its wood was used for the instruments of death; therefore Shakespeare calls it "double-fated." On Sundays, contrary to the canon against loiterers, the idle youth used to gather at this tower corner and under this tree, much to the annoyance of passers-by, who were too often the subjects of their witticisms. The carved figures to the waterspouts are as formerly, and besides them are two heads, the one on the west and the other to the east of the south porch. These two figures are interesting. The former is looking down the main pathway to the church, with the left hand holding the robe over the breast and the right hand shading the eyes, anxiously watching for the coming worshippers; the latter, overlooking the main portion of the graveyard, has a mingled aspect of sorrow, sympathy and hope, as though it extended these to the weary ones who came to weep at the graves of their dead. The tombstones appear old, but are not really so. The atmosphere soon darkens them, lichen covers them, and they speedily chip and crumble away.

I named Couching street; let us return thither and pick up a few reminiscences there. Years ago I used to puzzle over its etymology. Had Osney Abbey belonged to the Crutched Friars, I should have been tempted to think it was a corruption of their name; and once I came near fancying it might formerly have been Crouch for the Croce of Doomsday. These, however, were no more satisfactory than the suggestion of one who thought it meant Sleepy street because it was so quiet. In Old English there was such a word as *couchen* or *cowchyn*, meaning "to place or set together," and possibly, as the houses or cottages which compose this street were built up till they became continuous, the name was thus given. Be this as it may, Couching is a narrow, still street with rough pebbles most of its length for the sidewalk, one or two inns, a few shops, some private residences and a malt-house. At the back of the houses on the south side of the street are gardens opening into a lane, beyond which lie open fields running up to the rolling hills a mile away. At one end of this lane a plank serves as a bridge into the Henley road across the babbling brooklet already mentioned; the other end leads into the highway up to the White Mark. In the street and in the lane Chanticleer and his company scratch for a living, and a pig occasionally seeks for garbage. Little occurs in this neighborhood to disturb the restful monotony. When a trap rattles over the hard road or a hen cackles, most of the old ladies run to the windows to satisfy their curiosity; and when the constable succeeds in taking a drunken man to the lock-up, close by, they become so excited as to need something stronger in their tea than either milk, sugar, water or the uninebriating herb itself. At the time the prince of Wales was married, and a brass band from Wallingford played "All among the Barley" as it passed through the streets, the Union Jack waving in its glory and a goodly company of men and boys following and shouting with soul-stirring vigor, it is said it took so much hot water, sugar and brandy to calm the nerves of the people and to allay their heart-throbbing loyalty that the town was in danger of being left without a drop of distilled liquor in it. Such a crisis has never been reached since. Most of the ancient inhabitants of the place keep a little on hand against emergencies and hysterics, and before this is exhausted the new railway, which seems to have little else to do, replenishes the supply.

It matters little into which house we enter in this street; each will furnish us with a picture more or less pleasing of quiet life. Here is one, a comfortable-looking two-story brick domicile, a bay-window on each side of the front door, and, opposite, the bonnet-like chimney of the malt-house. The street door has a knocker and a bright brass handle; it is also panelled and has sufficient projection over it in the way of a pent-house to bring the rain-drippings exactly on the middle of one's umbrella when standing underneath. There was design in this last feature: a tramp on a stormy day would avoid getting wet through for the sake of a crust of bread or a crusty refusal. Inside is a short passageway or hall, on the right side of which a door opened into the parlor, and on the left a door into the sitting-room, through which one passed into the kitchen, and hence into one of the sweetest of gardens. At the end of the passage a flight of stairs neatly carpeted led to the three or four upper rooms. Thirty years since, for three hours in the forenoon and three hours in the afternoon, a number of respectable young ladies and gentlemen, sons and daughters of the best of the local society, met in the parlor for instruction in the rudiments of a polite education. The terms were not high—one guinea a quarter, and a crown extra for French, music or good manners. A shoulder-board for the young ladies and a cane for the young gentlemen were the means of disciplining the juvenile mind and body into the ways of rectitude and industry. The former went the round of the girls every day, and their time devoted to it was in proportion to their numbers. If there were twelve of them, each spent half an hour a day standing up and holding in proper position the instrument for making square shoulders; if there were six, each had an hour a day. The girls were, therefore, interested in keeping up the numbers and attendance. At the same time the one undergoing the gentle process had to commit to memory a page or so of Mrs. Magnall's questions or one of the psalms of David, the book being placed on a desk before her. Frequently a weaker girl could not complete her time, but it was so arranged that during school-hours the board was always in use; a stronger pupil took her place and filled up the spare minutes in addition to her own share. The good lady who managed the establishment had gone through this process herself in the days when the French Revolution was upsetting things on the Continent, and she knew the value and the benefit of such a training. Only in this way could the backs of young ladies be fitted to the straight-backed chairs of the period. As to the young gentlemen, the discipline of the cane fell to the lot of one in turn each day. The more boys there were, the longer the interval between the individual's portion. About eleven o'clock in the forenoon, when the potatoes were peeled and the pudding was in the pot ready for dinner, the lady of the school took the victim for the day out into the kitchen. Everybody knew the purpose—the boys by experience, the girls by information. Very little was said. The youth followed the instructions given, adjusted his clothing and extended himself full length upon a bench. All that followed was without fear or favor. The red eyes of the lad when he returned to the room showed the immediate effects; time has made manifest the permanent results. Every lad who came under the tuition and training of this school turned out well, and some have made positions for themselves in the world.

The school was popular, for the lady at its head had been a governess in the family of a great bishop and wrote a neat Italian hand. She was a maiden of many years' standing, short and stout, with a kindly face and a profusion of curls, dignified and exact, and, withal, humorous and lively. She wore a silk dress and a heavy gold watch-chain, and about her there was a fragrance of lavender which suggested the wardrobe and the herb-garden. It was commonly reported that once she had suffered shipwreck. This was in the Irish Sea, and was confirmed by one of the boys, who said that the paper of an old geography locked up in her bookcase had the blue tinge of the sea and left the taste of salt upon the tongue. Any way, she had travelled both in Ireland and in Wales and was a well-informed and well-read woman. That she was a Tory goes for the saying: her romantic spirit led her to love the days of chivalry and the traditions of the Church. Many a tale she told of valiant knight and holy bishop, of gay tournament and adventurous voyage, while her eyes glistened with enthusiasm and her voice quivered with emotion as she spoke of the battle of Roncesvalle and the dauntless Roland, of Runnymede and the noble Langton, of Drake and of Raleigh, and, above all, of Bonnie Prince Charlie. There was not a boy who heard her that did not wish to become crusader, reformer or navigator, and to perform deeds as marvellous as those of a Robin Hood or a Robinson Crusoe; there was not a girl who did not wish she had been Mary queen of Scots, or at least the lord mayor's daughter whom the apprentice saved from drowning in the Thames. They forgave her for making them recite the collect and the gospel for the week first thing on Monday morning, and as the girls forgot the shoulder-boards in the fairy's wand, and the boys the cane in the knight's lance, so all agreed that for a story of good times and of old times their mistress could not be equalled.

Occasionally the exercises of the school were varied by an afternoon's outing. Sometimes the destination was that delightful hill known as the Cuckoo Pen. This required an early start, as it was some three miles distant. At one o'clock the school assembled — about twenty, all told — and gravely and demurely walked through the streets two and two, the eldest girls first, after the girls the boys, and in the rear the good old lady carrying a large parasol and reticule. Up Couching street, by the town-hall, round the butcher's shop and up the road to the White Mark. No talking, no laughing, no breaking of the procession till the foot of the hill was reached, but then in the grass-covered road by the chalk-pits, where wicked young men used to play cricket on Sunday afternoons, the most unrestrained mirth. Gayly and lightsomely the school wended its way through that wide shady lane, past Bacon Hill, to the Cuckoo Pen. How merrily the young folks chattered and sang, now racing over the thick sward, now plucking wild flowers or blackberries from the hedges, and now jumping leapfrog, skipping or playing ball! I see them now as I saw them one bright August day a quarter of a century since. There are our three Pyrton boys, gay, lively youngsters, the eldest nearly fourteen;

there is our pretty Eva, the daintiest and sweetest of all the maidens. There are other boys, but none so noble as Arthur from Pyrton; there are other girls, but none so queenly as Eva. Through the gate at the foot of the hill they rush; up the steep sides they clamber. There are steps cut in the steepest places, and the moss and the grass are soft and slippery. On the summit is a fine copse, another a little farther back, and behind that and stretching far away into the valley between the hills a thick greenwood. The view from the top is fine, and on the edge of the first copse there was a double-trunked tree in the deep fork of which one or two of the more venturesome boys used to sit. In front of this tree all assemble, and after a while the cake and the ginger-beer arrive. The soft winds fan the rosy cheeks and cool the tired limbs; some of the youngsters wander in twos and threes into the wood, some gather moss or catch grasshoppers, and some roll down the hillside over thistles and through furze. There is Ben almost in the top of that big beech tree, his white trousers soiled with green off the bark, and there is Eva, the little puss, not ten years old, sitting on the ground with a boy by her side and her hand in his. "Will you marry me when you grow up, Eva?"—"Yes, if you will be a doctor like papa." Here comes George with a paper box full of grasshoppers, and Arthur with a fledgling which he has caught. Everybody runs to see the bird. "Poor thing!"—"Feathers scarcely grown!"—"Cruel!"—"Let it go!" and, somehow or other, there is a chilly feeling comes over all when the captive is taken back to the neighborhood of the nest and released. On the way home everybody walks slower and there is less noise.

But, though tired, each scholar owns that an afternoon on the Cuckoo Pen is about the best fun that can be in this world, and the next morning even the shoulder-board and the French verb are easy, and the boy whose turn it is to become acquainted with the cane thinks flagellation uncomfortable, to be sure, but nevertheless bearable after a day of such rare delight.

In the room on the other side, opposite to that in which the school met, might be seen at any time between seven and nine o'clock in the forenoon, and after five till a quarter-past ten in the evening, another old lady, sister to the maiden-mistress in the parlor. She was not the opposite of her sister, but the same sort of person, only on a reduced scale. Her tastes, ideas, sentences, habits and the rest were the same, only less magnificent. She could not teach French, but she could make excellent elderberry wine, and, as every one knows, elderberry wine, warmed and spiced, with biscuit or toast, is better on a wintry night before going to bed than the most correct speech of Paris. Her sister wore silk; she, having the house to look after, used prints and stuffs. Both had spectacles—the one gold rimmed, the other brass covered with flannel. She was a treasurer of antiquity. The sofa under the window at the far side of the room was made before men ceased to write " 1700 " at the top of their letters. Over the mantel was a picture of a Rebekah at the well, a very English scene as old as the sofa, and above it were three or four bulrush-heads which had not been removed for a generation at least. A curious portrait of an old lady who died actually one hundred and three years old—traditionally, one hundred and thirty—placed beside one of a rosy-cheeked boy of five, brought into contrast "crabbed age and youth." A desk made in the year 1827 out of a yew tree reputed at the time when cut down to be at least five hundred years old was one of her greatest delights. That tree may have furnished some of the archers of Agincourt with their bows, and it may have been planted from a tree which was young when Harold sat in the throne at Westminster. Her spare time was spent in thinking over the possibilities of that tree, and doubtless many a pleasant vision passed before her. In two things she had received a fuller development than her sister: she had a belief in ghosts, and she was fond of the garden. The former she sought to propitiate by saying as little about them as possible; to the latter she gave four or five hours of every fine day. She had plum trees, apricots and vines, gooseberry- and raspberry-bushes, strawberries and clusters of carnations, roses, gillyflowers, daffodils, daisies, honeysuckle, and even potatoes and cabbages. It was a frequent observation of hers that for beauty lilies in a vase, and for usefulness parsnips in a dish, had no equals. Life flowed on easily with the sisters, and little came in to disturb their peace. Once in a very long while one of them went up to London, but there were no charms in the city for them. Now they lie side by side near the east end of the chapel at the parish church.

Before we leave this house let me take you to a room up stairs looking out toward the hills. The walls are covered with designs of roses—old-fashioned, indeed, and highly colored, but the trailing vines run up from floor to ceiling, green leaves, mossy buds and brilliant blooms, with a suggestiveness as true as that the highest art could give. Everything is scrupulously clean, the carpet, of wondrous devices and faded tints, the figured dimity on the bedstead, the rush-bottom chairs, the chest of drawers with the oval looking-glass on top, the candlestick and the snuffer-tray, the black-oak coffer,—all as dustless as they are homely. There is but one window in the room, for the house was built when windows were taxed. It opens after the manner of the old lattices and has the small lozenge-shaped panes. Inside, softshaded curtains hang on both sides of the recess, in which is a low seat under the casement, cushioned and fastened into the wall; outside, a grape-vine twines its tendrils and sets its leaves thick all around, hiding the wall and the woodwork, and in the autumn rich purple clusters are within reach of the hand. But it is the view from the window that is the chief delight. Whenever I see it, I am reminded of the Pilgrim at the House Beautiful: "When the morning was up, they had him to the top of the house, and bid him look south. So he did, and behold, at a great distance, he saw a most pleasant, mountainous country, beautified with woods, vineyards, fruits of all sorts, flowers also, with springs and fountains, very delectable to behold." I do not say that the picture is as lovely as that of the Delectable Mountains, but seen in the glow of the early sunlight it is not altogether unworthy of comparison; indeed, it is probable that from such a scene Bunyan drew his inspiration. There lie the hills—graceful lines against the horizon, the green of the fields and woods making more intense the white of the chalk-pits and roads. At the foot of the Mark are the wheat- and barley-fields; and when the July winds gently pass over the wide reaches of tall grain, sweeping it into waves like those of some seawaters, they look like rich plush smoothed by a soft hand. What says the old song?

> "Come out! 'tis now September:
> The hunter's moon's begun,
> And through the wheaten stubble
> Is heard the frequent gun;
> The leaves are paling yellow
> Or kindling into red,
> And the ripe and golden barley
> Is hanging down his head.
>
> "All among the barley,
> Who would not be blithe
> When the free and happy barley
> Is smiling on the scythe?
>
> "The Spring she is a young maid
> That does not know her mind;
> The Summer is a tyrant
> Of most unrighteous kind;
> The Autumn is an old friend
> That loves one all he can,
> And that brings the happy barley
> To glad the heart of man.
>
> "All among the barley, etc.
>
> "The wheat is like a rich man
> That's sleek and well-to-do;
> The oats are like a pack of girls
> Laughing and dancing too;
> The rye is like a miser
> That's sulky, lean and small;
> But the free and bearded barley
> Is the monarch of them all.
>
> "All among the barley, etc."

Sing the good old lines to the accompaniment of the guitar in the open air of the closing summer twilight, with a "pack of girls" and their swains, happy-hearted and sweet-voiced, to join in the chorus, and a strange delight will be yours for the time and a pleasant memory yours for ever. Then you will enjoy with deeper zest and fuller inspiration the picture of the fields of grain. A pleasant sight it is to see the harvest-moon shining on the standing shocks of corn; pleasanter, to see the poor and needy leasing after the reapers. How strange appears the one tree in the middle of yonder field, thick with leaves and casting a deep shadow in which the sheep rest during the noontide heat, but seemingly lost in its solitude! There are nuts in the high hedges for squirrels and truant boys, and sloes and crab-apples. In the deserted rooks' nests among the elms far away toward the Nettlebed road the fierce and indolent sparrowhawk sometimes rears its young, and excites at once the fear of the smaller birds, the desires of the town-lads and the ire of the gamekeeper. How gently the clouds rest in the blue sky! And the earth seems to sleep in its calm and lovely splendor—no care, no sorrow, quietly doing its work and not suffering the mind to dwell upon the winter of nature nor upon the storms which try the human heart. Standing in the window there, the eye rests upon a landscape full of interest, a scene never to be forgotten, and the soul is refreshed with the vision of beauty.

But we must away to other parts of this interesting town. Once in a while a Punch-and-Judy show comes and exhibits near the town-hall. There is then much excitement—even greater than that caused by the monthly visit of the "scissor-grinder." The latter fairly rivals the travelling tinker, who does a fair trade for two reasons—first, because of his handiness at mending old pots and kettles; and secondly, being a gypsy, he is suspected of a capability of stealing fowl by way of revenge for not having work given him. If he cannot have bread honestly— Well, that is what some think. The children are half afraid of him because gypsies have been known to steal boys and girls and make acrobats, and sometimes aristocrats, out of them. As to the grinder of scissors, he is commonly supposed to live somewhere in the neighborhood, though where nobody knows. He is even suspected of being an itinerant preacher, but the weight of opinion is rather in favor of regarding him as a pretty straightforward sort of man. He is quiet, low in his charges, sober and respectful. For a penny he will sharpen all the cutlery of a small establishment. He also mends umbrellas and sells paper windmills. When he comes wheeling his little machine down the street, boys run after him with their pocket-knives and women with their scissors, and as the sparks fly from the tiny grindstone everybody looks on with profoundest interest. But he shines only in the absence of the sun. The luminary of luminaries is the puppet-show man. Here in this open space in front of the White Hart—one of the best inns, by the way, in the country—he goes through the tragedy of Punchinello. Between the acts he performs on a primitive musical instrument consisting of a row of small pipes fastened in the front of his coat. This "wind-organ," being level with his mouth so that he can use it at his convenience, and if need be beat a drum at the same time, produces music similar to that which is obtained by blowing over the open end of a key. Occasionally he uses a jewsharp;

AN OLD-TIME ENGLISH INN.

sometimes, a cornet; less frequently, a violin. If he has any artistic vanity, it is helped by the lusty cheers of the crowd; his pocket is filled with their pence. Only let Punch kill the devil, and every man in the company will give the "price of a pint."

You see in the cottage doorway the housewife trundling the mop. It is skilfully done; so is the way in which she balances herself on her pattens. The cleaner she keeps her stone floor, the higher her respectability. That is one of the aims of her life. She has two others —viz., to bring up her children as she thinks they ought to be brought up, and to grow the finest flowers possible. Compare the little fellow sitting on the upturned bucket by the door-scraper, munching a slice of bread covered with treacle, with the fuchsias and geraniums in the window, and you can judge of her success. Speak to her; yes, sir, independence is one of the characteristics of the English peasantry. She will answer you with respect, but not with servility. You may be richer and know more: that she will admit; but you are no better than she. Praise the boy or the flowers, and you will see the healthy blush on her cheek deepen with delight.

The curate is an important person in most country parishes. It is a mistake to suppose that he does all the work—some small portion of it is undertaken by the rector—but he receives most of the popularity. The people always regard him as an ill-used, under-paid and sadly-neglected individual, and not a few things of a severe and spiteful nature are said concerning the ecclesiastical superior who treats him so badly. The young ladies think constantly and kindly of him, especially if he be single. They are not turned aside from their admiration for him by anything less than a soldier, and, as a fact, the moment a red coat comes into the parish the black coat is forgotten. However, the curate's day comes round again. He is there all the time, and can play croquet, drink tea, quote authors, shape compliments, make sonnets, explain difficulties and do all sorts of odd things, while his appearance on Sundays in a snow-white surplice with the hood of soft rabbit-fur lining is "just too lovely for anything." To say that he flirts is going too far, but he succeeds in making every girl in the parish think her chances are the best. In many places he is the only youth a girl of taste and education would care for; and if he cannot marry all the maidens of the neighborhood, it is not his fault. As a rule, when he does take unto himself a wife, she is from another parish, and then his resignation speedily follows. Unfortunately, his chances of promotion are not invariably good. If poor and of lowly origin, he has small hope of being anything else than a curate. Talents except of the very highest and rarest order go for little: influence is everything. Many of the ablest workers the Church of England has remain curates all their life, and many of the most inefficient, useless, parish-killing clergy have rich livings from the outset. As a training when young nothing can be better than a position under an able and sympathetic rector. The lack of responsibility is then helpful, and none can feel that more than the man who, full of zeal and life, has from his ordination been committed to the care and management of a large parish. Young men can then make mistakes without doing any serious damage. Once upon a time a curate was called to solemnize marriage for the first time. He got confused, confounded, and opened the book at the wrong place. He did not understand why the people smiled when he began, "Hath this child been already baptized or no?" The clerk put him right; some of the young ladies said he was in love with the bride. It was the more provoking because, according to his own confession afterward, he had gone through the service the night before with the clerk and the rector's cook—both relics in the seventies—as subjects.— No; the story is not of this young fellow talking to the butcher at the corner. He looks as though he could as easily take first oar or bowler as perform the most difficult ecclesiastical function. I fancy he would keep cool even if he had to baptize a child, as was once certainly done, by the name of "Anna Miranda Morea Maria McRunnaho Donahue Bridget Dashiell."—But why speak of curates? Because Watlington needs something to keep it alive, and I know of nothing better than a curate. He could at least teach the people that when in mourning they are not obliged to drink black tea.

Crooked streets, old houses, shops with tiny windows and with bow-windows, residences hid away behind high walls and seen only through great iron gates, walls built of flint with brick facings and broken glass bottles along the top, cobblestones and pebbles under foot, antique taverns, a gentle, drowsy, restful, self-satisfied life,— that is Watlington. The waves of Time's sea, great and mighty as they roll in this our present, break and exhaust their strength on shores far away. Only a few spatterings of spray driven by the wind reach this place—just enough to let its people know that something great and ancient has been washed away, some mighty change effected.

CHAPTER VIII.
Thame.

> "And I liked their yew-cut alleys,
> Framing vistas of the valleys,
> And the church-tower and the lea,
> And the stately trees whose shadow
> Fell at eve o'er park and meadow
> Century after century."

A WARM morning. The hills lie quivering in the haze of the almost cloudless horizon, and three hours before noon the cattle in the fields seek the shadow of the beeches and the traveller moves slowly under the overspreading elms by the roadside. In the little town of Watlington the streets are mostly deserted; a few women are marketing at the butchers' stalls or the grocers' shops, and here and there a schoolboy drags his weary way to the place of flies, rods and Latin declensions. By the old market-hall stands a wagon; the busy chickens pick up the crumbs which fall from the horse's feed-bag. Up the road toward the White Mark a team is moving slowly; the dog paces gently on, too lazy to run after the pigeons, and the driver is lying on his back, half asleep, on the top of the load. Everything indicates a hot, quiet day—one of those days when the wind is warmer than the still air. Fortunately, the roads are not dusty enough to make walking unpleasant.

Two of us set out in the road running at the foot of the Chilterns—that is to say, the turnpike-road, for there is another parallel with this, higher up, grass-grown and unfrequented. The lovers of romance and of solitude may find their hearts' delight amid chalk-pits and sheep-walks, on mossy knolls and under gnarled and twisted hawthorn-bushes. Bacon Hill, bare of trees, but bristling with furze, and the Cuckoo Pen, with its noble copses on brow and side, are on the right, Chinnor and Stokenchurch farther on, and Shirbourne and Lewknor, already mentioned, in the way. At the cross of the Stokenchurch road—one of the great highways to London—is the "Lambert Arms." This was once a busy, well-frequented inn, a hostelry flourishing and famous in the days of yore; now it is decayed and deserted and has been turned into a "temperance hotel." It is sad to look at the old house with its faded sign and dim-paned windows and recall the times when coaches and postboys gave to it life and wealth. Horses were changed here; belated travellers found a warm welcome and a hearty hospitality; when the wild wintry winds swept across the country-side and deep snows lay on the ground, the open blazing hearth became a refuge worthy of a king; and mine host held that nowhere else on the highway could hungry guest find better cheer or thirsty soul purer and stronger ale. Traditions run of poaching hereabouts, and this lone house near to the estates of gamekeeping squires, with easy means of getting rid of stray pheasants and partridges, favors the idea. No doubt Sam, the hostler, knew how to snare a hare, and also knew where to hide it under the straw.

"Did you ever hear of any highwaymen in these parts?" I ask of my companion.

"They were common," he replies, "in years long ago, and some have said that Dick Turpin relieved two or three wealthy men of their purses near to the woods at the foot of the hills yonder; but I doubt if Dick Turpin was ever in this country."

So do I, but the road is lonely enough now, not a cart, horse nor man to be seen. How exciting when the coach, mud-splashed and creaking, came up to the inn with its story of robbery! Away ride horsemen to raise the hue and cry and, if possible, to find the thieves. The roads are bad, heavy, full of ruts and holes in which the horses stumble and send the yellow water in all directions, and before anything can be done night sets in and the difficulties become insurmountable. Then the searchers come back again for supper and for the moon to rise, the parish constable from Lewknor in the mean time having arrived on the scene to assume official charge of the proceedings. As his qualification for office consists in his being full of years and of rheumatism, he does very little beyond ascertaining the facts of the case and pronouncing judgment thereon. He is looked upon as an oracle by all who know him; no pagan ever listened more reverently to the augury of his priest than the men and the boys around these parts did to the utterances of the crooked and aged Dogberry. Once a rotund and rubicund coachman strange to the road and some distance gone in his cups, and therefore scarcely responsible, declared him to be an old woman; but some standers-by promptly beat him into grief, and would have beaten him into jelly had he not acknowledged his mistake. No more was said on that occasion, and we can imagine no more was done on this; and both constable and highwaymen remained comparatively unmolested.

Farther on is Kingston, an old-fashioned village with quaint straw-thatched cottages. There life peacefully slumbers, and the advent of a stranger in the quiet lane-like streets sets gossip and conjecture agog for a week. The blacksmith was standing, with arms folded, in the doorway of his shop talking to a woman picking currants in a garden across the way. They, a cow tethered by the roadside and some birds flitting from hedge to hedge were the only signs of a busy world; all else was still. Once a lark sang his rich sky-song in the clear sunlight, but the melody melted away in the heat, and the echoes seemed to fall wearily to the ground. Beside the way were many noble oaks and some remarkably fine clumps of giant beech trees. Wild flowers in abundance grew in the thick hedges and meadow-grass; roses of almost every hue vied with hollyhocks and dahlias to beautify the cottage gardens. At times the fragrance of the bean-blossom was stiflingly sweet and by its all-pervading strength suggested hounds thrown off their scent.

A pleasant walk of a mile across the fields brought us to Aston. Here we visited the parish church. It is built, as are most of the churches of this neighborhood, of flint with stone ashlar facings, and has lately been restored. The exterior is not promising, a sundial dated 1772 alone attracting attention. The parish clerk, an old man nearly ninety—so he told us—kindly unlocked the door and showed us around the inside of the building; a holy-water stoup at the door indicated its pre-Reformation origin. There is a number of tombs and mural tablets. Set in the wall in the north transept is an interesting monument to the memory of Lady Cicil Hobbee, who died in 1618. It is the figure of a lady, dressed in ruff and black robe, kneeling with clasped hands before a lectern on which lies an open book. On the top of the sculpture-work is an hourglass. In the opposite transept is a mural tablet, in Latin, of about the same date. In the aisles and the nave are vaults covered with inscribed stones to the memory of local celebrities, principally Coles and Thornhills; they are also of the early part of the seventeenth century. Going up into the chancel, one steps upon an old stone in which a life-sized figure is deeply cut. The lettering around the outer edge is difficult to read, but I believe it is in Norman French; if so, the tomb is of early Plantagenet date. Another stone tomb, partly within a low ornamented recess on the north side of the chancel, is also interesting. It must be of great age, but some worn carved work on the top alone remains. I could not ascertain anything of its history; only, a bench for the choir now hides it from the general view. Down in the nave are two small brasses almost obliterated, but still displaying a man and a woman in long robes and with hands clasped in the attitude of prayer. There are several modern tablets on the walls in the lower part of the church, and under the belfry are plainly-painted tables of the benefactors of the parish and the nature, value and object of their benefactions. The old font remains. The ancient figures in the clerestory are characteristic; they severally express Age, Youth, Sorrow and Mirth—typical of the worshippers upon whom they look. On the altar are candles and cross. In the yard rank grass hides many of the graves, and thick ivy the headstones An inscription, of 1826, runs:

> "Weep not, my Wife and Children dear,
> I am not dead, but sleeping here;
> My debt is paid, my grave you see:
> Wait but awhile, and you will follow me.
> A sincere Friend, a Husband dear,
> A tender Parent, lieth here."

Possibly neither wife nor children would feel much cheered by the fact that they would follow him; at any rate, there is something uncomfortable in the dead man's saying such things. That fourth line is very mean, contemptible and unworthy of a good-natured ghost.

Leaving this quiet and sacred spot, we had a delightful walk of about two miles across the fields to the "Barley-Mow," near Sydenham. This is the best way of seeing rural England. It is possible to walk from one end of the country to the other by footpaths, and the reward for doing so is very great. The haymakers were busy in the meadows through which we passed; in some fields sheep were grazing and cows meditatively chewing the cud; birds were singing, hedges blooming, and by the side of the tiny brook the brightly-tinted kingfisher darted from willow to brier and tall reeds and brilliant red poppies swayed gently in the warm wind. It was amusing to watch the stately, ludicrous walk of the rooks across the grass; as they carefully raise each foot, and give their body a slight and consequential tilt in doing so, they look absurdly grave and make one think of dignified black-robed monks, fat and full, tenderly picking their way barefooted through thistles or fallen holly-leaves. Some of the meadows were traversed with trenches, and in the springtime or during drought the whole land is lightly flooded: an abundant hay-crop is the result. At the Barley-Mow the ancient-looking landlady gave us some very poor ginger ale and enlivened us with a few reminiscences of her sleepy roadside inn. The tap-room is quaint, with high, worn settles and well-cut deal tables; an old-fashioned fireplace with mantel-piece near the low, smoke-hued ceiling; the walls covered with prints of prize pigs and racehorses and some bills of agricultural fairs. The hostess wore a dress which had seen better days—possibly when she was a gay maiden, forty years since; its color, that of an aged crow, dusky, mingled russet and gray, and its shape such as a novice had devised and constant, if not judicious, patching had perfected. Her whitened tresses were caught in the strings of an old black cap; a yellow collar with a bit of violet ribbon adorned her neck, and her feet were not like those pretty mice of which a golden ballad sings. In the autumn and winter evenings a goodly company of villagers tests the warmth of her hearth and the strength of her ale. Then Dick the ratter tells his stories of ferrets and weasels, at which Tim and Jack open their mouths wider and wider as the interest becomes deeper and deeper, and others tap their empty mugs approvingly on the table. A song with a rousing chorus, repeated over again and again, brings under the window the policeman, who devoutly wishes he could join the merry throng and discreetly takes himself off about the time of closing up. At fair-time and on market-days, when people pass more frequently along the highway, many stop here and refresh themselves with pure home-brewed or genuine Dublin stout from the local maltster. Close by is a large house, unoccupied; a woman hanged herself there, and her ghost now haunts the place. Our landlady had not seen the apparition herself, but, as she put it, "there be such things, you know, and lots of folks hereabouts have seen her." The horseshoe over the door sufficiently protected her from witches and the like—though, to be sure, she had once been frightened out of her wits by a travelling fellow with an electrical machine, and went to church three or four Sundays running afterward. He showed her little fellows dancing under a glass and several strange, unearthly tricks, and finished by getting her to touch a tiny handle at the end of a wire. If she ever came near seeing stars and spirits, it was then. She jumped and screamed; then she bundled him out of the front door and knelt down and said the Lord's Prayer three times, had a strong cup of tea, scrubbed out the tap-room, and thought more seriously of higher and better things. The man had a wife—a neat, trim sort of a woman—and she came afterward to get the carpet-bag which he had left in his hurry.

"I urged her to leave such a wicked man," said the landlady, "for he was an imp of Satan and would do her no good; but the blinded thing told me he was an experimenter after somebody's heart and he had never spoken an unkind word to her. Oh, the devil snares some folks!—Now, do take another glass; you will need it this hot day. No?—Well, she told me she was once a servant-girl in some outlandish place where they have fish pies—down Cornwall, I believe—and he was a mechanic with an idea, a real, good fellow, poor, and therefore obliged to travel for a living, but kind as the sun itself and bound to get out his idea. What the idea was I don't know; it had something to do with telegraph-wires. He went exhibiting his machine in gentlefolks' houses, and turned over many a honest penny. But I was scared, and I thought it best to keep to my tea and say my prayers for some time. Sevenpence, sir. Thank you. That is one, two, three, four, five—one shilling. Call again. Wish you a pleasant walk, but the weather is enough to roast a duck with the feathers on."

We passed through Sydenham, another quiet, trim village, with a modern church. There is evidently no right of way through the yard, for the gate was locked. Possibly there was nothing to see there, or the people are not to be trusted with free access to the graves of their dead or the house of their God. Another walk across the fields by shady hedgerows brought us to the road running from Towersey to Thame, and in a little while we reached the old familiar town. There was the railway bridge just as it was built some twenty years ago; there, the school-buildings in Park street, musty with age, decay, old books and pleasant and unpleasant reminiscences.

About thirteen miles from Oxford and forty-four from London is this ancient and interesting town. It is near the eastern edge of the county of Oxon, and its northern end begins on the banks of a brook bearing the same name as itself. At this end is Old Thame, and from that the town has grown almost entirely along the main highway; so that it principally consists of one long built-up street toward the south, with a few smaller ones and some lanes branching off a little way on the eastern side. The two sides of this street are bent outward like a long-bow, gradually widening for about half a mile, and then as gradually narrowing in for another half mile. In the widest place an irregular pile of buildings, consisting of shops and the town- or market-hall, has been erected. Not far to the south of this brick island in the street is the house where John Hampden died. The extension has been longitudinal; the growth, slow. The railway-station is at the extreme south, about a mile and a half from the ancient parts near the river, and, though thereabouts the buildings are mostly new and the town has suffered further elongation in its attempts to embrace—or, at least, to touch—the vein of steel which connects it with the world's great arteries of trade and commerce, there is no remarkable increase of material prosperity or of city-like bustle. Life flows on in its calm, peaceful way; the streets are clean and still; the houses and the gardens seem to sleep in their quiet, antique dignity; the people move leisurely about, sipping the honey from the flowers of business or of gossip and wisely taking their time, for they can live but once; and all who go there soon feel that they have been happily left behind by the rush of time's waters, if not, indeed, carried by a reflex tide a long way back into the ages of the past. If happiness is to be found in repose and contentment in inactivity, then the three thousand souls who dwell in this place ought to set an example to the world; and doubtless they would do so in a manner both becoming and worthy if the world would but open its eyes and see them. But, alas! like the traditional gems or flowers which pass their days unseen in ocean depths or bosky dells, the town which is so dear, and so justly dear, to its own inhabitants, is unknown to fame and almost to the maps; and when some stranger afar off chances to hear of it, and further and more wonderfully chances to look it up in a gazetteer, he passes it over with a sort of contemptuous sigh: "Umph! An old out-of-the-world, dead-and-alive place." And that, gentle reader, may be your sentence, though, if you be gentle in the truest sense of that term and will have patience to follow me along, you may end in agreeing with me that there is much that is delightful and lovely in that same old time-stranded town.

Let us first look at the church. This is a noble and historic edifice, many parts of it of great age, cruciform, with a mighty tower rising minster-style from the interstice of the cross. It stands on a slight elevation a few hundred yards from the slowly-flowing Thame, with the vicarage a little nearer the river and the remains of the old prebendal house, now a private residence, a short distance farther along the stream. Around the sacred structure is the graveyard, filled, contrary to the usual custom, with tombs and mounds on every side. As a rule, none who died in the peace of the Church were buried in the northern part of the yard; that was the region where the sun never shone and the bleak winds of winter swept over unhallowed graves. In the brightsome east and the sunny south lay the dead who slept the peace of paradise, and there in the early spring and through the long summer and into the late autumn loving hands brought offerings of flowers and loving hearts uttered the prayer that God would give even more light to his own who rest in him. And when the snow was on the ground and the Christmas joy reigned in the land, then, too, fond ones remembered those who had gone before, and placed a wreath of evergreen holly on their graves, token of perpetual love, and dropped the rich red berries on the white winter ground, spots of blood, as it were, even like unto the stains which fell from Calvary. No doubt here the people did as elsewhere, for in the old time there was an affectionate and ever-present clinging to those who had passed beyond the veil: they were never forgotten; and there was a right of way through the churchyard, so that at any time the living might enter God's acre and offer up a Paternoster beside the grave of their heart's treasure. But at Thame—possibly because of the buildings toward the north—the general rule of not burying in that part does not obtain. The dead fill up the available space, so that a new portion has been added to the eastern end. I know other churchyards where the north is used.

The main approach to the church is from the south side through a lovely avenue of lime trees. Such avenues are common in England, and, though this is not so glorious as some—say that at Stratford-on-Avon —yet it has stood for many generations, and along its noble path processions have moved hither and thither, now of rejoicing and now of sorrow, at one time of high ceremony and at another of humble town-worshippers. The appearance of the church inside is of mingled satisfaction and of various periods. The building has escaped restoration, so the old pews and galleries, the three-decker pulpit with the sounding-board and the tables of the Ten Commandments, the Creed and the

Lord's Prayer over the altar, remain. With the unsightliness of the last century come in bits of late mediæval belongings. Near the door is the antique alms-box, and a little farther in the old font, both probably of pre-Reformation age. There are no crosses or candles in the building, the tendency of the parish being to an extreme Protestantism, nor is the image of St. Thomas of Canterbury, which once occupied an honored place, to be seen. Ancient rood-screens separate the nave from the chancel and the transepts or chapels. The tombs are many and of extreme interest. In the centre of the chancel is a massive and exquisitely-carved monument to Lord and Lady Williams, dated, I think, 1559. It is cut in marble and alabaster, and he and she lie in full-length effigy, their feet resting against a greyhound and a horse and their bodies wearing the costume of the period. The whole is railed in and covered with a dingy red curtain, which is drawn back for the benefit of visitors. Lord Williams was a vigorous and violent mediævalist, and had no sympathy with the reforms which had taken place under Henry VIII. and Edward. He took a prominent part in the suppression of the new practices and was a leading spirit in the martyrdom of the prelates at Oxford. No doubt, when he saw the ashes of Latimer and of Ridley, he thought the end of their work was also near; nor may we deem him and others who did as he aught but honest and earnest men—more desirous, indeed, in their conversation and love to defend and maintain the ancient faith and customs than in their zeal wantonly to cause reverend prelates and tender women to suffer the pains of death. But the irony of fate is written across the times. Lord Williams rests within the sanctuary where once he heard the mass sung and beheld the glories of the worship he loved, but over his tomb an office is said and words are preached which he denounced and resisted. A bitter opponent of Protestantism rests in a Protestant place of worship; a Protestant place of worship shelters in its most sacred precinct a bitter opponent of Protestantism. The singular thing about the tomb is that the feet are toward the west. I can find no reason for this unique position, and conjecture is useless.

Lord Williams, however, was not wholly occupied in the suppression of Protestantism. His was an active and a public life—partly that of a courtier and partly that of a country gentleman—and seems to have been graced with the virtues of generosity, kindliness of spirit and nobility of mind. In the reign of Henry VIII. he was keeper of the king's jewels, and also one of the commissioners for the dissolution of the monasteries, possibly visiting the abbeys and the priories of Oxfordshire with John Tregonwell in the autumn of 1536. By his purchase, in 1539, of the ancient seat of the Quartermains, at Rycote, his position and authority in the county were increased, and in 1553, when Lady Jane Grey was forced by her ambitious friends to receive the crown, he gathered some seven thousand men and at Thame and elsewhere boldly proclaimed Mary to be the rightful queen. A few days later he and his Oxfordshire men accompanied the daughter of Catherine of Arragon in her triumphal progress into London, and his royal mistress recognized his fidelity by making him a peer of the realm. It was to him that Queen Mary entrusted the princess Elizabeth when she sent her as a prisoner from the Tower to the royal bowers of Woodstock. At that time the life of the future Virgin Queen was dark and doubtful. Only by the barest chance did she escape execution in the Tower; and when the tidings came that she should be separated from her servants and go to Woodstock, she considered herself in great peril and was filled with mournful dread. But Lord Williams, while he fulfilled his trust with honesty to his sovereign, showed unusual kindness to Elizabeth. Possibly he remembered the beautiful and witty Anne Boleyn, and was moved to pity by the wrongs and sorrows of the comely daughter of his old king. When asked if treachery were purposed, he sturdily exclaimed, "Marry, God forbid that any such wickedness should be intended! which rather than it should be wrought, I and my men will die at her feet." When in their progress they reached his house at Rycote, he gave her a princely and hospitable entertainment, treating her, in the presence of a noble company of knights and ladies, with the honor due to her exalted rank. Free was the mirth and loud was the song that night—May 22, 1554. The lord of Rycote had converted the old manor-house into domestic offices, and close by had built a large and glorious mansion—verily, a palace. In hall and in kitchen boundless hospitality was displayed. The drooping spirits of the princess revived; and when some one warned the generous host of the possible consequences of his thus acting toward the queen's prisoner, he warmly replied "that, let what would befall, Her Grace might and should be merry in his house." Nothing remains of the noble house at Rycote; the male line also ceased in the lord lying in the alabaster tomb; and whether the zealous and loyal man at the last softened toward the professors of the new faith I know not—only, in 1559, when dying, he sent for the godly John Jewel, lately returned from exile, to visit him.

In the chancel are other tombs—among them, partly let into a recess in the wall, one to Sir John Clerke, dated 1539. There is also a brass to Edward Harriss, 1597, and high up, hanging from the wall, is the helmet of one of the Clerkes, with vizor and all complete. Visitors are told it is the one which Sir John Clerke wore in the ancient wars—an indefinite statement, but perhaps referring to the Battle of the Spurs. In the chapels are also tombs of great age and interest. In that on the north side is one, altar-shaped, to Sir John Dormer. On the top is a brass of himself and his two wives, and at their feet are brasses, arranged in three groups—one of which has been stolen—of his twenty-five children. It is of the year 1502. In the south are even greater attractions. In one corner, high up in the wall, is carved a full-length figure of an ecclesiastic. It may possibly represent a bishop, but whether originally built in the wall or removed from some position in the floor I do not know. The robes, the features and the hands clasping a book to the breast are plain, though the stone is much worn and of great age. There is an aumbry underneath it, implying the former existence of an altar close by. Probably the tomb to the Quartermains, dated 1400, stands upon the site of this altar, if, indeed, the tomb may not have been used as the altar itself. The figures on this tomb are in good preservation. On the brass around the edge of the marble slab may be read the piteous appeal to the visitor of his charity to say a Paternoster for the repose of the souls of those who lie beneath. Near by is a similar tomb to the Greys, but some vandal long ago stole the best part of the brasses, and the date is therefore uncertain.

As one looks upon these monuments of men who lived their life centuries since, one realizes more than ever the strangeness of time. They once frequented this sacred building; they were the great men of the neighborhood—worthy, let us hope, of the distinction—and to their dependants, whose names are forgotten and whose dust has long since mingled with common earth, kind and forbearing. With hawk on their fist and hound at their feet or clad in coat of mail and armed with sword and lance, they came to worship that God who is the Father of us all. List to the lordly walk along the echoing aisle, and think of the life and power, the proud authority and noble dignity, which are manifest in every step! They once saw these same walls, rejoiced in this same sun and felt these same emotions; now they lie in mouldering dust, and the immortality in sculptured tomb and charitable bequest which they had fondly hoped would have been theirs is fast passing away. The idle tourist reads their names, the greedy poor receive their doles, but without interest in them, and even the congregation worshipping beside them and in the sanctuary which some of them may have helped to build or to beautify forgets them in its prayers, or, if it chance to think of them, regards a petition offered up to God on their behalf as superstitious and vain. Yet once masses were offered up and prayers were said at these altar-tombs, and, rightly or wrongly, people sought to realize the communion of saints as unbroken by death.

It is worthy of remark that in old time epitaphs rarely —possibly, never—referred to the moral qualities of the deceased in any but a deprecatory way. Generally speaking, the name and the titles only are given; sometimes the words are added, "miserable sinner." It was left to the last century to indulge in rhapsodies such as the following. This paragon of perfection, by name Robert Crews, died in January, 1731, at the age of sixty years:

> "He was an Humble, Obsequious Son,
> A Tender, Affectionate Brother,
> A Peaceable, Benevolent Neighbour,
> He kept up the good old Hospitality,
> His Liberal Table was spread to ye Hungry,
> His purse open to the Necessitous,
> Generous without Affectation,
> Just in His actions and Sincere to His Friend,
> A Pattern of Patience, Humility,
> Charity, Good Nature and Peace."

Look up into the lofty clerestory and observe the well-preserved and admirably-carved figures; the sculptured stone speaks of many things. In the nave first comes one placed over the pulpit, as if looking to see that the people are giving all attention, and opposite to it is one with hands crossed on the breast, as if accepting the truth and resigning the soul to it. Then come a crowned king on one side and a mitred bishop on the other; then an angel with clasped hands in prayer, opposite to one with open hands in benediction; afterward another king and bishop as before, and next to these an angel playing a harp, and on the other side an angel playing with cymbals. In the west-end corners are, on the south side, an angel holding a pen in hand, as though to record the shortcomings of the congregation, and on the north side another angel, pointing to an open book—perhaps the Book in which is written the way of life and forgiveness. In the south aisles are also heads, much worn and some almost gone, but there is one denoting Mirth and another Sorrow. Doubtless Age and Youth, Wisdom and Folly, were also depicted. Many of these figures look down upon the worshippers, and here as elsewhere it must have been something, in an age of art and faith, for the people to look up from their devotions and behold these faces, so full of meaning and expression. Surely they were unto them as messengers from the King! By the side of the door, in the old stone porch, are also heads, now barely decipherable, but no doubt once full of the expression of welcome to the incoming worshippers. There are also some at the great windows—angels peeping out of God's blessed sanctuary to watch over the loved ones who sleep in the still yard outside. Nor is the interior alone in this respect. On the high northern wall of the nave, looking toward the north-west, is a figure in splendid preservation. It is gazing skyward eagerly and expectantly, with every feature of the face marked with sweet and longing expression. Possibly it may denote the desire for the Divine Presence to abide with the brethren who in past days lived in the religious house in that direction, or, as possibly, the looking for the procession wending its way therefrom to the holy sanctuary. As the warm rays of the July afternoon sun lighted upon it, it seemed in its grace and loveliness to breathe forth a benediction over churchyard, tree-tops and river-meadow, even such as angels breathe when from the battlemented walls of the Golden City they look down upon the distant plains of earth. There are also huge grotesque faces—evil spirits fleeing from the presence of the Lord, utilized by the old builders for waterspouts, belching out of their gaping mouths the floods of ill, and in two or three instances used by the sparrows in which to build their nests. A sundial has the significant word "Jerusalem" across its face.

The associations of the place sacred both by time and by purpose must needs be many. It is a privilege to walk where holy feet have trod, and to look upon things which once met the gaze of those who have long since been with God. The church is the centre of a town's history. Here generation after generation met and worshipped. In life they worked together; in death they lie side by side. From the font to the grave each walked the same path, knew the other's hopes and sorrows, had a common interest in the things around him. The house of God was the home of all, and rich and poor met together because the Lord was their Maker. Before the church porch they gathered as the bells chimed for service and talked over the events of the past week; within, they listened to the words that should make them wise for ever. What a blank in the old life there would have been without the church, itself the symbol, the witness, of unity—the shrine to which the many feet wended their way! Time seems nothing amid such surroundings; the past melts into the present, the mists of ages lift, and the eye beholds armored knights, cowled monks, buskined yeomen, foresters, artisans, laborers and men-at-arms as in the bygone days they thronged these consecrated walls. There were old men and women bent and gray with years; stalwart, hearty folk of middle life; lovers young and hopeful—my brave Harry and my rosy-cheeked Margery; and boys and girls, thoughtful, mischievous, playful, good and bad—just as we see them now. As I stand before the eastern window and the great bell in the tower utters its slow and heavy toll, heralding some one to the grave prepared beyond the lime trees, I think, though dissimilar in outward things, yet in essentials how alike the ages are! There are few nobler or more interesting buildings than that old church of Thame.

Under the southern wall is the tomb of a good and holy man who some years since was vicar of this parish. Ere long the inscription thereon will be obliterated, for in this English atmosphere stones speedily become darkened and lichen-covered, and the new appears as the old. As we pass from the church down the narrow lane which leads into the High street of the town we may recall the kindly clergyman whose memory is dear to many of his former parishioners. This building on the left hand is the grammar-school. It was founded and the house built in the year 1569, and might have been as great as Eton or Harrow had the Fates been in its favor. The endowment is considerable, and a quarter of a century since the school had four or five masters and one scholar. Some of the masters were very good cricketers, and, as the mind of their solitary pupil was like unto a narrow-necked bottle, they could not occupy their time in forcing into him the wine of wisdom or the syrup of knowledge. While all, therefore, received their allotted stipends, one did the duty. The ecclesiastical commissioners made a change in this happy state of affairs, and now many of the townsmen avail themselves of Lord Williams's foundation. This was the Lord Williams already spoken of, and it is not unworthy the attention of those who profit by his beneficence that he by no means approved of the views which for three centuries have been taught in his school. His money has gone to make men after the pattern of those whom he helped to burn at Oxford. Peace to his soul, that is his punishment. And the good vicar, the Rev. Mr. Prosser, whose name I write with a tender reverence, was one who through a long and faithful ministry stood up manfully for the Protestant character of the Church of England. It would not have daunted him if Lord Williams had come out of his marble tomb with a score of his men-at-arms and haled him to prison; he was ready to die as Cranmer had done. Not that he was a bitter controversialist. He sought to soften men's hearts with the doctrines of Christ rather than to inflame them with the passions of party. It was more by his gentle, loving example, his kind words and peaceful counsels, than by violent denunciations or pessimistic utterances, that he won souls. Yes; were those old timbered houses on the other side of the Atlantic, there would be a sign giving particulars concerning them. He visited his people and discharged his duties with a fidelity akin to that of Chaucer's Poor Parson, and among those in paradise are doubtless many who throughout eternity shall rise up and call him blessed. I see him now, with his hand on a little curly-head, teaching the boy the words, " God so loved the world that he gave his only begotten

Son." When the text is learned, the lad will be richer by sixpence and will have a lesson to remember for life. The wants and the cares of his flock were his own. To the troubled he gave sympathy; to the needy, alms. It was rumored among the Baptists—who were of a kind known as Particular—that he believed in doctrines of grace, and would have preached them only he was afraid of being sent to prison by his bishop. Other dissenters in the town, however, used to say he had too much sense to believe anything of the sort, and the only fault they had with him was that he preached with a manuscript and took tithes. The tithes were as small as the sermons were long, so that his income was not to be compared with his outlay. Dear old man! in the simplicity and goodness of his heart he would have preached the whole of the longest day in the year if thereby he could have saved one poor child out of heresy and schism. He has gone to his rest, and the church is as he left it, and it will be some time yet before Lord Williams will turn over in his tomb to the *Introibo* of the Mass or to the majesty of the Gregorian tone.

The High street is very still this warm day, and, indeed, except when the market is being held, it is seldom otherwise. There are some old houses, but not many of great age. The inns look respectable and clean, and thrive as much upon village visitors as upon the townspeople themselves. The best hostel in the place has the Transatlantic cognomen of the "Spread Eagle," but the sign looks as though it were painted some time before Christopher of famous memory turned his vessel's prow toward the Western strand. They who desire English cheer good and solid, native-grown mutton and deep foaming ale, can have it here. The mahogany underneath which the traveller will rest his wearied legs is massive and suggestive of club dinners. The guests all sit down to the one table and eat and drink in silence; John likes to do one thing at a time: "Shall I not take mine ease in mine inn?" An hour and a half at the Spread Eagle will make a man happy as a king and supremely indifferent to earthquakes, taxes, gnats, newspapers and policemen. There are some shops—grocers, drapers, haberdashers, stationers, and the like—but the front door rings a bell when it is opened, so as to bring the elsewhere-occupied shopman to the counter. This suggests small custom. The chapels belong to some of the moderately-thriving tradesmen, who attend and control them until they themselves have gained a higher social position, and then they go to the parish church.

Up an intricate back lane was once the meeting-house of the Baptists—a highly-respectable folk, but, like the conies, feeble and abiding in retired places. It was not necessarily choice which drove dissenters to build their chapels in such out-of-sight holes and corners, but the unfortunate exigences of circumstances. No one would imagine there was any such place up this long, winding alley. Before an adverse force could get to the trembling worshippers warning could be given them, and they could scatter themselves in the neighboring gardens and back yards. The house was a square one, strongly built, with its roof shaped like a pyramid. Inside, it had a gallery at one end and at the other a pulpit near the ceiling. High pews, stiff and bare, typical of the stern religious convictions of the congregation, filled the building. There was no musical instrument, not even a tuning-fork, and the hymns—very long and very tedious—were given out and sung two lines at a time. An old farmer fervent in piety and simple in taste for many years ministered to the flock. He needed no paper and no preparation for his sermons: all he did was to stand the big Bible up on its back and let it fall open at any place by chance; then the first passage his eye lighted on became his text, and he went on for upward of an hour and a quarter. Frequently he spoke to edification; and when he had exhausted the wiles of the devil and the wickedness of the world, he had always the enormities of the Church of England to fall back upon. It is probable that he thanked God every day of his life that Providence had created the Church for his special benefit. Certainly, had it not existed he would have been without a subject two-thirds of his time—unless, to be sure, Satan had manifested himself in some similar ecclesiastical form. The farmer-preacher was popular with his people. The only time their affection for him was shaken was when an aged sister saw him speaking in the street to that man of evil the parish curate. He seemed to be on good terms with him—a thing bordering dangerously upon the unpardonable sin and not to be endured for a day. But when the anxious flock knew that their pastor was only cross-examining the curate on the idolatrous and profane doctrine of baptismal regeneration with a view to exposing and refuting that abominable belief, they were satisfied and complacently quoted one to another, "Wise as serpents!" The trouble which seemed to weigh most with the good old man was the apparent oblivion in which the vicar sank him. No matter how much he spoke against the Church, the Church went on as though he were not. This was provoking, of course, for there is little satisfaction in knocking about a man who will not strike back. At last the congregation decided to leave the house where it had met for upward of a century, if not for two centuries, and to build a chapel in the light of the sun and the town. It stands farther up the main street, and from the day it was first occupied to this the members have been unhappy. They were better off in the old place. They tried to bury their past; they did, indeed, bury their ancient pastor, and they have grieved over the grave and quarrelled over the will ever since.

I remember attending a service in the old chapel many years ago. It was in May, when the apple trees in a garden close by, seen from the gallery, were in bloom. The building was filled in every part; some, indeed, occupied the pulpit with the preacher. A stranger delivered a special sermon, but the occasion I have forgotten. He had a clear, earnest voice, an impassioned delivery, and, though evidently uncultured, was well read in the Scriptures and in the Christian experience. It was late in the afternoon, and the long, low sunlight swept across the still and intensely attracted congregation, a strange, soft weirdness making one realize mysterious things. The text was from Habakkuk: "God came from Teman, and the Holy One from mount Paran. Selah. His glory covered the heavens, and the earth was full of his praise." The Divine Presence was not only described: it was felt. As the preacher went on with graphic force to speak of the glory and the praise the people were wrapped in silence and emotion. There was no stir, no restlessness; no one seemed to breathe. The shadows lengthened, the sunlight died away, gloom stole over the land, but the people listened on and looked upon the streaming glory from Teman and the dazzling radiance from Paran. Then the preacher sat down, but the stillness was unbroken. In awe and wonder people waited in the gloaming, as if expecting to see the darkness pass away and God appear. The spell was relieved by some one beginning the " Praise God, from whom all blessings flow," and instantly the large assembly rose to its feet and sang aloud. How the old building echoed with the sound of many voices! And all went away feeling that for once—perhaps only for once in this life—they had seen the glories of the land beyond the silent stars.

Stand with me for a few minutes in the shade near this pond in the street, and before we take ourselves to the station let me present to you two or three more of the old inhabitants of the town.

This stout ancient gentleman in the knee-breeches and broad-brimmed hat standing at the corner of East street and High is one of the honored and honorable members of the community. He is a Quaker, and through his long and useful life has been both an ornament to his society and a benefit to his fellow-men. The only weakness known to the public of which he has been guilty is writing what he is pleased to call poetry; but in this he is not singular. A neighbor and tenant of his, a sawyer by trade and a dog-fancier by way of amusement, is fond of writing obituary and satirical lines. Whenever any one of consequence in the neighborhood dies, or whenever the zeal of the Wesleyans—against whom he has a violent antipathy—breaks out in extraordinarily volcanic-like fervor, good John Potter leaves his log which he is sawing and, accompanied by two or three of his favorite dogs, goes to the "Cross Keys," there at the corner, and with mine host Howlett's strong ale soon reaches a stage of spirituous and poetic exhilaration. A few hours later, in his back parlor, redolent with divers aromas— for his wife makes ginger beer and takes in dyeing and is as fond of cats and jackdaws as he is of dogs—the worthy disciple of the Muses may be found driving his quill, scratching his head, swearing at the world in general and at the partner of his joys in particular, sipping his potion of porter qualified with an unknown quantity of Scotch of unknown strength, and thus evolving slowly and painfully stanzas, rhymes and fantasies which shall be the wonder of the world when the world has nothing else to do but read them. Fortunately, a policeman lodges a few doors away, and the poet's wife and that guardian of the peace take John off to bed before any serious damage is done. The next morning both the author and the poem are ready—the one for the saw-pit and the other for the press; and when the latter has done its work, a copy is sent with Mr. John Potter's compliments to our good friend the Quaker. It has been said—but neither you nor I can believe it as we look into his calm, honest face as he stands there looking up into the poplar trees to see which way the wind is blowing—that the Quaker snorts and fumes and exhibits emotions of a dangerous tendency when he receives and reads his neighbor's effusions. He has even been charged with throwing the copy behind the fire, and then, being uncertain as to some line but faintly remembered, and his curiosity growing greater as his memory grows less, has sent to ask Mr. Potter to do him the favor of giving him another copy. The sawyer-poet is flattered and delighted: his rival is doubtless impressed; he has pleasure too extensive to be set forth in an ordinary foolscap sheet of paper in acceding to his request. A few days later, and within an envelope John finds the copy with emendations and criticisms crushing and severe, and a request that he will pay up the five weeks' arrears of rent without further delay—even more crushing and severe. But John is not vanquished. The poem is dedicated to some local patron; and when it is presented, John receives a guinea —perhaps two guineas, for the gentry are careful to encourage incipient genius and do not wish to have the misfortunes of Goldsmith or the tragedy of Chatterton repeated—and armed with that John calls upon his landlord, gives him a piece of his mind and pays his rent in full.

Our Quaker, however, is not harsh, though his treatment of his brother-genius may seem so. He is kind to his tenants; and when they bring their rent he gives each of the children an apple or a dose of camphor and nitre. The latter is in cases where he thinks medicine is needed, and it is always taken, because he is a great man and a wise man. He also lends books to the good boys of the neighborhood. He quarrels with no one, and, as he and his wife are the only Quakers in the town, his dining-room does for a place of worship; and some evilly- and carnally-minded folks have said that the two Friends have sat there in silence the whole of a Sunday afternoon, not uttering a word and only bobbing their heads at each other. Be this as it may, he always pays his tithe and treats the parson with respect.

The old man is charitably disposed. As he comes

down the street toward us he stops to speak to that woman who in sun-bonnet and shabby black dress is going in the opposite direction. She keeps a bakery not far from here, is a Baptist, and looks upon Quakers and people of that stamp as self-righteous Pharisees and not much better than ignorant and worldly churchmen. But she has a son who has brought her trouble—woeful trouble not to be spoken about—and were we nearer we should hear the kindly Friend's customary greeting: "Is thee well to-day?" See! without waiting for a reply he slips a gold coin into her hand and passes on. She looks at it; a tear comes into her eye; a vision of hope passes before her; and she lifts up her heart to God that he will bring that man into the truth, save him from his legalism and will-worship and make him an heir of glory.

Farther on, nearly opposite where we are standing, is the barber's shop. Mr. Simon is a tailor by trade and a Methodist by profession. His shaving and haircutting is an extra accomplishment, done because there is no one else at this end of the town competent to reduce stubbly beards or to make a feather-lock on a boy's crown. He is a deliberate man: he walks, eats, talks, snuffs, snips his scissors, sneezes, in a deliberate way. When he is serious, as at prayer-meetings or when shaving some unknown stranger, he is very deliberate. He has frequently prayed down two inches of tallow candle, and not a few of the brethren have wished that Brother Simon's piety would run a little faster and his devotions keep within one snuffing of the candle; but the sisters think him exactly and edifyingly right. When engaged in controversy, as is often the case, he is somewhat of

Sir Roger de Coverley's turn of mind, and thinks there is much to be said on both sides of the question. On only two things are he and the principal man in the Baptist chapel fully agreed—first, that the Church is a nest-bed of popery and wickedness; and secondly, that the parson and the Quaker are good men, but not after God's own heart. The Baptist man is a butcher, and they deal with each other, but they have never prayed together for Church, parson or Quaker, because the one is doubtful if the other has true saving knowledge, after all. How a man can say he loves God and not take to election and immersion is the problem on the one side, and how he could love God and take to them is the problem on the other. They have discussed the question over and over again, but without any further result than making the tailor-barber threaten to buy no beef from the butcher, and the butcher declare that he will neither send his cloth to the tailor-barber nor come himself to have his hair cut. But the breeze passes over, and each generously forgives the other; only, when the Baptist remarks that he will pray for his erring brother that he may see the light, Brother Simon replies more deliberately and freezingly than ever, "I rather think you had better pray for yourself."

Now, if there was any person in Thame or in the region round about of whom Brother Simon had a complete and wholesome dread, it was the district visitor. When she died, he said "Thank God!" with a full and grateful heart. She was an indefatigable lady of middle life, full of zeal and discretion and a loyal and patriotic churchwoman. Within her part of the town she visited every house regularly once a fortnight. She knew nothing about dissenters and honestly refused to recognize them. Were they not all English people? and therefore did they not all belong to the Church of the English people? So she visited Wesleyans, and nursed sick Baptists, and gave presents to Independent boys and girls, and lent money to everybody, irrespective of sect or denomination. Her influence was, therefore, very great, and, though she would no more think of going into the Baptist meeting-house than she would of going into the Red Lion bowling-alley, she was much beloved by every one. Even the Quaker approved of her, and, being somewhat of a genealogist and antiquary, thought of trying to ascertain if she were not a descendant or a relative of a good Quaker family; but when he intimated this to her and she warmly repudiated the possibility, he gave up the idea. Only Brother Simon could not endure her. When she called, he treated her with scant courtesy, and the tract which she left he carefully stuck high up behind the looking-glass, so that no one might see it and she might have it unread when she called again. She had a strong objection to those personal appeals which at one time were characteristic of Wesleyans, and she told our friend that she thought such very rude and vulgar—that, as at a table no polite host would press his guest to take that for which he did not care and had declined, so no minister having self-respect would force upon people that which they did not desire. Religion, she added, was not like medicine, to be given as mothers give children castor-oil—with a spoon and a rod. But as Brother Simon had never in his life dined with a gentleman and was in the habit, when he had a guest at his table, of making him eat as much as he would hold, after the manner of the plebeian English, he did not see the force of the objection; and, as for castor-oil, he always gave it to his children with black-currant jam. The district visitor was doubtless without the light. She was lost in the Church; poor soul! she was gone. He had heard of two or three young men who had been very near the Lord's vineyard led off by her persuasion to attend the Litany service at the parish church on Sunday afternoons, and of no less than seven girl-probationers who had gone one after another to be bishoped. It was an outrage, and he gave it out as his deliberate and conclusive judgment: "That lady's a proselytizer; I say it knowingly, and I say it dee-leeburatelee. As sure as her dress has flounces and her hair is done up in curls, her soul has all the phalacteries of Pharisaism and her mind has all the crookedness of the kingdom of Satan."

The sun is fast dropping behind the trees, and soon the train for Oxford will be due. This street on the left is the highway to London. The stage-coach rolled along that road less than thirty years since, and there was a something sweeter than the whistle of an engine in the winding notes of the postboy's horn. How cheerily it sounded in the clear, frosty air! Letters and strangers from great London far away! Well, forty-four miles was a long distance in those days, and the man who had been there was thought something of a traveller. The pound of real gunpowder tea, at fourpence or sixpence an ounce, which he brought back lasted a long time and was considered a luxury proper only for sick folks and for Christmas. Taken with milk, it was good; with the least drop of brandy, excellent. There are birds' nests in the hedges on that road, and a mile or so from here a footpath leading down to the river, where perch and pike abound. I know a good soul—even such a one as Izaak himself—who has drawn many a wriggling eel and weighty jack out of that water, a man whose heart at the sight of rod and line leaps as the trout to the fly on a summer day. There are no game laws relating to fish, only the question of trespassing on the land; but it is not every one who has the skill to profit by free access to the river. The fish in these old streams are cunning and wary and up to most devices of the angler. Among the flags and the rushes on the banks are frogs such as the sharks of the fresh water love, and under the willow-bark are grubs and caddis which are as irresistible to a carp or a chub as he is himself to a finny or a human epicure. In the late afternoon you may often see some one with rod and wicker basket turning up this street, bent for that same quiet stream.

This Park street, through which we pass to the railway-station, was a glorious place to the schoolboys when hid within a November fog. Then the vision was limited by the thick yellow mist, and shrill voices cried their "Halloo!" and "Tally-ho!" and nimble feet ran hide-and-seek. English people are tenacious and assertive of their rights—even English boys. A funeral of a little fellow was once wending its way down this street to the parish church. Four schoolmates carried the small coffin and the friends walked behind: hearses were unknown in that part of the country. Last of all came a maid and the only brother of the deceased. He was crying bitterly, not only for the loss of one dear to him, but also because the physician concluded that cherry turnovers were the cause of the untimely mortality, and he therefore should have no more. He was very fond of his brother; he was also very fond of cherry turnovers. However, a short distance down the street, another boy—one who was not invited to the funeral—came up to our weeping lad and wished to walk beside him. This was a privilege to which he had no right, and he was instantly and decisively ordered off. He declined to leave; the nurse remonstrated, but the dignity of the funeral was in question, and grief gave way to threats and feelings of violence. That evening, in a back lane, under some elder trees, two boys had a fight. When the mother of one of them came with her bruised and black-eyed son to the father of the other, his opponent exclaimed, "It was my funeral; he had no right to follow my brother or to stick himself in."

That building on the right, behind the row of laurel-bushes, is the Royal British School. It is not of famous reputation, nor do I know that any of its scholars have reached any position of eminence. You might find some of the old boys wheelwrights and policemen—possibly, one a gamekeeper. Nevertheless, it was largely attended in days of yore, and was remarkable for two things—a May-pole and a master. The former stood in the yard, here on the south side. Yes, it is gone, like many another good thing, but on the first day of the month of flowers it was adorned with festive and floral glory. The whole town turned out to keep May-day then, and there was a May-queen, sometimes the prettiest girl in the neighborhood, and sometimes, when no girl would act, the prettiest boy: sex made no difference. Old folks came to look on; even the Quaker, though he was not sure such things were right—possibly only expedient, to please the youngsters. And the master! Now, it is the master of whom I wish to speak, and as we walk on I will tell you about him. He took part in the fun, you may be sure, and everybody thought he was only a boy grown old. His accomplishments were varied. First of all, he was a Welshman and knew how to pronounce a word with eighteen consonants and only three vowels in it. Then he was a musician and could sing a song and scrape a violin. And lastly he was an economic and, as he was very poorly paid, knew how to make a decent living out of poverty. Where thrift is an object, it is well to have it taught by experienced teachers. Besides these gifts, he was a small man, very fond of potatoes and geography —he would hoe the one and talk about the other at the same time—had a wife, dabbled in local zoology, rode a dandy-horse, the precursor of the bicycle, read Sir Walter Scott, knew a little carpentering, kept rabbits and canaries and was looked upon with respect by all who knew him. The masters at the grammar-school did not know him, and therefore could not be expected to think anything of him; but their pupil did, and, not altogether liking his solitude, used to mingle with these ruder boys, and, all things considered, got a fair amount of pleasure out of life. It was he who advised the rubbing of the master's cane with a lemon. During a mid-day recess it was done, placed in the sun to dry, and in the afternoon when applied to a boy's shoulders it split into fragments. It was he also who knew the intricacies of tit-tat-too and how to win all the fellows' taws. Nobody could make whistles out of willow-sticks as well as he, and nobody else could talk Welsh with the master. The latter thought him a clever and promising lad and gave him many a hint concerning kidney potatoes and the use of the Latin subjunctive. It was rumored that they had frequently gone fishing together, and some one said that their intention was some day to go to New Zealand and buy a farm. That was absurd on the face of it, for the master stopped at potatoes and knew no more about fox-hunting—which is an essential qualification to good farming—than the man who was sent to the moon for gathering sticks on a Sunday.—Here is the train! Oxford? All right. Grand old place, Thame. Full of interest; church worth going many a mile to see. Tired? Warm day and a long walk. Never mind; draw the blue curtain aside and let the last sunbeams in.—Well, yes, the old schoolmaster is dead. He died years ago—some said studied to death and some said starved to death, but there is no telling. Teachers were not paid much in those days, and the wonder is there were any teachers at all. Common people did not want their children to know more than plain reading and writing and the rule of three. They had been happy on less, and fine schooling was not for the likes of them. Now that is all changed. Education is the order of the day. Ploughboys have a chance to learn Greek, and girls whose mothers washed dishes at twopence an hour can embroider and play the piano. It is enough to disturb even Lord Williams and all the old squires at Aston Rowant. And what will be the end? You cannot have wait on you at table a fellow who knows the rudiments of Sanskrit and all about conic sections, nor can you have to scrub your floor or to starch your collars a woman who can speak Italian and criticise Matthew Arnold. When everybody knows as much as you know, what will become of you? Electricity, eh? Nonsense! Talk about electricity after a day spent in the country and a town whose only idea of a track of lightning is the trail of a snail across a cabbage-leaf! In America we have the negro and the Irish to do our heavy labor and the Chinese to do our washing, but what have you in England got? No, the people here are dull; we have seen more to-day than half the inhabitants hereabouts have seen in a lifetime. But they are going to wake up; the schools are doing wonders. If the old master were to come back, he would shake his head and say, "Alas! alas! Teaching the boys political economy and the girls botany! And where is that obedience which only can make boys men and girls women?"

Oxford again. Woodstock, Chipping Norton, Moreton-in-the-Marsh. A few miles' drive in the clear, bright moonlight, and then we sleep amid lavender and shadows.

CHAPTER IX.

The Pilgrimage to Canterbury.

> "And specially, from every schires ende
> Of Engelond, to Caunterbury they wende,
> The holy blisful martir for to seeke,
> That hem hath holpen whan that they were seeke."

No loyal churchman visiting England is likely to forego the pilgrimage to Canterbury. That is among his first duties, and is one of his chief pleasures. There is the cradle of English Christendom; there, the throne of the primate and patriarch of the Anglican communion. If he seek but to gratify his love for history and art, here he will revel in associations and surroundings of rare and multiform nature, and in the splendor of religious imagination and skill will feel as Mohammed did concerning Damascus: "After Canterbury, only paradise."

Our journey thitherward was made in a pleasant sunny morning. We could not, indeed, travel in the happy, leisurely way of dear old Chaucer's pilgrims, but the run by rail from Charing Cross through the glorious Kentish land—the country where the roses are redder and the grass is greener than in any other region in the kingdom—is of satisfying charm. The district is rich in fertile fields, thick hedgerows, noble trees, great hop-gardens and pretty towns and villages. There are several tunnels—one two miles and a half long—within the first thirty miles. The road by which mine host of the Tabard led his guests is far to the north of this, and it is only the lack of time which compels one to avoid that long-honored highway to the shrine of the blissful St. Thomas.

But this, notwithstanding, does not keep the mind from Chaucer. The morning sunlight, soft and roseate, falls upon the open volume of *The Canterbury Tales* in our hand—open, but, alas! unread. Away fly the thoughts to the days when the Third Edward sat upon the throne of England, and, though many things, such as printing, railways, telegraphs, and sundry other inventions, have changed the appearances and conditions of life, yet one feels that nature and the inner and deeper flow of human existence remain very much the same. Man lives and loves the same, works, rejoices, sorrows and dies the same, through all the ages; and the mysterious and monotonous life moves steadily on through the centuries and the millenniums, not so much changing itself as changing all around it. If there be one author more than another who convinces us of this fact, and in bringing us face to face with the men and the women of his day and generation shows us that they are of the same flesh and blood as ourselves, it is Geoffrey Chaucer. There is no more graphic picture of English life in the Middle Ages than that which he has given us. He introduces us, indeed, to a world differing widely from our own—a world in which manners and customs appear strange and the charm and the power of the age of faith and of chivalry are still vigorous and enchanting. Much that goes to make up our modern civilization was then unknown. Warriors wore their armor and their coat of mail, and fought with bows and arrows, battering-rams and lances; ships spread their white sails to the winds and thought not of the days of steam; the minstrel strolled through the land from village to village, from castle to castle, and told the gossip of the court and the country, and sang his lays of heroes to admiring villains, retainers, churls and gentlemen; and the English people lived in a great wilderness-land with here and there roads running through the mighty primæval forests, and fens undrained, and hamlets built of wood and mud, and serfs bound to the soil, and abbeys hid away in woody glens, and quaint, busy towns, scattered along the river-banks or the great highways, for ever struggling for their rights and working out the beginnings of England's urban and commercial splendor. But, in spite of all the differences, Chaucer teaches us that one feature changes not, and that is man. His characters are such as we may see any day of our life, or, to put it another way, were we transplanted to that age we would be the same as they whom he describes.

Chaucer was born in the city of London about the year 1340. His father was a wine-merchant with sufficient wealth and influence to give his son a good education and introduce him to the society of the court. In his lifetime our author served in the camp, the custom-house and the Parliament; he tried his military prowess on continental battlefields and his diplomatic skill in foreign lands; he mingled with the great and the learned, the witty and the wise, of his own and of other countries, and thus obtained a personal knowledge of human nature and character. He was a large, corpulent man with a small, fair and intelligent face, downcast, meditative eyes and a shy and weird expression of countenance. Though a diligent student and somewhat hermit-like in his mode of living, yet he loved good and pleasant society, enjoyed the pleasures of the festive board, entered heartily with his roguish genial humor and quaint fun into mirth and merrymaking, and was beloved by all who knew him. As a poet he does not stand beside the other princes of the art, Homer, Dante and Shakespeare, but he is among the first of those who come after them. Few can describe a scene or a character better than he, tell a more admirable story or write a truer or more melodious line of verse. "His best tales"—if I may use the words of a master-critic—"run on like one of our inland rivers, sometimes hastening a little and turning upon themselves in eddies that dimple without retarding the current, sometimes loitering smoothly, while here and there a quiet thought, a tender feeling, a pleasant image, a golden-hearted verse, opens quietly as a water-lily, to float on the surface without breaking it into ripple." Chaucer has little or nothing to do with those fields in which Dante and Milton suffered their imagination to roam with such magnificent and sublime freedom. They lift the veil that hides the Unseen, and display, now to our delight and now to our horror, the mysteries of the eternal past and of heaven and hell. They lead the soul through darksome, gruesome avenues and fearful, awe-subduing scenes full of shadows and suggestions that chill the blood and distress the mind. The faithful reader of the *Divine Comedy* and the *Paradise Lost*, while delighted with the glowing and finished imagery and the vast and splendid creations, will remain suspicious of the truth and half annoyed at the thought that the scenes before him are painted upon clouds, to be driven and scattered by the winds of reality. He will admit the general facts, but will question the verity or the verisimilitude of the poet's coloring. This is in itself a defect of art perhaps inseparable from the kind of subject with which Milton and Dante dealt, though the latter, being the more skilful artist and the greater poet, has it less marked than the former. What I mean by this is, one can go with Dante through the Inferno and Paradiso almost, but not entirely, thinking it to be true and real; with Milton this power to absorb and to entrance exists in a much less degree. But Chaucer avoids mystery, and therefore avoids these difficulties. There is not in his work—unless, possibly, it is in some of his renderings of legendary or foreign stories—a single impossible character. His creations are of flesh and blood —of such flesh and blood as those of Shakespeare and those of our every-day life. There is no question of truth or of falsehood: that does not arise; and as an illustration of this it may be noted that to this day it is uncertain whether the prologue to the Canterbury Tales be fact or fiction. Defoe had the faculty of presenting fiction as truth—his *History of the Plague* and his *Robinson Crusoe* are remarkable instances of this—but I think, admitting the art, no one would maintain the reality. Certainly, a company of learned men would not sit down seriously to consider the fact or the invention of the hero of juvenile life. Here and there the robe is thrust aside and the void appears. But you may try your best with Chaucer's prologue, apply to it every canon of criticism that you like, and you will utterly fail to decide that it is not true and literal.

What a group does the poet present to us in his Canterbury pilgrims! How vivid and how real they appear! All sorts and conditions are there—men of war, ecclesiastics, shipmen, merchants, tradesmen, servants, farmers and women of both the world and the Church. Their idiosyncrasies are described and an individuality is imparted with true dramatic power. Once master the description of any one of them, and that one for ever remains distinct in the mind. No one can forget Madam Eglentyne, the prioress, "that of her smiling was full simple and coy," so expert in singing the "service divine, entuned in her nose full seemly," so gracious in her manner and learned in her language, and so tender-hearted that she wept over a mouse caught in a trap and fed her dogs with roasted flesh, milk and bread made of the finest flour. She had a long and well-proportioned nose, green eyes, a small mouth and a remarkable forehead. The goodwife of Bath, with her bold red face, her loud laugh and her remedies for love, was a very different personage. She wore sharp spurs on her feet, and, besides company in her youth, had had five husbands. But what strikes you is the distinctiveness of all the characters; each has a strong personality. The good parson, the physician whose "study was but little on the Bible," the brown-hued sailor, the merry friar, the fat monk, the gentle pardoner, the choleric reeve and the brave knight stand out in the company as never to be forgotten, as people whom we seem to have ourselves known and spoken to—old friends, indeed, as familiar, every one of them, as Sir John Falstaff, Samuel Pickwick, Esq., and the meddlesome old gentleman of St. Rowan's Well.

There is in Chaucer an absence of introspection and subjectivity, so painful in many poets and so popular with many people. It may seem a small thing for a man to look within or without—within, upon his own self, his thoughts, emotions, powers, sins, virtues, and so-forth; or without, upon the world of men and nature with its multiform life; but the result is great. Perhaps the most unhealthful tendency of certain religious types is this constant morbid looking within, dissecting and testing feelings, analyzing conceptions of truth and motives of vice and virtue; it is popular, but is neither soul-strengthening nor soul-developing. Its root is selfishness. As if self were the all-important thing in the universe, the most wonderful of God's creations and the object of his exclusive care! Under the plea of being spiritual and having adroitly fastened the epithet "moral"—which is supposed to imply awful and intelligent depravity—upon its opponent, it spends its time in taking care of dear self both for time and for eternity. As far as the world is concerned, it is not worth a thought, and may go on to ruin and to death. When you meet with one having this tendency, if you are fortunate enough in having a soul otherwise constituted, you feel that there is a great gulf between you. There is no touch, no affinity. You have no common ground of interest. To the one, self is but as a plumed seed drifting hither and thither on the autumn winds. Hence you read many writers, and you lay aside their books as being good, indeed, but not exactly what you want; you cannot get into them. But Chaucer is not of this kind. You read his lines, and you are at once face to face with things that are to you real and living.

Take his patriotism. Chaucer lays the framework of his Canterbury Tales in the country of his birth and his love, and in doing so he makes his framework thoroughly English. It is true Boccaccio had done the same with his tales: they are in themselves Italian and set in an Italian background; but Boccaccio's background is repulsive to an English mind. Florence is suffering from a plague of which the author gives a most powerful and ghastly description, and while the plague is devastating the city, filling its homes with bitterest sorrow and its streets with neglected dead, the Florentines are away in a country villa amusing themselves with the recital of tales, of the morality of which the least said the better. Of course Boccaccio's object was artistic, and he has made the contrast decided and terrible; but I venture to say that no English mind can endure a contrast so great and so awful. It is like dancing on the graves of the dead—like minstrelsy in the house of mourning. There is a heartlessness in the whole work: its teaching is heartless; the best, perhaps the only redeeming, story in the collection—that of Griselda—is a piece of heartlessness impossible except, perchance, in an Italian. Boccaccio was true to his natural instincts and to his age; so was Chaucer, and, thank God! England is not Italy. Our great poet has no black canvas on which to set his creations, no harrowing contrasts wherewith to produce his effects. Instead of a plague-stricken city, it is a pilgrimage of happy, light-hearted English people along a highway in the bright springtime through the sweet Kentish land to the shrine of England's national saint, Thomas à Becket. Twenty-nine men and women met at the Tabard Inn, in Southwark, and agreed to travel together to Canterbury and to beguile the journey with the recital of tales of adventure or legend. It may seem odd to us of the nineteenth century that such merrymaking should associate itself with a religious undertaking, but English people had not then heard, and they have not learned yet, that religion is not to enter into everything, and that in everything, even common things such as eating and drinking, there is not a religious element. They saw no incongruity between a gay journey and devotion to St. Thomas of Canterbury; joy and piety were both gifts of God. And note that devotion to St. Thomas. Of course most of us have been taught that he was a bad man, a proud, arrogant abomination—not one word of which is true—but we must remember that immediately after his death and for three centuries he was England's popular saint. The people thronged to his shrine. The cathedral of Canterbury was enriched by the oblations of the thousands who bowed the knee there. Churches were dedicated to him, not only in England, but even in Scotland and in distant Iceland. He was the beloved martyr of the Church of England—beloved in his own age and in succeeding ages, till at last there arose a generation that loved the patrimony of St. Thomas better than it loved his memory and desired rather his gold than his blessing. Since then Thomas à Becket has been esteemed the vilest of the vile, and the ten generations of Englishmen that honored him have been considered the foolishest of the

MERCERY LANE, CANTERBURY.

foolish and the blindest of the blind. But Chaucer did not foresee these latter days, and his faith in the national saint was strong and his devotion great. He has little sympathy with those who seek for foreign shrines; the "holy blisful martir" of Canterbury was enough for him—a spice of contempt for everything un-English so characteristic of our forefathers.

Yonder rises the cathedral high above the city around it, grander than when the pilgrims beheld it five hundred years ago. A feeling of laudable pride moves the soul—a moment in which one thanks God that one is a member of the Church which has its earthly centre in a structure so magnificent and so hallowed. The traveller enters the city through the west gate, built by Archbishop Simon of Sudbury, and the only city gate remaining. Hence he passes through St. Peter's street into High street, on the left-hand side of which he will find the narrow way called Mercery lane, down which the pilgrims went to the cathedral. Here they bought relics and tokens of St. Thomas, and some of the wealthier among them found hospitality at the Chequers Inn, at the corner of High street. In the present heavy, antique building some parts of the ancient hostelry remain, but, alas! instead of silvern and leaden images of the holy martyr, guide-books and baby-linen are now the staple articles of merchandise. There are in this day no sounds of joyous revelry, no busy throng of worshippers from all parts of Christendom, no signs that this was once the liveliest part of Canterbury; all is quiet, sleepy, dull—pleasantly and attractively so. Walk leisurely through the narrow lane with its old overhanging houses on both sides, and think of the days when thronging multitudes frequented the shrine of England's greatest saint. There, at the end, is the gate, erected in the reign of Henry VIII., leading into the precincts. The cathedral appears in all its massive splendor—a glorious pile the vastness of which can best be realized by walking around it before seeing the inside. The more one looks, the greater and more wonderful the building becomes. It grows as the minutes pass by. Gradually the fact possesses the mind that in bygone ages churches were built, not for convenience only, not merely for shelter against wind and rain, but that they might teach great lessons and hand on from generation to generation rich and profitable associations.

Before I speak further of this sacred edifice suffer me to prepare the way by imparting somewhat of the spirit which loves to linger amongst the glories of the past, and to see in architecture and in symbolism lessons of deepest interest and greatest value.

No one contends that buildings are essential to Christianity. The early Christians had none; their system made no provision for material temples. God was everywhere, and he could be worshipped everywhere —as well on the hillside, in the desert or by the ocean-shore as within the deftly-covered walls and beneath the ceiling of cedar in Jerusalem. They worshipped in secret, in the catacombs, the caves of the earth, the wilds of the forest and the little upper chamber. The missionary who preached the gospel in the open air presented the truth to his hearers as purely and as truly as did they who spoke in the basilicas of Christian Rome. The twining branches of the woodland trees or the blue vaulted sky itself gave him a roof as grand for the nonce as he could wish whose mind was full of weighty truths and whose soul burned with celestial fire. Upon a mound of earth or on a rough-hewn stone he placed the symbol of salvation, and as he pointed men to that and told them of Him who had died thereon hard hearts were softened and proud knees bent in penitence upon the green sward or on the dusty ground. Many a soul-stirring sermon was preached and many an impressive service held in Nature's own grand sanctuary long before cathedral was seen in the land. Even in our own day an open-air service is not without its charm and power, while in cottage-rooms, on board ships, in factories and plain little chapels, Christianity still retains its converting, ennobling and beautifying strength. You will find the begrimed miner come from the gathering of two or three worshippers in a corner of the dark mine a better and a happier man; you will feel the divine afflatus in the little company who by the riverside in the summer evening have sought to speak one to another of the mysteries and the love of God.

But, for all that, a building in which the graces and the symbolic truths of architecture are displayed cannot fail to produce a beneficial effect upon the soul and to impart a fuller and a sublimer conception of Christianity. It was in the nature of things that with prosperity and influence changes should come. Art could not leave untouched the most beautiful conception ever given to man. So soon as Christianity drew to itself the culture and the wealth of Greece and of Rome, so soon the bridal-dress was placed upon the Bride of Christ. Intellect, imagination and genius went to the enrichment of the religion of Jesus; art, with the skill of a heavenly enchantress, helped to bring out its beauty and to express its thought. One cannot worship within a minster where the devout and loving imagination has wrought its mystic poem and not be moved. There is a something which steals upon the soul and fills it with reverence. The very walls seem to speak; the many-colored windows and the lines of stately shafts suggest thoughts of hallowed meaning. Fancy fills the mighty solitude with spirits from heaven's bright land, and their songs break upon the silence. The magnificence and the beauty bring one into unearthly scenes and pour into the heart sweetness and satisfaction akin to that which angels have. Such a building is an expression of God: his glory rests upon it; his presence dwells within it.

These religious edifices—the very embodiment of symbolism—are not only marvels in themselves, but also wonders of the age in which they were built. How they were conceived and constructed is a mystery. Our forefathers were rough, uncouth and coarse; they were ignorant and superstitious. Their towns and their villages were the haunts of misery and of distress. In the narrow undrained streets pestilence lurked; in the wretched cottages discomfort reigned. Yet in that past of poverty and rudeness and in those scenes of filthiness and want arose these beautiful structures, grander than Egyptian, Grecian or Roman temple, more artistic than aught we of the nineteenth century can devise. Nothing was left undone, no cost or labor was spared, that was calculated to move the spirit of devotion or to show honor to God. Earth had nothing too valuable for the purpose. Princes and barons gave of the abundance of their wealth; yeomen and serfs contributed according to their substance. Nor was it the mere love of display that led to this magnificence; on the contrary, in a rich symbolism they sought to perpetuate and to manifest their ideal of religion. Everything had a meaning and a purpose; everything was sacred and eternal. If on the outside walls of the church hideous figures were carved to denote the evil spirits fleeing from the abode of God's presence, inside the sweetest grace in pillar, arch and tracery suggested the beauty and the majesty of God's love and mercy to man. The ground-plan of the building was that of a cross, reminding man of the mystery of redemption, and oftentimes with a deflection in the lines of the walls at the east end, to denote the drooping head of the Saviour in his last moments. The spire pointing ever to the sky told of the unity of the faith and of the appealing prayer and constancy of the worshippers, while the bird of warning upon its top recalled the Master's solemn charge to his people. The nave by name and by form spoke of the "ark of Christ's Church;" the aisles, of the wings or the sails of the same. None but men possessed of a high conception of Christianity could have devised such lessons or produced such buildings. They must have realized something of the beauty of holiness, of the majesty of God, of the awfulness of eternity and of the sweetness of paradise when they sought to express those truths in the rough stone and the plastic clay.

And the effect of such sanctuaries upon them must have been great. When they knelt within the nave or walked along the aisles, they must have risen to heights of devotion they could not have reached in their own miserable homes. They must have felt that God was very near them; that here the angels brought comforting messages from the far-off land to the weary and the heavy laden; that within these consecrated walls the Lord Jesus was present for evermore. The light which streamed through the pictured windows came to them from no earthly sun, but from the throne whereon sat the Everlasting Glory, its tinted hues contrasting the beauty of grace with the coldness of nature. The faces which looked down from lofty clerestory were no figures cut in stones, but the spirits of the holy ones who from the highest heaven look back to the beloved friends of earth; those upon the windows, of angel-minstrels, of the King's messengers. The imagination, subdued and taught by the earthly temple, read therein the evangelical lessons of Christ. There was cast from the chancel-screen upon the nave the shadow of the cross beneath which all must pass who would enter the holy place. There were the seats around the altar, recalling the vision of the exile of Patmos. The orient rays resting upon the sacred place where in hallowed sacrament lay the body of the Lord spoke of the rainbow-circled throne where he sits crowned above all the kings of the earth. And, while the thoughtful soul was thus exalted to the higher world, there came the recollection that beneath this magnificence and glory was the silent crypt into which the flesh must enter, but from which the God of power shall bring back his own. These things, wrought so wonderfully by art, could not fail to touch even the man whose brain had devised and whose hand had executed. They educated and made nobler and better the mind, and taught the world that "the King's daughter is all-glorious within; her clothing is of wrought gold."

The devout Christian of the present day will not think that buildings of this sublime character are the webs which superstition weaves around the soul and which time hardens into fetters of iron, but he will see in them signs of mystic meaning, the fosterers of devotion, the interpreters of doctrine, the foreshadowings of heaven. They have served to mould his and his fathers' religion. They have aided his imagination and strengthened his affection. They have taught him that essential virtue of all religion, reverence. They have given him suggestions which have helped him heavenward and led him farther into the mysteries of God. The triumphs of Christian architecture, the grace and the charm which adorn the outer temple, must at least speak to him of that integrity of purpose and that symmetry of character which should beautify the heart wherein the Holy Ghost is pleased to dwell.

The same magnificence and symbolism that adorned the buildings extended themselves to the services. Doubtless the people loved ornate display, but there was a far deeper feeling than that. They may have gazed with wonder and with fear upon the mystic sanctuary where, amid the clouds of incense, white-robed choir and blaze of candles, the priest, arrayed in gorgeous vestments, consecrated the sacred Host, but they were in hearty sympathy and doubted nothing. They bowed with deepest reverence as the procession of priests and monks and singers, bearing cross and banner, holy relic or mysterious sacrament, passed by, reminding them of man's pilgrimage through this world. The organ sent its music echoing through the aisles, now in subdued strains of hushed supplication, now in thundering peals of glad praise, and with hallowed chant and well-sung anthem moved and softened the roughest nature and made the weary heart long to sing its song and mingle its voice with the great multitude above. Nor were these services rare things: they came daily, and many times a day. The churches were ever open, the lamp before the altar was ever burning. At no time, day or night, was silent the voice of prayer for the Church's safety, the nation's welfare, the preservation of travellers, the conversion of the heathen or the everlasting rest of the departed. In the monasteries the twenty-four hours were one round of devotion. Lauds, prime, tierce, sext, nones and compline were sung in every religious house in the land. At daybreak matins, at sunset evensong, brought rough hind and belted knight, rustic maiden and high-born lady, to their beads and their meditation. Ever and anon there broke upon the air the sweet melody of the murmuring chimes, telling of joy and gladness, or perchance the heavy, sad tone of the passing-bell, speaking of mortality and of the duty to pray for the dying. And even now, in these days of hurry and faithlessness, a sweet restfulness and a gentle awe steal upon us when, with the door closed upon the outer world, we stand within the ancient sanctuary. A holy peace falls upon the soul, the Divine Presence is felt, the knee bends and the heart in joyous emotion pours itself out to Him whom we may have sought in the world in fields and in gardens, but have found only in his temple.

Perhaps the highest inspiration which an edifice full of beauty and luxuriant in symbolic art can give is to be had in the calm, moonlit eventide. As the pale beams fall upon its walls, shading the outline of tower, pinnacle, nave and chancel and dimly realizing the tracery of the windows, the carved gargoyles and the arched doorway, the imagination sits upon Fancy's throne and begins its happy revellings. There are suggestions that the soul loves to encourage, thoughts that come to one like dreamy music in the gloaming. The silence of the place reminds one of the mysterious stillness into which all things living must enter. Not now, as in earlier hours, does the sound of chanting voices fall upon the ear like the roll of wave-floods on the beach; no brightness flows in streams of liquid beauty through the antique windows; no sign is there of the great world, so noisy in its bustle, so troubled in its life. There comes no melody of murmuring chimes, telling of joy and gladness, and no sad tone of passing-bell, speaking of mortality and of the duty to pray for the dying. The scene is impressively unearthly. In the deep shadows mingling with the soft light you see the mysteries which are ever and anon thrown across the gospel-page—mysteries which we cannot fathom, and would not if we could. As you turn away you realize the grace and the power of the system which demands such a tribute of beauty, you gain an insight into the spirit of symbolism, and more than ever the fact of religion and the ideal of Christianity impress themselves upon you.

Nor are the associations of Christian buildings less calculated to deepen and to strengthen the religious spirit. The comparative changelessness of the building helps to this end. While things around are passing away, while generation follows generation and the seasons run their courses, these sacred walls remind us of the permanence and the stability of religion. Sunday after Sunday, year after year, the eye rests upon the same hallowed surroundings and the beating heart is hushed in the same solemn stillness. Here worshipped others of our race—men and women who have long since passed into the Eternal Presence. Here hymn was sung and prayer offered long, long ago, as to-day. Here, now as then, the echoes of the gospel die amid the sweeping arches and within the dark bosom of the groined roof. It is the same as ever. And in olden time, when the dead were laid to rest, sometimes within the consecrated building, sometimes in the yard around it, and sculptured monuments and jewelled shrines commemorated departed worth and grandeur, there was that which brought home very closely the fact of mortality and the doctrine of the communion of saints. They who lay in the fast-closed vaults or in the green-clad graves were the links which bound not only the present to the past, but also earth to heaven. The rudest spirit was hushed when in a place hallowed by associations such as these; the most irreverent could not but bow the head when walking along aisles which once had been trodden by those whose ashes were mouldering beneath the lettered pavement. Nor could the thoughtful man think of the time when he would be borne within the temple, or look upon the spot where he would be laid to rest, without tender emotion—emotion which could be stilled only when the eye fell upon some object which taught that Jesus is the Resurrection and the Life.

It is impossible to wander in such an Eden of pleasant delights as I have sought to suggest here in the very shadow of Canterbury without thinking of the times in which lived the men who wrought these structures. It was not the building only, but everything else, that marked the reality of those ages of faith and devotion. Maxims such as these were enjoined upon all Christian men: "Arise early, serve God devoutly and the world busily; do thy work wisely, give thine alms secretly, and go by the way sadly." Letters of those days are interesting for the deep reverential spirit of their greeting—perhaps too often formal, but still a quaint, sweet form. The knight was charged by the dignity of his order to uphold the rights of maidens and of widows, truly to hold his promise to his friend and his foe, to honor his father and his mother, to do no harm to the poor, but to be merciful and to hold with the sacrifice of the great God of heaven. Nor were the clergy ignorant either of necessary doctrinal truth or of their duty to the people. They taught the people at least the stories and general truths of Scripture, and undoubtedly sought, according to the light they had, the good of the Church and the nation. In a period strongly marked by caste they moved between the court and the cabin, from the mansion of the peer to the mud hut of the peasant, and endeavored to soften the pride of the one and to better the hard lot of the other, and to bind all together in a true Christian brotherhood. The monks, too, were far from deserving that wholesale condemnation which later times passed upon them. Early members of their orders had gone out into the wilderness and the barren places, far away from the haunts of men, where they might worship God in peace and live in solitude. The richest and the most beautiful of modern abbey-lands had originally been desolate, uninhabited and worthless. In some deep sequestered glen, the home of the wild boar, the bittern and the crane, or beside the waters of some almost unknown stream, or by the shore of the great, lonely ocean itself, they built their house and their sanctuary, and lived roughly and rudely by the labors of their hands. Here they gradually gathered around them a village of artisans and laborers, who depended upon them for support and protection. The most liberal hospitality was given to all who needed it. The Fathers cared for the poor and the sick, administered justice and kept good order on their estates, and supplied the neighboring villages with the ministrations of religion.

CHAPTER X.

In the Cathedral.

"I lift mine eyes, and all the windows blaze
With forms of saints and holy men who died,
Here martyred and hereafter glorified."

WE enter the sacred edifice by the south-western door —a porch built by Thomas Chillenden, prior at the beginning of the fifteenth century, and covered with niches in which are placed famous characters connected with the history of Canterbury. A scene of splendor bursts upon the vision—a prelude, as it were, to other scenes of greater glory and of more soul-stirring emotion. The view up the nave toward the east is enhanced by the cleanness of pillars, roof and walls. The white stone has not been darkened by smoke or by age, though four centuries have passed since Archbishop Chicheley finished the work. The lofty pillars, massive and exact, appear in their long avenue as giant trees of the forest, supporting arches of noble sweep, the triforium and clerestory of delicate detail and the roof which bewilders with its distance. Some have thought that the steps leading up into the choir detract from the effect; it is only for a moment. The design of the building as a whole dawns upon the mind, the magnitude of the nave and aisles becomes every moment more impressive; and if disappointment there were, it speedily passes away in wondering surprise at the daring splendor of the art and the completeness of the work. If from the choir beyond the great stone screen the melody of pealing organ or chanting boys steals echoing down the church, emotions are awakened which subdue the soul and suggest exalted things. Up the steps we pass, under the central tower—a beautiful structure open to the top and worthy of much attention. In front is the entrance to the choir, to the left the transept in which St. Thomas of Canterbury was murdered, and to the right the south-west transept, leading out of which is St. Michael's or the Warriors' Chapel. In this chapel, among other tombs, is one, half in and half out of the church, said to contain the body of Archbishop Langton. As a proof of the high esteem with which the people regarded the hero of the Magna Carta, when this part of the building was erected and the line of the wall fell exactly upon his grave in the cemetery the architect built over it an arch rather than disturb remains so revered. It is doubtful, however, whether the archbishop was buried here at all. A story runs that when young he and a village maiden were lovers, but for some cause or other they were separated; he became a churchman, she a nun. In time he reached the rank of archbishop, and she that of abbess. Then they met again, and continued in intimate friendship till they died, when they were buried side by side in a country churchyard a few miles away. Whether this be legend or no, certain it is that her tomb has been identified and beside her lies a man. Somehow or other, this story of love draws us closer to the great cardinal than even that which he did at Runnymede. In this same chapel is a monument of marble and alabaster,

CANTERBURY CATHEDRAL.

very fine to look upon, to the memory of Lady Margaret Holland and her two husbands. She lies in full-length effigy between her two lords—one, the earl of Somerset, who died 1410; the other, the duke of Clarence, who died 1420. She died in 1440. At their feet, as usual, animals are sculptured. These generally indicate the characteristic of the deceased; *e. g.*, an eagle, courage; a hound, fleetness; and a dog, fidelity.

The choir is contained between the pillars dividing it from its aisles on either side; here, as in the holy place, service is daily held. Another flight of steps leads up into the presbytery; another, to the altar rails; and still another, to the jasper pavement on which stands the high altar. Several tombs of archbishops are on both sides of the presbytery; that to Archbishop Chicheley, on the north side, is too remarkable to be passed by. Beneath a rich canopy of carved stone-work, supported by exquisitely sculptured pillars, in the niches of which are small elegant statues of white marble, rests the body of the prelate who built the nave. The monument was erected in his lifetime, and he left a large endowment to All Souls' College at Oxford to keep it in repair. On an upper, altar-shaped slab he lies in effigy, clothed in his splendid pontifical robes, so well done as to seem almost living. Angels support his head, and at his feet are two monks holding open books. Underneath, on another slab, lies the effigy of a skeleton partly shrouded, and also so well done as to appear like actual death. The contrast is startling—the archbishop in his glory, and the archbishop in his shame.

We pass back again to the steps under the tower and turn to the north-west transept—the place of the martyrdom. It has been changed since that dark December evening, seven hundred years ago, when was shed the blood which made it sacred for ever. Against the north walls are the tombs of Archbishops Warham and Peckham; the latter, of bog-oak, is in good preservation, though six hundred years old. To the east is the Dean's Chapel, formerly called the Lady Chapel, in which are several monuments to the deans and some books on which the titles have been placed, not on the backs, but on the edges of the opening leaves. These, however, are as nothing beside the interest of the martyrdom itself. The story is too well known to need repeating. Suffice it is to say that the memory of the man who dared to die for rights which he deemed sacred was precious in the hearts of Englishmen from the day his blood was poured out on the cold stones till the day when a king coveted the treasures which the ages had heaped upon his shrine. Nor has the spirit of admiration and of justice so passed away that none are left to think of him with honor, and even with love. He fell pierced with many wounds. In the darkening twilight the murderers escaped; and when the news spread through the city, the townspeople ran to the cathedral. The glimmering torches showed them the body of the archbishop lying in his gore before the altar. They began to weep, and, while some kissed his hands and his feet, others dipped linen in the blood with which the pavement was covered. Ere long the trembling monks buried the body in the crypt. The royal proclamation to the contrary was useless: Becket was a martyr and a saint from that very night. If Henry feared him when living, he had much more cause to fear him when dead. The thunderstorm which burst upon the city as the murderers fled was at once the sign of Heaven's anger and the awakening of an enthusiasm which lived for centuries. Miracles were wrought at the tomb; pilgrimages became popular. An altar was erected upon the spot of the martyrdom, and here the greatest of the Plantagenet kings married Queen Margaret. Edward IV. gave the great window of the transept, wondrous in workmanship, wherein were seven glorious appearances of the Blessed Virgin and St. Thomas himself fully robed and mitred. This was mostly destroyed by a Puritan iconoclast.

From the martyrdom we proceed along the north aisle of the choir, past the north-east transept and the chapel of St. Andrew, beyond which is the treasury, up the steps by which the pilgrims went, into the chapel of the Holy Trinity. This is immediately beyond the high altar, and here, in the highest and most beautiful part of the cathedral, was the shrine of St. Thomas. The tile pavement against the west screen was given by the Crusaders; it remains, but every vestige of the shrine is removed. An evidence of the multitudes who visited it is in the worn stones: the bare knees of pilgrims hollowed out a semicircle before the saint. Close by is the tomb of the Black Prince, and hanging aloft are the helmet, the coat and the gauntlets which he wore at the battle of Crecy, half a millennium ago, his popularity attested in his being buried near the most sacred spot in England. Henry IV. with his queen, Joan of Navarre, is also buried there. Beyond this chapel is the corona, the most eastern part of the cathedral. Here is the plain tomb of Cardinal Pole, the last English archbishop who recognized the papal supremacy. In the ancient black marble chair have been enthroned the rulers of England's primatial see, the patriarchs of English Christendom. Thoughts press fast upon one another in such a place, but even as the sunlight outshines the stars the surrounding vision blots them out. Look down the mighty and magnificent edifice raised to the glory of almighty God and through long centuries a centre of the nation's life. No description can convey the impression of that vista; no picture or poem can impart the fact of its splendor. The vastness of the structure and the beauty of the conception overawe the mind. Through the windows, marvellous in tracery and rich in colored glass, falls the soft and tinted light, its warmth and loveliness of hue suggesting the contrast between the outer and the inner radiance, between the realm of grace and the region of nature. The long lines of sculptured shafts rise with noble dignity and impressive stateliness to support the lofty and majestic arches. The eye passes down through the Trinity Chapel, where once thousands and tens of thousands knelt before the hallowed shrine of the martyr; on beyond the high altar and the presbytery into the choir, where holy service is chanted at the rising and the setting of every sun; and farther on, beyond the richly-finished screen, into the great and glorious nave—a very forest of noblest architectural splendor, where like tall and mighty trees set in a royal avenue of wide-arching beauty pillar after pillar rises and sends aloft its moulded branches into the groined and distant roof, glory upon glory, strength upon strength, as though the builders, filled with divinest power, sought to outdo the work of Nature, and to show to the Lord of all that human hearts and human hands could do that which the rocks and the forests, the sun and the frost, the shifting winds and the flowing waters, could not do. In the mellowed radiance fading in the misty distance, and in the holy awfulness of the voice of God speaking through man in the lines of the poem wrought in stone, the mysterious sweetness of the Divine Presence makes itself felt. Heaven may have that which is grander, more suggestive, richer in form and color and more truly an expression of all that the mind conceives to be beautiful and sublime, but earth has not. The King's daughter is all-glorious within, and the great Anglican communion wants no grander centre, no nobler mother-church.

The rich, delicate carving, the simplicity and dignity, the costliness and rareness of material, the most thoughtful, consummate poetic and religious art, show that the best of all has been given to the Lord of glory. But much of what was once here has been taken away. The wealth of gold and of precious stones that once adorned the sanctuary and the shrine was stolen to replenish the exchequer of Henry VIII. Even the jewels about the head of the Black Prince were dug out and appropriated. Never were the desires for the purity of the faith and the wealth of the Church more curiously blended than in that age, and no one seems able to say which was greater—the hatred of the men of those times for the clergy or their love for the lands of the Church. Beautiful as Canterbury Cathedral is, there comes upon one the feeling that it has been stripped of its richest glories and is not what it was in the first days of the sixteenth century.

There is little difficulty, standing here in Becket's Crown, in repeopling the place with the men of earlier days. The picture of pilgrims walking barefoot or crawling on naked knee up the stone steps in the north aisle to the shrine of St. Thomas soon becomes vivid. They brought their offerings and uttered their prayers to him who they hoped would intercede for them before the throne of God. Sometimes a nobler penitent came—a prince with a rich retinue and with costly gifts. Kings and emperors worshipped there, people from all parts of England, and even from the lands beyond the seas. As an illustration of the popularity of this pilgrimage, we may note that in the fifteen days' jubilee of 1420 no less than a hundred thousand persons knelt before the glorious shrine of St. Thomas, and the offerings in money made that year amounted to nearly six hundred pounds—a sum probably equal to about eighteen thousand pounds at this present day. Miracles were wrought there, and revelations made. Some of the windows, dating from the thirteenth century, remain, and are unrivalled both for delicacy and harmony of color and for accurate execution of design.

The central thought of Canterbury is undoubtedly the martyr, and yet the building is full of the associations of other men who helped to make England what she is and whose names are enrolled in the annals of her fame. They looked upon these very walls and trod these very stones. Many of the archbishops are buried here, but only one king, and he has a chantry on the north side of the Trinity Chapel.

We wander down the south steps and look into the chapel of St. Anselm, in the entrance of which is the tomb of Archbishop Mepham, and from which a pleasing glimpse of the choir presents itself. Hence we find our way across the building to the entrance to the crypt, and on descending we first visit the Lady Chapel—St. Mary's of the Undercroft. This is a singularly attractive spot. It is directly under the high altar in the cathedral, and is divided off by stone screens of fine workmanship. It was once rich in jewels and in gold; gold, Erasmus said, was the meanest thing about the place. Traces of the exquisite decorations remain. Figures, symbols and stars cover the vaulted roof. When lighted with lamps and tapers, the effect must have been great. Here service never ceased, day nor night. A curious shrine, down in the deep body of the church, symbolical of the affection with which men regarded her whom all generations call blessed. Beyond this chapel is the place where Becket's body lay for the first fifty years after his martyrdom. Here is the spot where Henry did penance and submitted his back to the scourge of the monks. Not far off is the tomb of Archbishop Morton, who restored the chapel of Our Lady. In the work about this tomb is an illustration of the rebus-play of the old sculptors. There are figures of a hawk and of a tun, the former lighting upon the latter. The arch is also adorned with roses, each surmounted with a crown. Of these the last one is cramped and imperfect, the artist evidently having tired of his work. In St. Gabriel's Chapel are some curious figures of animal-minstrels wrought around the capital of the central column—goats, etc., playing horns and flutes. The mural paintings are not obliterated; figures of angels and of saints are plainly visible. In the middle, over where the altar formerly stood, is a representation of Christ, singular in the right hand pointing downward. The blue-and-gold illuminations in the vaulting are also visible. This chapel was the work of a genius, and is not excelled by other work of the time, either in the cathedral or elsewhere. Another interesting feature of the crypt is the little French church, the home of refugees nestling under the protection of the great cathedral. Queen Elizabeth extended this hospitality, and from then to now the organization has held its own. It is not a part of the Anglican Church, but its pastor receives Anglican orders.

Days could be spent in this wonderful cathedral without exhausting its treasures of art and of association. Happy are they whose duty lies within its sacred walls and whose life is spent in its calm, heavenly atmosphere. They who visit have for ever recollections to sweeten and brighten the after-days. As we pass out of the church into the cloisters the white-robed procession winds from the chapel of St. Andrew through the dark aisle into the choir, and ere we look for the last time upon the vision of beauty, the storied windows, the shafts crowned with the circlets of vine and acanthus leafage, the silent tombs, the vast spaces of nave and aisle, there come the voices of singing choristers, and in the murmuring melody of evensong, sweeping in gentle waves of undulating sweetness, hope rises upon the wings of hallowed imagination and suggests the glories of the worship of the land which is very far off.

The cloisters are full of architectural and heraldic interest. In the groined roof are the armorial bearings of benefactors of the church, and, though sadly mutilated, some Romanesque arches, trefoil-headed arcades and ribbed vaulting indicate the former splendor of the monks' walk. Here the brethren spent some of their time in meditation, amusement and exercise, the bright green earth being restful to the eye and healthful for both body and soul. On the eastern side is the chapter- or sermon-house, a noble structure of several styles, from Early English to Perpendicular. Some traces of the former glory remain—the coloring and the enamelled work in the canopies of the raised stalls at the east end. Around the hall are the stone seats on which the brethren sat during chapter, the abbot's or prior's throne being conspicuous for its higher elevation and its greater finish. Here the community met to consult about the affairs of the church and the monastery, for Canterbury was a Benedictine foundation. The youngest brother first gave his voice and vote, and so on, according to age, till the most ancient spoke, and then the prior uttered sentences and censures and penances and scourgings were imposed, the delinquent standing out in the open space to receive punishment, perhaps to turn his back to the whip of the penitentiary. Sermons and lectures were given from the pulpit in the centre; no one then thought of using the church, so utterly unadapted for the purpose, for preaching. A light burned perpetually in this place, and the chapter met every morning. Sometimes a novice received the cowl or an officer was appointed; perchance a brother that night deceased was carried in on his blue bed with a chalice on his breast, and then with solemn dirge and requiem taken away to his long home. At the close of the meeting a wooden tablet was struck, and in the dull sounds the brethren were reminded of man's painful life, his sad pilgrimage and his sure death. No longer, however, are these things done. Times have changed; the monks are gone. One of the most interesting events of the year is the "speech-day" of King's School. Then the beautiful building is filled with scholars and their friends, addresses are made and prizes presented, ladies, gowned masters and scarlet-robed doctors look with interest and admiration upon the happy faces before them, and one wonders what the old monks would think were they in slow and silent procession to enter upon the scene.

Near to the chapter-door is the way, through walls fourteen feet thick, into the slype. Here, when a brother lay dying, the hollow sound of the clapper called his fellows to his bedside in the infirmary. They watched beside him, prayed with him and for him; the children of the almonry—sweet-voiced choristers—sang to him from the psalms of David; and when he passed away, he was gently and lovingly carried to join the silent brotherhood in the green churchyard.

We pass out of the dark entry, and find ourselves among buildings and remains of buildings which show the extent of this place in olden times. In the green court, on one side of which is the deanery, we linger to look upon some of the exquisite views of the cathedral. The quiet charm can only be suggested; neither pen nor pencil can do more. A few steps farther, and we are outside the sacred precincts. We wander around the wall—for the cathedral was enclosed and fortified—till we get back again to Mercery Lane; then through High street we proceed eastward to other historical spots.

Canterbury is full of interesting churches and other buildings; two, however, are pre-eminent—St. Martin's church and St. Augustine's College. The former of these is in the extreme eastern part of the city; the latter, halfway between it and the cathedral. On the way out the highly-respectable and the highly-dull character of Canterbury becomes more than ever apparent. One of the oldest churches is St. Paul's, founded in the thirteenth century, lately restored, and containing some interesting tablets. In the belfry is one to the memory of Sir Edward Master, once lord mayor of London, and in the inscription emphasis is laid upon the fact that he was the husband of one wife and by her the father of twenty children. Farther on is a long row of low-built houses called a hospital and founded by a John Smith in 1657. Farther still, leaving the great monastery on the left, is the little building which may in truth be called the cradle of all English Christianity.

A simple, unostentatious structure is this St. Martin's, rich in age and in associations, but void of architectural beauty. There are genuine bits of Roman work in the walls, showing that the more modern Norman work was done only in the way of repairs and restoration. On the whole, it is the very building in which St. Augustine celebrated the services of God thirteen hundred years ago, and it was esteemed old then. There Christians worshipped in the days of the Roman occupancy of Britain, and, though the English pagans fiercely swept out of the land the older civilization and religion, there divine worship was destined to be offered again without interruption, even as at this time.

The story of St. Augustine is as well known as it is

ever fresh. When he and his monks passed up the way from Ebbsfleet to win the kingdom of Kent for their Lord, not only were they kindly received by Ethelbert, but in his queen, Bertha, they found a protector and in St. Martin's church a home. This was for a time the headquarters of the mission; ere long both king and people were converted to the faith, and the land was given upon which was afterward built the abbey of St. Peter and St. Paul. In a once Christian church there the king of Kent worshipped the gods of the heathen; this he changed into a church again, and St. Augustine consecrated and dedicated it to St. Pancras. When we go back to the city, we will look at the ruins of this first abiding-place of the founders of the Church of England.

St. Martin's consists of a nave, a chancel and a tower. The entire length of the building is less than eighty feet, and the chancel is nearly a yard longer than the nave. The walls are about twenty-two inches thick, and are of stone, rubble and Roman bricks. The tower was built in the fourteenth century and is covered with ivy. In the choir floor appears an altar-slab about eight feet long and having the usual stigmata and crosses—one of the few stone altars which escaped utter destruction in the Reformation. It was, however, used as a monument, and is inlaid with memorial brasses. A Norman piscina in the south wall, possibly of Saxon date, wrought by itinerant masons from the Continent, is said to be the oldest in England, and there is an aumbry in the chancel of the fifteenth century. In the chancel is also shown a tomb said to contain the remains of Queen Bertha, but she was buried somewhere in or near the monastery. The font is one of the greatest objects of interest. Its age is unknown; ancient tradition affirms that in it St. Augustine baptized King Ethelbert on Whitsunday, 597. In the western wall, north of the tower, is a squint through which penitents could see the high altar; there are also near the altar traces of the priest's door and of the lepers' window.

The contrast between this plain, tiny edifice and the grand and glorious cathedral is very great, even as the brown shrivelled seed to the full-blown splendor of the flower. This is really the mother-church of our race. Through the changes and the chances of thirteen centuries we look back to the day when within these walls was gathered the handful of men who were to lay the foundations of a religious community that should spread through all the world and become second to none of the churches of Christendom. Stand in the western porch, in the gateway of the ivy-clad tower, on the ground where once stood St. Augustine, Queen Bertha, and many another Christian of the distant ages, and look upon the exquisite and inspiring landscape. That view is a type of the spiritual garden of the Lord, as refreshing as it is picturesque and as full of glory as it is rich in living green and pleasant memories. Under the yew tree close by lie the remains of Dean Alford, a man of varied gifts, at once a theologian and a poet, a musician, a carver and a painter, a preacher and a writer —more than all else, a gentle and holy servant of God. The lich-gate is a fine piece of work. Near to it is a cross on the front of which is carved the name " Hew Whyte;" on the back, " And Alys his wife." One passes away over sacred ground thankful for the mercy which has suffered one to see so holy a place.

The abbey of St. Peter and St. Paul was famous as much for the extent and the magnificence of its buildings as for the constant quarrellings of its members with the community at the cathedral. Among other causes of contention was that over the remains of the deceased archbishop. The monks of Christ church wanted him living and dead; the canons of St. Peter claimed his body for their own. Therefore, whenever a prelate died, the dispute arose, till at last the former prevailed. However, within the porch of the great church which in time was erected lies the dust of St. Augustine and his six immediate successors; but whereabouts the porch was no one living knows. Some parts of the building remain—the wall of the north aisle and some bases of columns, fragments of fallen arches and mounds. The old builders wrought well: a strong outer casing of good stone, then the interior filled with rubble, and finally molten cement, possibly near boiling, poured in. The result was a solid mass of unwearing masonry. To the east is the only remaining arch of St. Pancras church. Many parts of the monastery buildings are still standing —the tall towers, the beautiful gateway and some portions of the dining-hall and the chapel. The wealth and the position of the brotherhood were once great; they entertained kings and prelates and feasted six thousand guests at a time. Changes came, and in the end of the fifteenth century they had scarcely bread to eat.

Perhaps this was prophetical of the degradation to which the place itself was destined to fall. Henry VIII. appropriated it, converting the grounds into a deer-park and the buildings into a palace; Queen Elizabeth kept court here in 1573; Charles I. was married here, and

Charles II. was here entertained on his passage at the Restoration. The abbey and its precincts of sixteen acres enclosed by a wall passed to various lay possessors; it was finally neglected, suffered to go to ruin, and the people of the neighborhood freely appropriated its materials for building-purposes. Less than half a century since, this place, sacred for its memories and famous for its work, was woefully desecrated by having within its courts a brewery, a skittle-alley and a public-house. Gamesters, pleasure-seekers, idlers and riff-raff, drunken and irreverent, wandered at will over ground and within walls rich in the memorials of saints and kings and for ages consecrated to religious purposes. In 1844 the premises were bought by an earnest and devout churchman, Sir Beresford Hope, and converted into a college for the training of a missionary clergy; of the good which the noble institution has accomplished the hundreds of missionaries scattered throughout the world testify. The men of St. Augustine are to be found in Canada, Australia, Africa, India, and elsewhere; wherever found, they display a piety, an earnestness and a power unexcelled by any and worthy of their Alma Mater. Parts of the ancient buildings are utilized in the modern college; the same water-springs which supplied the old monks supply their successors. In the modern cloisters are painted on the wall the names of the graduates of the college and the dioceses to which they were sent; to the names of those who have passed away are added the letters R. I. P. There is a chapel in which these latter names are also reverently inscribed, and an altar where probably commemorative services are held. In the college chapel everything denotes good churchmanship; the altar is suitably furnished and appropriate vestments are used. In the hall under the library is the museum, in which is a fair collection of curiosities sent by the missionaries from their several fields of labor. Thus the beauty of holiness and the life of usefulness have come back again to the old monastery. There were difficulties in the way. It is said that when St. Augustine converted the heathen temple into the church of St. Pancras the devil was so annoyed at the change that he sought with all his might to overturn the building. He only succeeded in leaving the print of his talons in the walls of the south porch. It may have been the work of the ivy, but that is immaterial; let the legend stand: the cross won. So in this later regeneration right prevailed over wrong and light over darkness.

Our visit to Canterbury is at an end. Full of pleasant recollections, we take the train for London. In the same railway compartment with us are three or four boys of King's School on their way home for the holidays. What happy, jolly little fellows they are! How politely they offer us the newspapers they have with them, and with what free, undisguised delight one of them shows us his prize book! Their bright laugh rings in our ears, and somehow or other we forget the dark sculptured faces in the cathedral and see only the clear faces of these merry schoolboys.

CHAPTER XI.

At Stratford-on-Avon.

> "Here his first infant lays sweet Shakespeare sung;
> Here his last accents faltered on his tongue."

IT was on a bright, warm August morning that I started in the carrier's stage for Stratford-on-Avon. The road is one of the best and pleasantest in England, passing, as it does, through several villages and a country fertile, well wooded and highly cultivated. By this way it is next to certain Shakespeare himself travelled, as people have done for centuries, to London. As in his day, so now, the noble spire of Tredington church is a landmark for many a long mile, and the Stour wanders between the willows and through the fields by the roadside. There was a pleasant look of old-time life in the cottages and inns, at the latter of which the coach stopped to receive messages and passengers, and where the trimly-dressed hostess, full of sunshiny smiles and well-satisfied authority, or the wide-awake hostler or boy-of-all-work, gave the "Good-morning!" and sought for customers. To some of the travellers it was evidently a thirsty day, and, as the temperance movement has not to any great extent affected this part of the world, huge potions of bright, foaming ale were consumed at every stopping-place. The driver was happy and obliging, ready at all times to have a chat or to give information; three or four of the passengers were merry, and enlivened the journey with odd rhymes, humorous stories and witty repartees. One old fellow, full of fun and beer, puzzled a boy who went riding awkwardly by on a horse by asking him "if he would not be safer riding inside." The lad stopped to scratch his head and to think. In the meadows the haymakers were busily at work; here and there the forge-fire gleamed out of the dark shop, and the anvil ceased to ring as the leathern-aproned smith, holding the hot horseshoe in his pincers, stopped to look at us; the birds darted out of the hedges at the crack of the whip or the bark of the dog; carriages, horsemen and pedestrians passed us looking cheery and bright as the day itself; and, now out in the open road, now under the cool green shade of overhanging trees, we rolled over our ten miles, feeling that, after all, there were some pleasures connected with stage-travelling which railways cannot give.

The sun was high toward noon when we entered the remarkably clean and pretty town on the Avon. What a delightful out-of-the-world place it is! And what strangely-sweet emotions fill one's soul as one remembers that this quiet, contented burgh, with its beautiful surroundings, prosperous-looking people and antique spirit brooding over all, was once the home of him whose glory is the glory of humanity and whose thought permeates the world! Here he was born; here he loved and lived; here he died. Stratford is all Shakespeare, and the town appears calmly conscious of the fact. It may have an older history, running back, as it does, beyond the days of the so-called Saxon Heptarchy, full of

ANN HATHAWAY'S COTTAGE.

interest, and possibly of romance, but all else is forgotten in the one mighty thought of Shakespeare. Even as the sun at its rising dims the stars whose brilliancy made the night-sky splendid, so this man, full of most marvellous power, outshines all who lived before him. Doubtless the place always had attractions, but

> "Fairer seems the ancient borough,
>   And its sunshine seems more fair,
> That he once has trod its pavement,
>   That he once has breathed its air."

Beyond the town and across the meadows, some twenty minutes' walk, is Shottery, the village-home of Ann Hathaway. There is no difficulty in recognizing the cottage, the pictures of it being very like. It is at the far side of the little village, its end to the lane-like road and its front largely hidden with honeysuckles and roses. It is of the dark timber framing filled up with bricks and plaster commonly looked upon as Elizabethan—or I might almost say Shakesperean—with deep gables and roof thatched with straw and dotted with moss and lichen. A gate opens into the garden, and a narrow pathway partly paved with irregular pieces of stone and brick and running up two or three uneven steps leads therefrom to the strange-looking old door. The clumsy wooden latches, lifted with a string, the end of which is put through a hole and hangs outside, are still there. Nor are the oak pegs with which the framework of the simple structure was fastened together cut off. The appearance of the place, unchanged as it is for the most part, gives a fair idea of the houses of the well-to-do villagers three centuries since. Odd and unpretentious, it has, nevertheless, an air of homely comfort about it—a simplicity and a restfulness in which suggestions of happy, uneventful country life come to the mind as tenderly and sweetly as the matin-chimes murmur in the still summer air.

The old lady who lives there, a descendant of the Hathaways, was very genial and communicative in showing me around. The house inside is pretty much the same as of old—the ample and comfortable kitchen-room, with its chimney-place, in which are the old bacon cupboards, as it was when Willie Shakespeare courted sweet Mistress Ann. Here, possibly in this old chair or on that rude settle, he sat and told her the story of his love. These very walls, this antique panelled wainscoting, these low darkened beams of the ceiling and these stones of the floor, could they but speak, would repeat the assurances and the vows of the ardent youth. With some such lines as these he wooed:

> "Would ye be taught, ye feathered throng,
> With love's sweet notes to grace your song,
> To pierce the heart with thrilling lay,
> Listen to mine Ann Hathaway.
> She hath a way to sing so clear
> Phœbus might wond'ring stop to hear;
> To melt the sad, make blithe the gay,
> And Nature charm, Ann hath a way,
>   She hath a will,
>   She hath a way,
> To breathe delight, Ann Hathaway.
>
> "When Envy's breath and ranc'rous tooth
> Do soil and bite fair worth and truth,
> And merit to distress betray,
> To soothe the heart, Ann hath a way;

> She hath a way to chase despair,
> To heal all grief, to cure all care,
> Turn foulest night to fairest day,
> Thou know'st, fond heart, Ann hath a way.
>   She hath a will,
>   She hath a way,
> To make grief bliss, Ann Hathaway."

Some have held that the married life of these two was not happy, but the most reliable evidence goes the other way. Undoubtedly, Shakespeare found in Ann Hathaway a good and loving wife, and she found in him a true and noble-hearted husband. If in his will he left her only his second-best bed, it was probably because ample provision had been otherwise made for her. At any rate, the tradition runs that she earnestly desired to be laid in the same grave with him. It does not follow, however, because he was the poet of the world, that his sweethearting was more romantic, soul-absorbing, beautiful, than that of other men. It may have been utterly prosaic and commonplace: such, indeed, is the reaction frequently found in the realities of the life of one of rare imaginative powers; but, somehow or other, as you walk about this old cottage, you feel that it was not that. The full, deep eyes of the man indicate a warmth and depth of soul, a force which would gather the very sweetness of roses into a sweeping wind of irresistible passion. And Ann? What was she? Great geniuses make sad mistakes, but one does not like to think of the master-reader of human character doing so in this respect. Doubtless she was a comely village-maiden—not a sylph such as Miranda or a glowing beauty such as Juliet, but a true, homelike Warwickshire damsel, even such a one as sweet Mistress Page.

Well, here in the venerable cottage she was wooed and won by Stratford Will. There is no reason to doubt the tradition that this is the very house, though, when one has carefully examined all the evidence in its support, it is not so absolutely convincing as one would like it to be. The feeling, however, is not confined to Ann Hathaway's cottage: it comes up again in no less a place than the room in which the poet is said to have been born. Such scepticism is wicked, perhaps unreasonable, but it underlies most of the traditional testimony, nevertheless.

In a room up stairs—the best bedroom of the Hathaways—is an old carved bedstead probably of Elizabethan age; there are also several chests and a stool of the same period. The pleasant old lady already mentioned showed me a sheet woven and made three hundred years ago, when by such work the maids of the family earned their title of "spinster." It is neatly spun and has a line of inserted embroidery up the middle. The flooring, the walls and the beams of the house are unaltered; the queer little staircase, the diamond-paned dormers, the small low-ceiled rooms, the rude latches to the heavy, worm-eaten doors, the veritable old furniture and the wide fireplace with its cosey corners have an interest delightful and absorbing. Judging from the house, the Hathaways were plain and fairly well-to-do people. In front of the cottage is the old well, which tradition says is as it was in Shakespeare's days—when, perhaps, Master Will drew a bucket to save Mistress Ann the labor. From the little garden my agreeable guide gathered me a small posy of flowers—not, I presume, the lineal descendants of the flowers Ann Hathaway tended, if she tended any, but surely such as she and her Will saw and plucked as they rambled arm in arm through the lanes and the gardens of this sweet village. There are still the flowers and the herbs which were popular in the olden time—rue, thyme, lavender, marigold, rosemary and celandine—and in the orchard, full of knolls and hollows, are apples, pears, cherries and plums. From the seat near the cottage door much the same scene now presents itself as the lovers beheld long, long ago—the hills of Ilmington to the south in their woodland glory, the spire of Stratford church peeping up over the elm trees, and here and there ancient cottages with their sun-browned thatched roofs; a gentle land where life peacefully flows through time undisturbed by the ambitions of mighty cities—like, indeed, unto the silvery Avon as it restfully meanders amid the bright green meadows. The walk across the fields to Stratford is very pleasant. I could get no certain information as to the age of this footpath, but for long after the poet's time the Shottery people continued to attend Stratford church, and there was naturally constant communication between the village and the town.

On re-entering the town I passed along the chestnut walk and soon found myself at the old grammar-school. This was founded in 1482 and is a plain building of two stories, the lower of which was the guild-hall, where the citizens met in council and where plays were sometimes performed, and the upper the schoolroom. It is easy to picture Shakespeare wending his way to this fount of learning, plodding over his lessons as with slow steps he approached and ascended its stairs, and then listening, as boys everywhere listen, with more or less attention to the instruction given by the prodigiously-learned schoolmaster; but such a picture depends solely upon imagination. It may not be autobiographically—for Shakespeare may have been a ready and an industrious scholar—but the melancholy Jacques speaks of

> "The whining schoolboy, with his satchel,
> And shining morning face, creeping like snail
> Unwillingly to school;"

and it may have been the recollection of his pedagogue, his Sir Hugh Evans, that led the poet to say of Malvolio, "He does smile his face into more lines than are in the new map, with the augmentation of the Indies." I have no doubt the wool-stapler's son went here to school; I have also no doubt the Stratford people have been generous in their discovery of traditions, and have made leaps at conclusions possible only to intellectual acrobats. These old, overhanging, black-beamed houses, however, have an interest apart from Shakespeare: they speak of that grand old world in which lived he and many of the noblest and the mightiest of England's sons.

Joining the grammar-school is the chapel of the guild of the Holy Cross, "a right goodly Chapell," as Leland describes it, dating from the time of Henry VII., but looking very worn and much older. The iconoclasts of the Reformation and of the Puritan ages did not leave it untouched; some of its images were destroyed and its mural paintings were whitewashed over. Among the latter was a remarkably fine picture of the martyrdom of St. Thomas of Canterbury and a series upon the history, and especially the invention and the exaltation, of the holy cross. The antique porch with its quaint gargoyles attracts attention. On the left-hand outside corner of this doorway is the singularly grotesque head of a man with his fingers in the corners of his mouth, stretching it open as schoolboys sometimes do, so that the water may spout through. A few years, and age and weather will have entirely obliterated this bit of odd humor. The building is in the Decorated style, and in its fine old tower is said to be one of the sweetest bells ever made by man. This bell uttered its " sweete and perfect sownde " not only for divine service, but also to gather the members of the guild. As everybody knows, the guilds were the friendly societies of the Middle Ages, and their usefulness as bonds of social and commercial unity and their care for the poor and the needy made them popular among the people. In this place not only the grammar-school, but also a row of ancient almshouses, testifies to the benefit and the charity of the local guild. However, Henry VIII. confiscated their property throughout the kingdom and appropriated their wealth to distribute among his friends and to his own purposes. A crueler or a more ungodly act of vandalism was never perpetrated in the name of religion.

Across the street is the "New Place" where Shakespeare lived in his latter days, and where he died. Here we may picture the poet, beloved and laurel-crowned, resting in his quiet home-life amidst congenial surroundings and visited by cherished friends and acquaintances. The eventide of his life, so uncertain are its details, seems filled with the calm, misty glory which dims and yet makes radiant the objects upon which it falls. The house was in Shakespeare's time one of the most important and largest in the town. It had an orchard and a garden stretching down to the Avon. Now a few pieces of the foundation alone remain; the rest was pulled down in the last century by an amiable clergyman, but the true reason therefor is wrapped in mystery. The garden is beautifully kept—the garden in which the poet walked and entertained his friends, and through the trees of which he saw the walls and the tower of the guild chapel. Sit down within the tree-shade on one of these rustic benches—or, better still, on the green-sodded bank itself—and think of him who once trod this very ground and whose flowers once grew in this very soil. Here rare Ben Jonson may have walked arm in arm with him, perchance across such another velvety lawn as that one, and here were told stories and came to life creations which shall for ever hold man spellbound. In the darkening twilight, when the sweet chanting of the evensong from the neighboring chapel lingers in the summer air as in days of yore, and the sky is bright with sprinkled splendor, this is the spot to realize the force of Lorenzo's lines:

> "How sweet the moonlight sleeps upon this bank!
> Here we will sit and let the sounds of music
> Creep in our ears: soft stillness and the night
> Become the touches of sweet harmony.
> Sit, Jessica; look how the floor of heaven
> Is thick-inlaid with patines of bright gold:
> There's not the smallest orb which thou behold'st
> But in his motion like an angel sings,
> Still quiring to the young-eyed cherubins;
> Such harmony is in immortal souls;
> But whilst this muddy vesture of decay
> Doth grossly close it in, we cannot hear it."

A great many tourists were here at the same time as myself, looking with great reverence upon these remains of the man all men adore. I only hope that they, and others such as they, will think kindly of the pilgrims who in mediæval times frequented sacred shrines. This modern age regards the visit to the town of Shakespeare as the right thing, and the reverent pilgrimage to his grave and the gazing upon his relics as highly commendable; it looks back upon the journey to the tomb of Edward the Confessor or to that of Thomas à Becket as rank superstition.

It is twenty years since I made my first visit to the poet's birthplace, in Henley street, but my interest in that sacred spot has grown with time and is as fresh as ever. What a centre of the world's homage! What multitudes have entered this old cottage! The eye no longer rests upon the ancient Tudor tenements of the neighborhood with their dark timbers, gables, jutting windows and signboards, nor upon the undrained and badly-paved streets where pigs wallowed in the mire and fowl scratched among the garbage; but this house remains to link us with the past and with this same Shakespeare. I suppose he sat on that seat in the great roomy fireplace, looked out of this oddly-glazed window and played on this floor. Any way, this was the scene of his childhood—a dark old place, but no doubt very comfortable in bygone days. Up stairs is the room in which the poet was born. Does any one doubt its being the very room? The world believes it implicitly, yet the minor facts of Christianity rest upon a foundation which is as eternal rock compared with the evidence for this tradition. It is, however, highly probable that the tradition is correct: who could reasonably question, if it occurred in this house, that the birth would be arranged for in the best bedroom? The walls and the ceiling are covered with autographs—an evidence of the intense interest the world has in this small chamber. There are also some names scratched on the window-panes. This way of immortalizing one's self is now denied the public: visitors are required to write their names and their residences in a book prepared for that purpose. There are a few odd pieces of furniture in the room, but there is no proof that they have any connection with Shakespeare. When the bare unsightly walls were covered with arras, the place presented a more comfortable appearance than it now does. Other rooms, heavy beamed, low roofed and dimly lighted, suggest pleasant visions of the simple Stratford family. An old desk, massive and cumbersome, is shown; it is said to be the one Shakespeare used in the grammar-school. It is interesting for that tradition, and he may have sat at it in common with other scholars; but it is even more interesting as affording an illustration of the universality of schoolboy nature through all the ages. It is whittled and carved in true style, covered with initials and devices even such as would become our youth of to-day. The portrait in the iron safe up stairs is said to be genuine. Many others are shown in the museum, each different in some respects from the others, and yet all noticeably agreeing in the high, wide forehead and the full, clear eye. In this same museum—an adjoining cottage opening into the kitchen-room of Shakespeare's house—are preserved the early editions of the poet's works, books illustrating them and his life, documents in some way connected with him, and many other relics, some of them very full of interest. The tradition of the Bidford drinking-bout and the crab-tree slumber is carefully preserved by pictures, etc. The very chair from the "Falcon Inn," in that village, in which Shakespeare sat at his revels, is shown. It is old enough to have served for that purpose, but, unfortunately, there is little certainty of the truth of the legend. This Bidford was famous in those days for its company of ale-soaked topers, and, as drinking-matches were then common, one Whitmonday—so runs the story—some Stratford men, Will Shakespeare among the number, went to that place to test its nut-brown ale and to challenge its boast of the championship of England. The "topers" were away on a match at Evesham at the time, and only the "sippers" remained to defend the renown of their village. The Stratford men soon found that they were no match for their opponents, and, being anxious to get home while they had some strength and skill left, beat a hasty retreat. When half a mile on the way, they were quite overcome, and were obliged to lie down under a crab tree by the roadside, where they slept till next morning. Some would then have returned to the attack, but the youthful Will had had enough of "drunken Bidford." There may be some allusion to such drinking-matches in the resolve of Slender: "I'll ne'er be drunk whilst I live again, but in honest, civil, godly company, for this trick; if I be drunk, I'll be drunk with those that have the fear of God, and not with drunken knaves." The story, though long believed by Stratfordians and not altogether improbable, is, most likely, a fabrication—alas! in spite of the fact that the crab tree kept its place till the winter of 1824. As one wanders about the house so fragrant with associations of deepest interest one feels that the strangest thing of all is that of a man so great as was this man we really know so little.

From Henley street to the parish church, dedicated to the Holy Trinity and retaining its ancient collegiate privileges, is a walk of ten minutes. A noble lime-tree avenue leads up from the gateway to the principal porch. Some portions of the sacred edifice are Early English and Decorated, but the best parts are Perpendicular. The clerestory of the nave is remarkably well lighted with Decorated windows unusually large and close together. In the north aisle was once a chapel dedicated to the Blessed Virgin; in the south, one to St. Thomas of Canterbury. Now in the former are several altar-tombs, mostly of the Clopton family and having upon them some well-executed recumbent effigies. The chancel was built in the latter part of the fifteenth century by Dr. Thomas Balsall, dean of Stratford, and is a perfect and beautiful specimen of Perpendicular work. There, inside the altar-rails, is the grave of the poet. Not long since it was outside, but the constant press of visitors began to wear away the stone, and so the rails were moved forward to a lower step. What can I say of this sacred spot that others have not said? Here is something tangible of Shakespeare—something that brings home to you the fact of his existence. In his marvellous work you overlook the fact of his personality: the creator is forgotten for the nonce in the loveliness and the might of the creation; but as you look upon this plain slab with its oft-repeated inscription you realize the very truth of him who is *primus inter pares*—the prince through all the ages,

outshining even the pure glory of Homer and Dante.—
Sweet Will! grand as thou art in thine unapproachable
splendor, thy majesty greater than that of the kings
whom thou hast made to live in thy wondrous lines,
how dear thou art to the hearts of all men! No; none
shall touch thy sacred dust: thou shalt sleep in peace
till

> "The dreadful trumpet sound the general doom."

Is not the fact that Shakespeare is here buried a sufficient refutation of the story invented by some one that he died a papist? Over his open grave was read the office of the Church of England—an act which would not have been done or been allowed by either Anglicans or Latins had he been a member of the Roman obedience. In that age of bitter Protestantism neither his position nor his talents would have overcome the scruples of his townsmen—intensely Puritanical as they were—and led them to honor him as they did.

In one of the graveyards of Fredericksburg, Va., there is a relic to which we may here direct attention. It is a slab of red sandstone, on which may be deciphered these words:

> Here lies the body of
> EDWARD HELDON,
> Practitioner in Physics and Chirurgery. Born in Bedfordshire, England, in the year of our Lord 1542. Was contemporary with, and one of the pall bearers of William Shakespeare of the Avon. After a brief illness his spirit ascended in the year of our Lord 1618—
> aged 76.

On the one side of the poet's grave lies his wife, once sweet mistress Ann, and on the other side his favorite daughter, Susanna, wife of John Hall. His daughter Judith is also buried there. Other graves and tombs are close by—beside the altar a monument to Shakespeare's friend, John Combe, and on the south side of the sanctuary one, much defaced, to the builder of this part of the church. On the wall over the west end of the latter monument is the famous bust of Shakespeare. This was erected perhaps earlier, but certainly within seven years of his death, and, as it is generally admitted to have been worked from a cast of his features, it is the only known trustworthy representation of him. Here may be seen his fine, full, round face, towering brow, light-hazel, large-orbed eyes, auburn hair and beard, expressive lips and well-set chin. The signs of genius are there, if they have ever been expressed in the countenance of man. The scarlet doublet and the black sleeveless gown in which he is clad bring him before us as he was when on high-days and holidays he walked along the streets of London and of Stratford.

The timber roof of the chancel is fine; at the ends of the beams are well-carved figures holding armorial shields on their breasts. At the corbels on which these beams rest are also sculptured figures in stone which join the smaller figures at the end of the mouldings over the window arches. The three figures in a row, recurring several times, have a singular effect. The great Perpendicular window in the east, resplendent with the glory of stained glass, and the American window, in like manner glorious, are very good; and the doorway on the north side, near the altar-rails, once leading, I believe, to a great charnel-house long since pulled down, has at the terminations of its arch-moulding—or, rather, had, for they are nearly obliterated—carvings of St. Christopher and the Annunciation. The niches and the *miserere* seats are deserving of notice; also the old carved pews. In the south transept is the font in which Shakespeare was baptized, also an altar-tomb dating about 1593, with an inscription in Hebrew, Greek, Latin and English. It is needless to record the several inscriptions relating to the poet, but the following is a copy of that belonging to this tomb:

> "Heare borne, heare lived, heare died, and buried heare,
> Lieth Richarde Hil, thrise bailif of this borrow;
> Too matrones of good fame he married in Godes feare,
> And now releast in joi, he reasts from worldie sorrow.

> "Heare lieth entomb'd the corps of Richarde Hil,
> A woollen draper beeing in his time;
> Whose virtues live, whose fame dooth flourish stil,
> Though hee desolvèd be to dust and slime.
> A mirror he, and paterne mai be made
> For such as shall suckcead him in that trade;
> He did not used to sweare, to glose, eather faigne,
> His brother to defraude in barganinge;
> Hee woold not strive to get excessive gaine
> In any cloath or other kind of thinge;
> His servant, S. I. this trueth can testifie,
> A witness that beheld it with mi eie."

Dugdale preserved the following copy of verses inscribed on the tombstone of Susanna Hall, but afterward obliterated to make room for the record of a certain Richard Watts:

"Heere lyeth y⁰ body of Svsanna wIfe to Iohn Hall gent: y⁰ daughter of William Shakespeare, gent: Shee deceased y⁰ ijth of iuly A⁰. 1649, aged 66.

> Witty above her sexe, but that's not all,
> Wise to salvation was good Mistris Hall.
> Something of Shakespeare was in that, but this
> Wholy of him with whom she's now in blisse.
>   Then, Passenger, hast ne're a teare,
>   To weepe with her that wept with all?
>   That wept, yet set her selfe to chere
>   Them up with comforts cordiall.
>   Her love shall live, her mercy spread,
>   When thou ha'st ner'e a teare to shed."

The external appearance of the church in grace and dignity well becomes the mausoleum of Shakespeare. It is cruciform, the battlemented tower, surmounted by a modern spire, rising from the intersection of the nave and choir and the two transepts. Outside the chancel, at the heads of the buttresses and along the panelled and embattled parapet, are many grotesque figures—toads, dragonflies, fish, etc. Such representations of natural objects on the outside are not uncommon in churches of this and of earlier periods. Sometimes they are grotesque, sometimes fairly accurate representations—birds, beasts, reptiles and fishes. Possibly the intention of the old artists in putting these figures outside was to indicate that the animal creation was external to the realm and object of grace. They are rarely—never in a grotesque form or otherwise than as symbols of some virtue or personage—placed inside the building, and yet, on the other hand, designs of flowers seem to have no restrictions: if anything, they predominate in the interior. Flowers, however, in themselves so beautiful, are the fittest and the sweetest symbols of that which is heavenly and divine. They are fragments of glory—cast-off bits of celestial material which ere they fell to earth were touched by the sweeping robes of angels, and thus received a beauty and a hue, alas! such as can only be evanescent in a world such as ours.

The sweet Avon flows gently by this noble house of God, and the meadows beyond look lovely in their summer dress. In the churchyard are many old tombstones. The orthography of one on the south side of the church struck me as peculiar. The inscription is to the memory of two women who died in the spring of 1699, aged, respectively, eighty-seven and thirty-seven years. Whereabouts they are buried I do not know, for the stone has been removed from its original position to serve as a sort of curbstone where it now is. This desecration, so suggestive of an unsympathetic spirit and deserving of every condemnation, is not uncommon in the old English churchyards, though it is possibly confined to the utilitarians of some few generations since. My transcription is carefully exact: with the exception of the *k* in "Stroks," which is a capital, it is precisely as it is engraved on the stone.

> "Death creeps Abought on hard
> And Steals Abroad on Seen
> Hur darts are Suding and hur arous Keen
> Hur Stroks are deadly com• they soon or late
> When being Strock Repentance is to Late
> Death is A minute ful of Suden Sorrow
> Then Live to day as thou mayest dy to morow."

Curious ways of giving dates also attract attention. Of

a woman it is said she died "in the 40 Second year of her age." Sometimes the old gravestone-cutters chipped out the tens first and then the units; thus, for 34 we find 304.

There is a right of way through the churchyard, and the walk by the Avon is exceedingly pleasant. On a stone near that walk is the name "Davidona," unique in my experience and not mentioned by Miss Charlotte Yonge. There is an old stone seat—I fancy it was once a tomb—where visitors may sit in the shade of the trees and look upon the river and the fields beyond. How softly the warm beams fall through the leafy branches and play like bright-robed seraphs amongst the graves and on the cool, tiny wavelets! There are a few trees farther down to suggest the willow-shaded stream of Ophelia; the fish leap to the fly in the sunshine and merry ripples play around the boats with young men and women rowing hither and thither. Such a restful summer scene as this Shakespeare must have looked upon; nay, he undoubtedly wandered up and down that gentle river, peering into its banks for the holes of otter and of rat, seeking to catch pike or perch or trout, perhaps going over love's sweet story to his dear Ann of Shottery, and perhaps dreaming out some of those creations which must be the wonder of the world till the end of time. It is all Shakespeare. The green grass, the willow and the lime trees, the sunshine, the glittering water, the noble church, the fields so fresh and living, the birds that flit from bough to pinnacle and from wall to tree,—everything speaks of him. If elsewhere nature is the expression, the robe, of Deity, here nature is filled with the spirit of the man to whom God gave a supreme,

THE AVON AND STRATFORD CHURCH.

magnificent and unique gift. Who visiting this consecrated place does not for ever after read Shakespeare with the greatest interest and the fullest appreciation?

Apart from the places associated with the poet there is nothing of much interest in the town. A few old houses remain—very few, considering—and one looks with pleasure upon their gabled roofs and the black timbers. The streets are very clean and well kept; the shops, small and tidy. There is an appearance of prosperity: Shakespeare is evidently to Stratford what Becket was to Canterbury, or, to put it differently, the one made and the other is making the trade and the life of their respective towns. The constant presence of visitors from many lands gives to the people something of a cosmopolitan polish and politeness; their speech is fairly free from provincialisms, and they have as full and as just an appreciation of the distinction which their town has received by having greatness thrust upon it as they have a bright and attentive disposition toward both business and pleasure. I made several purchases, and in one shop bought a pair of "Shakespearean" gloves. The pretty twelve-year-old girl who sold them amused me by blushingly and naïvely saying, "Of course, sir, if they don't fit, we will change them." She did not understand that in a relic the matter of size is of little consequence.

Four miles from Stratford is Charlecote, once the home of that Sir Thomas Lucy to whom Shakespeare gave an immortality of ridicule as Justice Shallow. The story runs that the poet, having fallen into ill company, made a practice of stealing the knight's deer, for which offence Sir Thomas naturally sought redress in prosecution. Shakespeare was followed closely and severely, and in the spring of 1585 he resolved to leave his business and family in Stratford and to seek shelter in London. But before he left Warwickshire he wrote a bitter ballad upon Sir Thomas Lucy and nailed it on one of the posts of the park gate. Only one stanza of this ballad has been preserved, and, to say the least, there is little or none of the Shakespearean ring about it:

> "A parliament member, a justice of peace,
>   At home a poor scarecrow, at London an asse;
> If lowsie is Lucy, as some volke miscalle it,
> Then Lucy is lowsie, whatever befall it.
> He thinks himself great,
> Yet an asse in his state,
> We allowe of his ears but with asses to mate;
> If Lucy is lowsie, as some volke miscalle it,
> Then sing lowsie Lucy, whatever befall it."

Passages in the *Merry Wives of Windsor* are said to contain allusions to the tradition, and to the unfortunate knight so severely lampooned. Possibly there may be some truth in the legend, though it should be remembered that the earliest mention of it is about 1707, that none of Shakespeare's rivals, who were ready enough to pick flaws in him, ever twitted him with it, that the punishment for deer-stealing was not, as the legend affirms, whipping, but imprisonment and fine, and, lastly, that Sir Thomas Lucy had no deer-park and no deer. Nevertheless Charlecote—or *Ceorlcote*, the home of the husbandman, according to the Saxon—is indissolubly connected with the poet, and they who visit Stratford should also go farther and see the ancient village. Well will they be repaid for so doing. Read these sympathetic lines from the pen of Charles Knight: "There stands, with slight alterations—and those in good taste—the old mansion as it was reared in the days of Elizabeth. A broad avenue leads to its great gateway, which opens into the court and the principal entrance. We would desire to people that hall with kindly inmates, to imagine the fine old knight—perhaps a little too puritanical, indeed, in his latter days—living there in peace and happiness with his family; merry as he ought to have been with his first wife, Jocosa (whose English name, Joyce, soundeth not quite so pleasant), whose epitaph, by her husband, is honorable alike to the deceased and to the survivor. We can picture him planting the second avenue, which leads obliquely across the park from the great gateway to the porch of the parish church. It is an avenue too narrow for carriages, if carriages had then been common; and the knight and his lady walked in stately guise along that grassy pathway, as the Sunday bells summon them to meet their humble neighbors in a place where all are equal. Charlecote is full of rich woodland scenery. The lime-tree avenue may, perhaps, be of a later date than the age of Elizabeth, and one elm has evidently succeeded another, century after century. But there are old gnarled oaks and beeches dotted about the park. Its little knolls and valleys are the same as they were two centuries ago. The same Avon flows beneath the gentle elevation on which the house stands, sparkling in the sunshine as brightly as when that house was first built. There may we still lie

'Under an oak, where antique roots peep out
Upon the brook that brawls along this wood,'

and doubt not that there was the place to which

> 'a poor sequester'd stag,
> That from the hunter's aim had ta'en a hurt,
> Did come to languish.'

"There we may still see

> 'a careless herd,
> Full of the pasture,'

leaping gayly along or crossing the river at their own will in search of fresh fields and low branches whereon to browse. The village of Charlecote is now one of the prettiest of objects. Whatever is new about it—and most of the cottages are new—looks like a restoration of what was old. The same character prevails in the neighboring village of Hampton Lucy, and it may not be too much to assume that the memory of him who walked in these pleasant places in his younger days, long before the sounds of his greatness had gone forth to the ends of the earth, has led to the desire to preserve here something of the architectural character of the age in which he lived."

In Charlecote church is the tomb of Sir Thomas and Lady Lucy. The former died in 1600—a man high in position and worthily esteemed by his neighbors. On the front of the altar-shaped tomb are the figures of Sir Thomas and the Lady Joyce kneeling in prayer. Upon the top they lie in full-length effigy, dressed in the costume of the period, with folded hands, and in the features of the old knight—well executed and probably accurate —we may discern a nobility of character far greater than a Justice Shallow could possibly have had. The wife's virtues are recorded on a black slab at the back of the tomb in the following touching and beautiful inscription:

> "Here entombed lyeth the Lady Joyce Lucy, wife of Sir Thomas Lucy, of Cherlecote, in the county of Warwick, Knight, Daughter and Heir of Sir Thomas Acton, of Sutton, in the county of Worcester, Esquier, who departed out of this wretched world to her heavenly kingdome the tenth day of February, in the year of our Lord God 1595, of her age LX and three. All the time of her life a true and faithfull servant of her good God, never detected of any crime or vice; in religion most sound; in love to her husband most faithful and true; in friendship most constant; to what was in trust committed to her most secret; in wisdome excelling; in governing of her house, and bringing up of youth in the feare of God that did converse with her, most rare and singular. A great maintainer of hospitality; greatly esteemed of her betters; misliked of none unless of the envious. When all is spoken that can be said, a woman so furnished and garnished with virtue, as not to be bettered, and hardly to be equalled by any. As she lived most virtuously, so she dyed most godly. Set down by him that best did know what hath been written to be true.
>
> THOMAS LUCY."

A husband who could say so much of his wife could not have been deserving of such obloquy as that heaped upon him by an idle story of a youthful poacher.

And now my day at Stratford began to darken for its close. In the still, warm twilight I set out on my return journey. The drive was full of pleasant thoughts and delightful reminiscences. The stone bridge of fourteen pointed arches over the Avon was built by a Clopton in the reign of Henry VII., and is still good and sound. Just on the other side is an inn named "The Shoulder of Mutton;" the old sign, battered and broken, retains on it a figure with some resemblance to that joint of meat. The tavern was long since of more importance than it now is. As we pass through the villages on the way we notice the great number of children; at one small place no less than eighteen, all dirty from head to foot, gathered in the road to look at us. As the night-gloom thickens the stars peep out one by one, faint streams of light are cast across the road from cottage candles, bats and owls sweep leisurely by, and the eye grows weary of peering into the darkness. Nature has robed herself for rest.

I ride silently along, half thinking, half dreaming, and, among other things, the old bridge over which we passed reminds me of the story of poor Charlotte Clopton. She was a sweet-looking girl—so the authentic legend runs—with pale-gold hair combed back from her forehead and falling in wavy ringlets on her neck, and with eyes that "looked like violets filled with dew." They who have seen her picture, which is still preserved, say she was full of grace and beauty. When Shakespeare was an infant, a plague broke out in the town and the neighborhood of Stratford, and from it this comely and noble-born maiden sickened, and to all appearance died. With fearful haste they laid her in the vaults of the Clopton chapel in the parish church. In a few days another of the family died; but when they carried him down the gloomy stairs into the vault, by the torchlight they saw Charlotte Clopton, in her grave-clothes, leaning against the wall. They drew nearer; she was indeed dead, but she had passed away in the agonies of despair and hunger. This fearful event, if it did not suggest, possibly helped the poet to realize, the well-known catastrophe of Romeo and Juliet.

CHAPTER XII.

To Edgehill.

"While the ploughman, near at hand,
Whistles o'er the furrow'd land,
And the milkmaid singeth blithe,
And the mower whets his scythe,
And every shepherd tells his tale
Under the hawthorn in the dale."

IT was on an October day in the year 1642 that the royalists and the Parliamentarians met on the battlefield of Edgehill. This fact has given an historic interest to one of the most lovely districts in the English Midlands, and attracts to the neighborhood many who are interested in the great struggle of the seventeenth century. There are also villages and hamlets scattered about this quiet region, both pretty and ancient, their names indicating early Saxon origin, and their peaceful life and their gentle beauty, as they nestle half playfully, half shyly, amidst the bright green trees, suggesting the simplicity and the happiness of Eden. Here one may still see England much as it was in the days of yore, and behold in their perfection the power and the charm of a rural life on which Nature has right royally bestowed some of her best gifts, and where the people are for the most part untouched by the realities of modern progress. Next to living in such an Arcadia, the best way to appreciate and understand it, to find out its secrets and to enjoy its delights, is to pass leisurely and contentedly through it on foot. It is no use to hurry through, riding or driving as if time were of consequence; neither meadow nor village, neither woodland nor hillside, will unfold its sweet mysteries to one who impatiently or thoughtlessly rushes along. Life is slow and quiet here, and they who cannot for the nonce enter into the same calm, steady spirit had better not visit the valley of the Red Horse nor climb the heights of Edgehill.

At Shipston the shadows were long and the streets were still when in the bright summer morning I set out on my ramble through this part of the country. It was not for the first time in my life: every step and every scene of the way was familiar and awakened pleasant recollections and associations. I passed over the millbridge, beneath which the boys still wade and fish for minnows and sticklebacks, as they have done for generations. The sunbeams flow through the willows on the bank and make the dewdrops sparkle and the tiny ripples on the clear water shimmer. A solitary frog plunges into the stream, the birds are twittering and looking eagerly for the early worm, and the cows in the meadow are busy at the mist-wet herbage. I cross the fields and soon reach Fell Mill lane, so called from a mill once used for felling cloth—an ideal lane, tree-arched, hedge-hemmed and grass-bordered. Here you may hear the full, rich song of the blackbird and the thrush; and if you will remain motionless for a while, you may see partridges feeding in the wheatfields close by, rabbits skipping in the green sward, and linnets, blackcaps and wrens nest-building or bathing in the road dust. The woodpecker taps away at the withered branch in the elm and the rat comes sniffling up out of the ditch, undisturbed by the bleating of the sheep in the meadow or the barking of the dog at the distant farmyard or the cackling of the geese on their way to pasture or to water. Earlier in the year the cry of "Cuckoo!" falls upon your ear, and in the late twilight the melody of the nightingale flows from the wayside orchard. The moment you stir all is changed: the rats and the rabbits run, the partridges whir away, the birds fly off.

As I walk on through the lane I meet two or three haymakers—stolid-looking, stiff-moving, carrying their scythes and rakes, and also their earthen jug of small-beer. I wish them "Good-morning" and turn into the road running across the fields, in which sheep and cattle and horses are grazing, past the farm known as St. Dennis, to Tysoe. In the still, bright morning the country appeared picturesque and pleasing. One could not tire of looking at the fresh green hedgerows, the tall tree-clumps, the fertile hills and the waving fields of corn. In the ponds which here and there occurred by the roadside ducks and geese were waddling or swimming and cows were cooling themselves and thoughtfully chewing the cud. Only once did I meet any one in the five miles between Fell Mill lane and Tysoe. Nor, indeed, did I wish to have the sweet solitude broken. Alone one can think aloud, hum over snatches of old melodies, recall passages of the poets, drop leisurely into desultory arguments with one's self, build castles as high and as glorious as the towers and the palaces of cloudland, take in the scenery around, and stop at one's own sweet will to behold this attraction or to examine that curiosity.

It was still early when I reached the little straggling village of Tysoe. The place is old; the church is said to have been built two hundred years before the Norman Conquest, and some parts of it may indeed be as ancient. Between the nave and the chancel is a small bell-cot or turret apparently as old as the rest of the building, and possibly in days gone by containing the bell which was rung at the consecration and elevation of the Host. In the yard, full of graves, is part of an old stone cross. These crosses are of frequent occurrence in ancient and mediæval churchyards. After service did the people of bygone times adjourn from the church to the space immediately around such crosses as this to hear sermons? The village is well supplied with arched fountains in the walls by the roadside. One of these fountains is surmounted by a cross and has running along the line of the arch the appropriate words, "Whosoever drinketh of this water shall thirst again, but whosoever drinketh of the water that I shall give him shall never thirst." Doubtless many a weary-hearted villager who has come here to draw has realized the strength of these words, to the comfort of his soul.

From Tysoe I passed along the road skirting the foot of Edgehill till I reached the Stratford and Banbury highway, leading directly up to the summit by the "Sun-Rising." This was formerly, in the days of stage-coach travelling and as far back as 1642, an inn of some celebrity, but it is now used as a farmhouse. Some who are now living remember when it was busy and prosperous, when "mine host" welcomed travellers to his friendly portals and hostlers, drivers, farmers and wayfarers made the old kitchen or tap-room a scene of riotous joy. Now the only signs of life visible were an elderly lady in a morning-wrapper and curl-papers writing at a table near an open window, and a pretty and comely damsel standing at another window thoughtfully looking down the hill for some chance being to come and break the matin monotony. Evidently she did not see a stranger every day; for when I asked her if the bridle-path on the opposite side of the road led to the " Tower," the rosy hue passed richly and softly over her cream-white cheeks and she answered me with a kindly tremulous voice. I wonder if such graceful maidens gladdened the eyes and the hearts of the Cavaliers in the days when they frequented this neighborhood? The bridle-path runs along the top of the ridge, now across a pleasant clearing and now through the shady greenwood, while the view of the wide plain beneath is very fine—such, so an old writer says, as Lot beheld in the valley of the Jordan before Sodom fell. I should have enjoyed it much more had it not been for the swarms of flies. If Pharaoh was plagued worse, I pity him. At times I was obliged to keep my handkerchief in constant motion, or I should have been eaten alive. The path is much used, for many initials and names are cut in the trunks of the beech trees on either side. Frequently I heard the prattle and the laughter of picnickers and down the hillside caught glimpses of groups of young men and women. Delightful is the charm of a day's outing in the country, and especially in such a place as this, where mossy banks and crystal springs and deep shades and glorious vistas together help to satisfy the mind and to please the senses.

I throw my blackthorn on the ground, take off my strapped wallet containing luncheon and guide-books, and sit down on a grassy bank within the shadow of the beeches to take in the magnificent panorama and to think upon the past suggested by it. On fine days the view extends—so it is said—into fourteen counties. On one side are the Malverns and on the other is Charnwood Forest. Coventry, Warwick and Stratford, with their spires and towers, are visible, and on the distant horizon rest the gray-black clouds of Birmingham. A well-wooded plain, set with picturesque villages and farms, threaded by the Avon, enriched with fertile fields and noble orchards, traversed by ancient roads and bordered by the glowing haze of a brilliant summer sky! The eye rarely beholds a more lovely or extensive landscape or one in which Nature has been more prodigal of her richest gifts—not, indeed, the romance and the splendor of the mountain and the forest, but the quieter graces of a low, level country in which prosperity contentedly smiles in the sunshine and beauty seems to move under the vision like tinted waves of some wide emerald sea. As I look upon the picture I remember the word of old: "And God saw everything that he had made, and, behold, it was very good." Yes, very good; and yet the ancient rabbis used to say that "God had taken of the dust under the throne of his glory and cast it upon the waters, which thus became earth." What, then, must be the land beyond the clouds? If this glorious scene is but the shadow of the heavenly splendor, what must be the substance? And yet down in yonder fields, now lying so calm and peaceful, the angry and sinful passions of man have arisen, brother has fought against brother and father against son, and the land has been defiled with blood.

In the pages of Clarendon may be found the best description of the famous battle. Near where I am now sitting the king viewed the progress of the struggle. In the plain below, the Parliamentarians, under the command of the earl of Essex, were encamped, twelve thousand strong. On the heights, of about equal strength, were the royal troops, one wing near the Sun-Rising, the main body where the Tower now stands, and the other wing commanding the road to Kineton. The key of the position was thus in the hands of the king; and, had his men remained on the hill and waited for Essex to attack, a decisive victory would in all probability have ended the conflict and changed the course of English history. The Puritans were stirred to vigor and zeal by the exhortations of their ministers. The red horse cut in the side of the hill opposite Tysoe became to them "the red horse of the wrath of the Lord," which he caused "to ride furiously to the ruin of the enemy." In the neighborhood the people, largely persuaded by the rebels that the Cavaliers were cruel and wicked and that they robbed and evilly treated the inhabitants wherever they went, hid their goods and sought to protect themselves against the coming of the king. "The very smiths hid themselves, that they might not be compelled to shoe horses." Through the day the two armies watched each other. An October Sunday, possibly the sound of the chiming bells in yonder towers came softly across the plain and some few pious souls on either side prayed that God would defend the right. At three o'clock in the afternoon the battle began, and the sun went down and a thousand and half a thousand men lay dead upon the field. They were buried where they fell; five hundred were thrown into a pit near to an elm-clump. Neither side had the victory, and neither side was desirous of renewing the combat. In the cold, frosty night the king's soldiers, shelterless and hungry, straggled into the villages to beg for food, but, as Clarendon puts it, many " were knocked in the head by the common people." Ere long the armies marched away, the ancient quiet returned, and the red coats of the king's men and the orange scarfs of his enemies were seen no more.

It is now an old study, that seventeenth century, and most people have long since ceased to hold exclusively with either side, but it is well to remember that the Puritans had no more a monopoly of the virtues of the age than had the Cavaliers of the vices. There were good men and bad men in both parties. The bad we may well pass by, but among the good none can forget such men as George Herbert and John Milton, the two poets of the period, nor Jeremy Taylor or Richard Baxter, two of its most eminent divines. It is true that Milton was a Puritan; it is also true that Milton describes the saintly Bishop Andrewes entering paradise vested in the robes of his order. Yet to the churchman and the royalist the bare thought of lifting up the hand against the Lord's anointed was abhorrent. Charles was the king; the crown had been set upon his brow and the consecrated oil had been poured upon his head, removing him from among men, making him on earth the vicegerent of God and rendering his person sacred and his will law. The divine right of kings may be set aside now, but it was held then, and held, too, by many of the purest souls and the most thoughtful minds in England; they, at least, could not understand how men dared to resist the prince. Others besides them could not understand men who would abolish the ancient Church of the land, with its bishops, ritual and customs, and turn the sanctuaries of God, where beauty dwelt with holiness and splendor cast its vestment upon righteousness, from temples of worship into places of meeting. Sermons were good, but services were better; and when the Puritan had the power—when he had poured out the blood of the king and the primate of all England on the scaffold, and thrust the bishops out of their sees and the parsons out of their parishes, and made it criminal for any to use the Book of Common Prayer—then were many hearts grieved and many souls oppressed. None can ever tell the full story of the cruelty and the wrong which the Puritan wrought in those days. He did in the seventeenth century what the papist had done in the sixteenth—persecuted the Church, condemned the Liturgy, exiled the clergy. Rome and Geneva have clasped hands against Anglicanism. No; Walker's *Sufferings of the Clergy* is quite as dependable as Neal's *History of the Puritans*, and John Evelyn is worth more than Samuel Pepys. If in the reign of Elizabeth, and again in the reign of Charles II., the Church sought to drive her adversaries from the land, she but did that which she was forced to do for her own preservation. Doubtless there was wrong on both sides, but as of seed cast in the ground the bad perishes and the good remains, so that which was of evil among them has passed away and that which was of God abides even in our midst.

The country-people here do not know much beyond the facts that there was once a battle and that Oliver Cromwell did wonderful things toward settling the grievances of the poor. Some of them have heard of Julius Cæsar, for one asked me the other day which came first in English history, the Roman or the Puritan. The man seemed hurt, as though I had detracted from the fame of Oliver, when I told him that the great Commonwealth man lived in the century before the last; he had heard of him all his life, and therefore thought he was a hero of far-distant times. But exactly what Cromwell did beyond upsetting affairs generally and satisfactorily, or what was actually done at Edgehill, the men who plough yonder fields or tend the sheep in these pastures close by have no idea. They know some ghostly legends, though, and in the dull October evenings, when the mists hang along the hillside and the gray shadows overspread the plain, they will hurry along these roads and paths, fearing and trembling lest they should see some of the dead ones who haunt the place. "Apparitions and prodigious noyses of war and battels," as an old writer affirms, have been seen and heard here; and though in a clear, warm August noontide it is not so easy to people the plain with "incorporeal substances" as it might be in the dim wintry twilight, yet there comes to my mind an old story told me long ago by one whose years began before the last century ended, and who knew from his boyhood every nook and corner, every legend and tradition, of these parts.

Among those who fought and fell in this battle—so runs the story—was a knight of noble birth and of brave and loyal soul. When living, he had made the welkin ring with his manly voice, and around his hearth clustered many a true and kindred spirit. No stint of hospitality was there in his day; no lack of free souls to hail the baron of beef and the tankard of mead. He is said to have been the last gentleman in the neighborhood who took his greyhounds and his hawk to church. Such a good man, beloved as he was by all who knew him and having died in the noblest cause for which one can die—that of king and country—ought to have rested contentedly in his grave; but no: for many years on the anniversary-night of the battle he was seen riding along the heights of Edgehill on a steed of fiery hue. Noiselessly the horse rushed hither and thither, and the rider—at times gesticulating fiercely with his sword, as though urging his troops to the front, and at times spurring his beast and bending forward his body, so as to pass swiftly on, but never uttering or causing sound, though clad in the armor of an earthly warrior— had a careworn, shrivelled visage which all who saw it said belonged to the nether realm. For weeks, till the winter's rains washed them away, the imprints of the hoofs in the soil glowed brightly in the darkness. Some had seen them; some, more venturous than others, had tried to touch them, but there was nothing, only they shone clearly and imparted to the fingers a strange trembling light. Nor was it only in this place that the knight of Edgehill appeared: people of reliable reputation declared that they had seen him in the market, both at Stratford and at Shipston, and that he had examined their samples of grain and asked the price. Others said that he had been seen kneeling before the altar in the church in which he was buried, and others, again, that he frequented the avenue which wound through his park to his ancestral home. Of course everybody was alarmed. Old people shook their heads and said little, and young folks cared not to wander abroad after dark. Even the rude and unbelieving Commonwealth man ceased his swaggering and said his prayers when he passed by any of the haunts of the warrior-soul. So long as the Puritans ruled nothing could be done—the spirits are not amenable to such as they—but years after, when a prelate sat once more in the chair of St. Oswald at Worcester, a well-remembered and successful attempt was made to "lay the ghost."

One midnight—so says the legend—the bishop and the neighboring clergy, accompanied by a large concourse of people, proceeded to the church, near the altar of which was the grave of the old knight, covered with an inscribed stone. It was a wild night. The rain fell fast, the daws and owls screeched in the belfry, the lightning flashed and the thunder rolled as though the day of doom had come, and the wind roared angrily as it shook the building and swayed the tall elms. The people began to imagine that the powers of darkness divined their purpose and were causing the elements to war against them, and a number of them waved yew-branches and rang the bells to drive away the evil ones. But the storm raged as fiercely as ever. When the bishop, standing on the altar-steps, solemnly adjured the knight to appear, there was intense and silent excitement as the echoes died away amid the distant arches, and every one trembled with fear lest the mandate should be obeyed. They who held the flaming torches stood as though ready to run, and even the clergy looked on with pallid faces. The charge was uttered again, and then again, three times, according to the form prescribed. Then came a blinding flash, then a very avalanche of thunder-billows, rattling like quickly-fired artillery, roaring like huge, breaking waves upon an ocean-shore; the wild wind swept through the nave, and, lo! in an instant all was still, and there in the midst of the terrified throng stood the old knight, his armor red with glowing fire, his head bowed toward the ground. No one moved; no one had strength or courage to run. The very men who over their ale had sworn that they had seen him time and time again were startled and stunned at the apparition. They looked with awe akin to horror; and some devoutly hoped that as a result of England's sin the power of controlling demons and spirits was not taken away from the ministers of grace.

At last the old knight spoke:

"What would ye with me? Why have ye disturbed my rest?"

"Because," said one standing close by, "thou canst not sleep in peace."

"Hath England peace?" asked the knight.

"It hath," the man replied. "The king's son sits on royal Charles's throne; the Church hath her own again, and loyal men till the land as in the old time."

"'Tis well," responded the knight. "Then why trouble ye me?"

"We fear to see thee in the dismal shadows," another said; "we dread to have one with us who belongs to another world."

"Thou thinkest I am worse than ye?" said the old knight, with a scornful laugh which seemed to drive life itself out of some hearts. "I go to church as often as any here."

"That dost thou, sir," the bishop exclaimed, jubilantly, "but thou leavest thy heart at home."

This rejoinder was unanswerable, for everybody knows that a ghost does not take his heart about with him. The knight was therefore in the power of the bishop, and by the law which obtains in such matters was bound to remain wherever he was laid. As a rule, spirits thus subdued were consigned to the depths of the Red Sea, where Pharaoh and his host abide in everlasting bondage; but sometimes the wishes of the ghost were considered, and he was allowed to choose a place for himself. Frequently the ghost would select his resting-spot among the roots of an apple tree or under a gate-post or a front doorstep, or near a spring of water, or in some other strange and unexpected position; from which we gather that ghosts were facetious as well as troublesome. The old knight saw his mistake, and bowed in token of submission.

"Where wilt thou that we lay thee?" asked the bishop.

"Give me thy blessing, reverend lord, and I will go in peace," the knight replied.

The blessing was given; the people looked to the spirit, and as they looked it vanished from their sight. From that hour one soul at least remained at rest. Nobody ever saw or heard the knight of Edgehill again, and doubtless he has long since passed into regions far from this of ours.

I remember how anxiously the ancient gentleman who told me this story sought to impress me with its truth.

Whether it were in the summer afternoon as we sat together on the wooden bench under the box tree in his garden, or in the winter evening around his fire before the candles were lighted, he would always add, by way of finally disposing of any possible doubt,

"There is Edgehill, and there was a battle; and what more can any reasonable man need?"

But time passes, and I have yet miles to go before my day's jaunt is over. From the spot where I have rested for the last half hour to the Tower is only a few minutes' walk. This building, erected about the middle of the last century, marks the place where the royal standard stood on the day of battle. It is a sham ruin, and as a sham ought to have no place in either heaven or earth. The view from its walls is splendid, and, as it is a public-house, refreshments as well as relics can be obtained there. As I got over the stile from the bridle-path into the road I asked a man who stood leaning against a gate if the place had any other name than that of the "Tower." He looked at me with grave stupidity; I repeated my question. A woman looked out of a cottage door close by, and said "Old Israel's deaf, sir." But even she was not able to give me any information.

I wandered on along the hot and dusty highway, the very road on which the king's army marched in the dusk of that October morning. On the way to Warmington, close by, are the remains of a veritable British camp. Here one may stop and picture the scenes, not of two hundred years since, but of two thousand. In those remote ages the land was a wilderness and its inhabitants were fierce, savage and heathen. With bow and sharp stone-headed arrows, and javelin, axe and club, they hunted the beasts of the forest or lay in wait for and struggled with their human foes. I fancy I can see them moving stealthily along through the tall grass and watching me with wild, restless eye from yonder bushy hedge, ready to spring upon me as I stand here. This was their village-home—a place of huts or wigwams made of poles and wattled work and thatched with rushes or covered with sods. A hole in the side of the simple structure served both as a chimney for the smoke and as a door for the inmates. Around were rough palisades and high earth-banks. The valle and the fosse of this camp still remain. In this open space the thick-limbed and skin-clad warriors, fearless of death and cruel as the wolves in the jungle-like woodland, listened to the decisions of their chief and prepared for battle. Their women, more degraded, worse clothed and dirtier than themselves, stood by to urge them on to deeds of blood. Doubtless the unkempt, brown-skinned boys searched the hillside hereabouts for nests in the spring and nuts in the autumn, and learned, as savages learn, by exposure and trial, the skill and the habits of their fathers. The soil, badly tilled, supplied the family with a few roots; cows and goats, half tamed and thriving poorly in captivity, gave them milk, and the forest furnished them with fuel. The only thing natural to us about the hut or the camp would be the cat. Puss was there, as happy and contented as she was among the Egyptians two thousand years earlier, and as she is amongst us to-day. This ancient camp was admirably chosen for military purposes, and, situated, as it is, at the extreme point of Edgehill, commands a wide stretch of country. Now, even as the bell-tones gently wafted from some village church near by proclaim that the cross has triumphed over the old heathendom, so the soft green robe which Nature has cast over the place declares that the hidden past has been forgiven and that peace reigns.

The road down the hill to Kineton is steep, and by a notice on a board at the top bicyclers are informed that it is dangerous. In the way I meet a heavily-laden wagon slowly coming up the hill. What ponderous wheels! and what mighty horses! The driver is clad in corduroys and smock-frock, with thick hob-nailed boots on his feet and a great wide-awake on his head. His hair is lank and long and his stubbled beard has not been cut for some time. He walks beside the team, his bending shoulders suggesting hard work rather than age, and the loud smack of his whip, with his "Coom hup, nu!" and his whistle, indicating both vigor and interest in his work. The broiling sun pours fiercely down upon him, but no sun could make him browner than he is or cause the perspiration to drop more freely from his face. When I pass him, he stops his wagon, getting a huge stone from the roadside to put under one of the hind wheels, and asks the time of day. It is past one. How far to Kineton? Three miles and a half from the Tower—the best part of three miles from here.

"Dear me!" I say, "and along that dry, unshaded road! It's enough to roast one, such a day as this."

"Us must expect 'ot waythur this tiime o' yaare," he replies, philosophically, and leisurely wiping his face with his large white-spotted red handkerchief.

"It's a hard pull for your horses up this hill," I remark.

"Them dunna miind it; uld Beetty aar ah gooōd un to goo, and Buuttarcoop ahn't ah bad un. And gooin' hup ahnt as bad as gooin' doon. Gooin' doon 'ill aar allus bad. Ah mon mah breeak 'is neeck gooin' doon 'ill, an' theen 'ee's dun fur."

I move on. Then I hear the "Gee hup, uld gaal," "Pool awah theer, maw luve," and the harness cracks and the wagon creaks, and on the heavy load goes round the turn in the highway and up the hill. It is not only in the moral sense that going down hill is bad—which sense the driver's words naturally suggested—but it is also bad physically. Try it in the blazing sunshine after a walk of ten miles, for the most part across soft meadows and through shaded woods. The hands become swollen, the legs get stiff and the feet feel as if they were going through the toes of the shoes. This was the most uncomfortable bit in my day's journey, but then pleasures must be expected to have their correlative pains, and what is a wearisome tramp of a mile or two, even down hill and along a sunburnt road, to compare with the delights of a stroll through the country-side? Besides, Providence is generally kind under such circumstances: some vehicle drives up with the horse's head in the right direction, and the cheery welcome to a lift makes one forget the heat and the toil. Here is my chance coming—a chaise with an elderly gentleman, fat, and therefore good-natured. Is he going far my way? I have not time to ask, for he stops his pony and inquires if I am going to Kineton. The very place, and off we drive together. He is from Banbury. Do I know Banbury? Rather: I ate Banbury cakes at the time I began to ride to Banbury Cross. It is a prosperous town, but in old days it was awfully Puritan. The story goes that a man there of that persuasion once hanged his cat on Monday for killing a mouse on Sunday. The church has no steeple, but the cheese has a reputation centuries old; Camden implies that it was good, but Shakespeare makes Bardolph speak of it as though it were thin and soft. No; I shall not be able to visit the place this time. I know something of its history: the elderly gentleman is disposed to antiquity as well as to adiposity. There was once a battle fought there in early Saxon times—that of the Wessex men against the Britons—about A. D. 550? Yes. So some have said, but it was in Wiltshire, and not here—at Byran-byrig, and not at Banes-byrig. I know nothing about that, but I am right in charging the Parliamentarians with pulling down the ancient castle after the royalists had held it under siege for three months, and before they surrendered were reduced to such straits that they ate up all their horses but two. People drive in for miles to the fair, where, among other things, they get some of the best beef and the strongest ale in the country and see the biggest woman in the world and the only original Tom Thumb. The latter individual seems to be ubiquitous and sempiternal. I have seen the "only original" in my day on both sides of the Atlantic; old folks have told me that they saw him three-quarters of a century earlier than I did; a ballad of the reign of Charles I. speaks of him as a hero of King Arthur's time, when he was swallowed by a cow, tumbled into a pudding, and was finally eaten by a giant; a village in Rutlandshire claims to be his birthplace and declares that he was served up in a royal pie; and lastly the folklorists come in and say that the whole story is a myth of Northern origin. Any way, they had the little fellow at Banbury Fair—had him for years—and the farmers and the gamekeepers, dressed up in their Sunday velveteen, and the laborers and the laborers' wives, and young men and young women, also dressed up in their best, used to look upon him with the greatest interest and believe all that the showman said concerning him.

So, chatting merrily about one thing and another, we jogged along the road to Kineton.

CHAPTER XIII.

Ober the Country.

"And the summer day ended, for late or long
Every day weareth to evensong."

WE found the little old-fashioned place all astir. It was the day of the annual flower-show, and the streets were gay with flags and noisy with the rattling of traps and wagonettes over the pebbles and the chattering of visitors from the neighboring towns and villages. There is not, as a rule, much excitement in such secluded districts, but the people somehow or other manage to make the most of life and to enjoy themselves. The "Swan" was filled with guests; the stables were crowded with horses and the tap-room was crammed with holiday-making and beer-drinking swains. Boniface—good-tempered, sleek, shrewd Boniface—was bustling about and making strenuous efforts to supply, and no doubt to suggest, the wants of his customers. On one side of the gateway was a little window or wicket through which the crowd who could not get indoors or who preferred the fresh air obtained a continual stream of brown mugs filled with foaming ale. Sounds of loud merriment, the scraping of a violin and fragments of a rude song came through the open casement with the red curtains and the brass bars. Here is a boy with a pint-pot in one hand and in the other a black clay pipe filled with the vilest-smelling tobacco trying to emulate the older ones around him, but the older ones say he ought to be thrashed and sent home to bed; so that he gets but poor encouragement. There, a half-drunken fellow kicks a poor cur out of his way, and the wretched beast yelps and the jackdaw in the cage screams. All is bustle and confusion, and the signs are that both the devil and Boniface will make a successful day of it; which juxtaposition of the Prince of Darkness and a man duly licensed by law to make his living in this way by no means implies that there is a league between them or that the one is as bad as the other. As I see the people of the inn driving their business I think of that scene in *Piers the Ploughman* where Glutton, on the way to church, is stopped by the brewster, who upsets his good intentions with the allurements of good ale, "hote spices" and the company of such choice spirits as Watte the warrener, Tymme the tinker and Hikke the hakeneyman.

I am shown into the parlor, my stout kindly friend having left me to my own devices. The house is old, with the yard, stables and wagonsheds usually belonging to hostelries of the kind. Inside there are narrow passages, winding stairs, dark recesses and rooms with low ceilings and mysterious-looking cupboards and closets. Care is needed lest one stumble over unexpected steps or old lumber partly hid in the prevailing gloom. In the room in which I find myself are a long table, a piano and some pictures on the wall of racehorses and stiff-looking houses. I ask for dinner, and the hostess, stout and mirthful—she seemed to be made of a smile from head to foot, a huge ripple—skilfully navigates me through dark and devious ways to a long room up stairs. Here she explains to me that the day is a bad one for a warm dinner, but she adds, pointing to the table spread down the middle of the room, that I can make a meal out of the cricket-club supper. Possibly. At one end of the table is a massive piece of boiled beef, at the other a gigantic ham, and at respectable intervals between poultry, pies, cheese, bread, etc. My dinner will not be missed. Having seated me in a chair, she puts into my hands implements in dimensions something akin to a scythe and a pitchfork and bids me help myself to the beef or the ham. Then I am left alone—in that long room with that mighty dinner. Neither cat nor dog shares my solitude; I can eat and drink in peace. There is a horseshoe over the door; evidently, the people believe in witches. I proceed with my collation and at the same time picture the scene which the room will present in the course of a few hours, when the hungry cricketers come in for their beef and beer. The twofold process refreshes me both in body and in mind. I throw myself back in the great arm-chair and half fancy I should like to be with the merry company. What speeches and what songs! The din of applause, of thumping the table, clapping hands and stamping the floor, will be deafening. There will be jokes and stories which will bring out the side-splitting laugh and the vigorous " Hear! hear!" And the fun will go on away into the night, till one and another will have slipped under the table or fallen over asleep or been led or wheeled off home. Then, about midnight—the magistrates allowing an additional hour after the closing-time usual on ordinary occasions—Boniface will turn into the street those who are left, extinguish the lights and lock the doors.

I spring up from the chair and the dream, for I have no desire to pass through a metamorphosis of that kind, and after satisfying the host's very moderate charges I start out to see the town. There is some dispute as to the etymology of its name. Some say it was so called from its extensive market of kine; others hold that it should be "King," and not "Kine," from the fact that here was formerly a royal palace or castle, and others, again, affirm that it was named after St. Keyne, the patron-saint of wells in general, and of one near the site of this palace in particular. These conjectures suggest curious questions of the origin and the history of the town into which one may not safely enter; only, as I walk slowly through the unpaved street, I fancy I see here an illustration of a "road-town." Many more such come to mind as I think of this one. The hamlets of Britain and of early England, as of all primitive countries, were mostly independent and isolated settlements in the wilderness, perhaps on the banks of a brook, perhaps in the midst of a dense forest. A clearing was made and habitations simple in structure and few in number were built. As time went on and the village grew in size and importance communication with other places beyond what a mere footpath would afford became imperative, and highways were accordingly cut through the intervening region. The town thus preceded the road, but, the road being made, other towns would spring up at desirable points along its course, a string of cottages stretching for some distance on both sides. As these, in turn, increased in numbers and in consequence, other ways from neighboring hamlets would be made through the forest directly to them, and then the village would naturally extend itself along the new way. In these instances the road would precede the town.

The church, yellow and ancient and of mingled Early English and Perpendicular work, with its "acre" of lichen-covered tombstones and grass-grown graves, stands in the midst of the place, and has a low square tower, a fine doorway and the effigy of a priest. There are a few stone houses, some of them of considerable age and with their moulded windows, clustered chimneys and heavy walls suggesting stories of days and people of whom one would fain know something. Farther on the way to Warwick, at the west end of the town, is the grammar-school, a modern and small institution, at the front gate of which, his arms akimbo, was whistling lazily a small boy with red-brown face and trencher-cap. He hoped to go to the flower-show by and by—perhaps as soon as he got over the Pons Asinorum or the Passive Voice of τυπτω. I love boys —that is to say, boys that *are* boys and not your precocious boy-men—and this little fellow appears to be after my own heart. Play cricket, pull an oar and ramble through the woods and by the brookside, my lad, as well as pore over Euclid and Æsop, and you will make your way in the world. Boys are to be found everywhere—good boys and bad boys—but there is no more beautiful sight under God's sun than the face of a pure, upright, soulful lad the blush of whose cheek sin has not touched and whose eye is bright with innocence and with unconscious courage. The boy bobs his head respectfully as I pass by, and I turn back to the side street leading to the Tysoe road, and soon come to the place of the day's festivities.

Three thousand miles away and in the depth of a Western winter, the freezing wind sweeping wildly over the fields of stainless snow and through the bare trees, making the dreary, bitterly-cold night more than ever Arctic-like, that scene, among others, presents itself to my mind clearly and pleasantly. In a large field by the side of the road and under great widespreading trees were erected several tents and booths. Beyond, a gentleman's house, with the rich velvety lawns set with shrubbery and flower-plots so common in England, appeared in extremely pretty form. The place was gay with flags and with brightly-dressed swains and lasses. Boys and girls were playing here and there; swings and merry-go-rounds were going; hucksters and toy-men were crying their wares; from the steps of his wagon-house Cheap John was holding forth upon the merits of a twenty-four-bladed knife of the best Sheffield make, all for a shilling—warranted pure steel, or possibly he may have said pure of steel; old folks were leaning against the gates or the fences gossiping, and a very good brass band discoursed pleasant music in short and suitable fragments. The village was too small to attract a wild-beast show or even a miniature circus, and so were absent two of the greatest pleasures an English country crowd can have—viz., that of seeing the lions feed, and that of listening to the stale witticisms of the clown. Even the "Punch-and-Judy" man—the most popular dramatic performer in the British Isles—was not there.

The people, however, were themselves an interesting study. Here was Long Tim, the sturdy wagoner, with

"A Gentleman's House Set with Shrubbery."

his Sunday shoes, brown trousers, red vest and black coat—the coat much too short in the sleeves and too tight in the back—and with him were his good wife and seven of his boys and girls, the other three being left at home with "Granny." Never-sweat Dave strutted about with a bunch of ribbons tied in his beehive-shaped hat, and with an imitation silver chain with an imitation bunch of seals and keys adorning his once-white vest. He had a cane and kept his eye on Mollie, who in a group of giggling servant-girls was the most remarkable for the length of her nose and for the gay scarf across her shoulders. Several strangers with the grime of "Smoky Brum" inlaid in the lines of hands and face and under their finger-nails were entertaining Hodge and his friends with stories of the town and with jokes without any point. There was a delightful air of rustic simplicity about the whole thing, and one could well say with Thomson,

> "thus they rejoice, nor think
> That with to-morrow's sun their annual toil
> Begins again the never-ceasing round."

The local gentry and the clergy intermingled with considerable freedom among the villagers, for, though the miserable democratic spirit of the age has crept like the sin-tempting serpent of old even into such Edens as this, men have not altogether forgotten that it is equally an honor for man to respect his betters and to treat kindly his inferiors. Ruskin says somewhere—I think it is in his *Stones of Venice*—that the secret of the present social discontent lies in the workman having been reduced to a sort of machine set to reproduce a given copy exactly and without variation—possibly, for instance, to do nothing but make heads of pins or to do nothing but sharpen their points—and thus, all invention and consequent manliness having been destroyed, he takes no pleasure in his task, but labors mechanically and frets his soul against all who are not in the like state of slavery. Hence the centres of rebellion against society are to be found in manufacturing towns, in such as Birmingham, where both masters and men work like convicts in the galleys and drag through a monotony of existence fatal to all nobility of soul or health of mind. In the rural districts there is more variety of employment, more personal interest demanded, and therefore more pleasure in the daily toil. That red-faced, thick-set fellow leaning over the mound—as they call a fence in this neighborhood—and listening to a dingy Black-Country man, will take a pride and a delight in shearing the sheep, ploughing the land and clipping the hedges. Possibly agitators have persuaded him that he is an ill-used animal, oppressed and wronged by those who are over him, but there is more change in his life, more opportunity of ingenuity and invention, more enjoyment of rugged health and Nature's gifts, than fall to the lot of most men in a higher sphere of life. If I wanted to find real happiness, I should not go to the palaces of cedar or the homes of the city-people, but to the stall of the apple-woman or the cottage of the farm-laborer. Here I should not expect to find high intelligence or extensive learning, but I should find a fuller appreciation of the joys and the pleasures of this world, few though they might be, and an inspiriting looking forward to those of the world to come. The people walking about these grounds have in their faces that which indicates the possession of a happy soul. And doubtless, when the parson comes among them, he will add to their delight by his encouraging nod, his kindly word or his cheerful smile to one and another.

In the tents are flowers worthy of this land of roses and dahlias, and vegetables vast in size and suggestive of epicurean joys. It is pleasing to see the interest every one in England takes in such things. Flowers grow there in such abundance and reach such perfection as to excite the surprise of the stranger. In the houses even of the lower classes some attempt is made at their cultivation and display, and many a woman points with pride to a scented geranium or a pot of common musk. The country-side is filled with wild flowers; the banks, with primroses and violets; the hedges, with May-bloom and dog-roses; and the meadows, with cowslips, buttercups and daisies. The peasantry are encouraged in their love for flowers by these local shows; and, though some may think more of the possible prize than of either Nature or the beautiful, or aught else, yet the greater number have a genuine affection for and a justifiable pride in their gardens and the fruits thereof. See how carefully they watch the pet flower, the table of cut roses and dahlias, the box of mignonette and the vase of carnations, lest any profane hand should touch them and mar their loveliness or rob them of their fragrance! How they watch the countenance of the visitor for some sign of approval, some lighting up of the face which will show his surprise at the perfect object before him! Its color, form, size, nature, habits and history will be spoken of and told so soon as you venture to express an interest in it. The good man will tell you from where he got the seed or the slip, what kind of soil he put it in, how many times he nearly lost the fruit of his efforts through the frost, the excessive rain or the ubiquitous and mischievous boy, and his confidence that except in London itself nothing finer could be had in the land. Why London is excepted I do not know, unless it be for its vagueness and mystery to country-people. His hope is now to get the first prize, and by and by to find a place in the squire's garden for his eldest son, who loves flowers with all his heart and can do a good day's work alongside of any lad of his own age in the village, and with as good a heart too. Few here have heard the legends of Narcissus and Hyacinthus as told by Ovid, or know that once the white rose tried to outrival the pure paleness of Sappho and blushed for every failure, hence the red; but their round faces broaden under the inspiration of the hour, and their affectionate interest creates a rude but genuine eloquence.

The people are evidently here for more than seeing flowers and vegetables. They move about over the sward and under the trees in a sort of rhythmical measure to the music of the band, or loll upon the grass in companies of twos and threes. Children toot with horns and play with whistles, and everybody is on pleasure bent. Fairs and wakes similar to this gathering have been held here for centuries, and ages back they who now sleep in the old churchyard up in the town took their part in them as gayly and as merrily as do the free-souled folk of to-day. Some of the young fellows will in the course of the afternoon handle a quoit or a bat, and later on the largest of the tents will be cleared for a dance. Possibly one reason why there is not so much heartiness in the pastimes of this generation as there was in the sports of past ages lies in the rapid increase of population. A crowd up to a certain point is necessary; beyond that it hinders genuine fun. A great multitude uncontrollable and made up largely of strangers, as great multitudes are, can be amused only as the spectator is amused: it cannot amuse itself in any true and thorough way. In a small place such as this the old-time conditions to some extent prevail, and, as the number of people is not too great to prevent them from knowing one another or to dampen their feelings, each is necessary to the common games and sports, and each enters into them. For some time to come the effects of to-day will be felt in pleasant recollections, and probably, also, in unpleasant stiffnesses, bruises and headaches. But my time is short, and I am able only to take a walk and a look around, to speak to one or two and then hasten on my way.

I continued my journey along the road toward Oxhill, a tiny village four miles from Kineton. For a good part of the way the road runs across open fields, here and there passing old farmhouses. These houses are built solidly of stone, the gable-end and blind-wall mostly to the road, and with bits of garden in the unused front yard and the court at the back. In the windows are flowers, and over the doorway jasmine and honeysuckle. It was pleasant to hear the cackling of poultry and the cooing of pigeons, nor did the watchdog lying grimly near the well scarcely prick up his ears at the sound of footsteps, though doubtless the first tread off the public path would have brought forth the warning bark. Nailed to one of the barns were dead weasels, stoats, rats and owls. At one gate a women with a sun-bonnet in her hand stood watching a boy holding a guinea-pig by a string tied to one of its legs. The little animal was not very lively, and nibbled at a cabbage-leaf as though it were tired of the warm sunshine, its master and everything else. The woman courtesied as I went by—possibly as much for want of knowing what else to do as for respect; the boy and the guinea-pig, not having either curiosity or reverence for the clergy, kept on with their several occupations.

Each of these solitary houses has its own history—possibly only the quiet, uneventful history common to such, yet one would give much to read the past of any habitation where man has dwelt, and to learn the passions, the hopes and the achievements of those who have occupied or been associated with them. Every life is interesting, every building instructive. The strong walls, the heavy doors and the narrow mullioned windows tell of more than defence against the weather: in days not so long since a lonely farmhouse needed protection against the tramp and the robber, just as in remoter times it had to be guarded against thieves, who more by force than by subtility took possession of that which they desired. Some of these were built when the recollections were still rife of people not only spoiled of their goods, but also turned out of their houses, and frequently maltreated and brutally murdered. Now the queen's peace is kept from one end of the land to the other, and men can lie down in confidence and sleep in safety. There are no gallows by the wayside with felons hanging thereon to intimidate the evilly disposed and to frighten the superstitious; nevertheless, the law has a strong arm—stronger than the oak gate or the spiked palisade, and more to be dreaded for its moral than for its physical effects. The bushes and the flowers in the garden, and the pigs and the poultry, the calves and the ducks, in the yard, indicate restfulness and somehow or other suggest happiness. I stand and wonder if the people who live there unannoyed and unperplexed by much that worries—even as a savage dog worries the sheep—the souls of people in busier spheres are really content and joyful. At any rate, they have a better chance of being so; only, such virtues depend more upon the self than upon the surroundings. I walk slowly along and think it over, at the same time regretting that the "Elegy" has been quoted *ad nauseam* and that the season of blackberries is not yet.

Many young people pass me on their way to the flower-show at Kineton, some walking and some driving. All are dressed in their best and their gayest, the taste for sober colors not having reached this neighborhood. It is a relief to see a man in something else than an undertaker's costume, even though he approach more nearly to Nature's tints and hues. The girls, with scarcely an exception, are fresh, rosy, plump and rugged, the pictures of sturdy health, but they are not, as a rule, more than good-looking. The refined, delicate sylph is rare in England; the women are mostly of the traditional apple-dumpling order. Dark hair seems to be more common nowadays than formerly, but some of these have the blue eyes and the flaxen hair said to indicate Saxon lineage, and some have locks worthy of the Virgin Queen herself.

A mile and a half beyond Oxhill is Whatcote, a drowsy little place with a quaint old church. It is called "Quatercote" in Doomsday, and for some time owned as its lord the abbot of Westminster. In the church is a memorial to a John Davenport who died in 1668, in the one hundred and first year of his age, after having been rector of the parish for seventy years and six months. The shaft of the ancient cross in the churchyard is now surmounted with a sundial, which of itself in a twofold sense indicates a change of time. The bells in the tower are said to be ancient and worthy of notice. Most of the villages around are of Saxon—or, to speak more correctly, of Early English—origin. The centuries have not disturbed them; they slumber even in this age of rush and excitement. Once in a while a cottage is newly thatched and somebody buys a bedstead or a table, but little else occurs from one year's end to the other to disturb the minds of the people. In a very long time a funeral or a wedding happens—possibly an election or an auction; and these are epochs from which events are dated—"Six years after Luke Lemons died" or "Four years after the fire," the fire having been the burning of two wheatricks and the roof of a barn. A stranger furnishes material for several hours' wondering gossip—who he is, whence he comes and whither he goes; if he has high heels to his boots or a string to his hat; what he is doing in these parts, and if he is likely to be anybody's relation. As he passes along the road the women run to the door or to the garden gate and look wistfully after him; the old man shelling beans on the porch steps stops, rubs his eyes, lifts his hat and wipes his brow; and the children jump up from their play in the dust, and, while some stand nibbling the corner of an apron or a pinafore, others run away and fetch mother to see the phenomenon. If you speak to any one, there is no sign in his face of the slightest interest in you; walking on, you may see scarcely man or woman, but look back suddenly, and you catch sight of a dozen heads of all ages eagerly peeping round hedge-corners or out of doors and windows to watch you and, if possible, to solve your mystery. The children are rather shy than rude, and as likely as not are off like a shot the moment you stop to speak to them. Rosy, rough-haired, chubby youngsters, dirty, every one of them, with clean dirt, two of them with the whooping-cough and holding on to each other as they pass through one of its recurrent onsets, some making mud-pies and others with a piece of clothes-line harnessing three or four together as horses,—there they are; well, the same as you may see anywhere any day. A lad of ten or twelve summers holding a handful of flowers and under his arm a huge cabbage stares at me with his mouth and eyes wide open. I am not sure whether he thinks I am a Dutchman or a goblin, but he looks as I have always understood cheese and beer are supposed to look at the former and wicked people at the latter. I ask him to give me of his roses; he turns pale either with fright or with pleasure, but he picks out one of the finest and offers it me. I give him a penny; what have I done? He blushes, smiles, regards me with favor and my gift with joy. Off run half a dozen boys and girls for flowers, and almost before I have gone as many yards one and another beg me to take them—on the same terms, of course. They do not know the tones and the ways of the London and Liverpool urchins—

"Please, sir," "No, no, thank you!"—and I can tell by their faces that, whatever they may have thought of me before, they are now well satisfied that I am barbarous and stingy. That will not do; a few coppers scattered amongst them, and I get three cheers.

I went into the village inn and enjoyed a glass of ginger ale and a chat with the landlady. The house is called the "Royal Oak"—why, I do not know, unless, possibly, after the famous adventure of Charles II., for the great tree in front of the door is certainly an elm. Long, long ago an oak may have grown there, and possibly a hostel has occupied the site for centuries; at any rate, the building has the appearance of considerable age. The low black ceiling, the deep recesses in the windows and the fireplace, the wooden settles and the clean stone floor, create feelings almost of veneration. In old English times, as there were occasionally female sheriffs and female churchwardens, so inns were frequently—perhaps mostly—kept by women, and even now in many such as this a wife or a widow holds the license and acts as hostess. My hostess has little to say and does not know anything about the sign; and when I tell her that innkeepers used to put out of their door a bush to indicate that they had good wine—though "good wine needs no bush"—she looked at me very unbelievingly. Signs are, however, curious things, and I remember one of the "Gate" at Brailes—it may be still there, for aught I know—and on it were the lines,

> "This gate hangs high, And hinders none;
> Refresh and pay, And travel on."

Five o'clock! I finish my ale and proceed.

Outside of Whatcote I came up to a man driving a heavy cart laden with barrels and parcels. On my asking him the way to Honington he invited me to ride with him on his wagon. I was glad to accept and to lodge my now wearied body on the head of a beer-cask. He was very talkative and opened up a long, unceasing harangue upon the troubles of the country, which seemed to consist solely of the unwise economy of some rich people who did not buy or rent the unused land of the neighborhood. Certainly there were many fields lying fallow by the way we drove. I suggested the competition of American grain.—" Not a bit of it, sir! There's money enough to overcome that, and there's no land in all America to beat this for growing wheat."

There are snake-tracks across the road; here and there is a cast-off shred of skin. We pass a man carrying wild rabbits strung on a pole across his shoulder; and when I tell my garrulous friend of the last-century custom in Edinburgh of a man carrying a leg-of-mutton shank through the street and crying, " Twa dips and a wallop for a bawbee !" at which the gudewives would bring their pails of boiling water and thus make broth, he laughed and said it was a better plan than that of people taking their dinner to the bakehouse. The man would have given his head to have known who was the stranger by his side; but, instead of that information, when we reached Honington I gave him fourpence.

Honington is a pretty village near the Stour and a convenient distance from the Stratford and Shipston highway, hiding amongst the noblest of trees and possessing an ancient lineage and a great antiquity. It has a church about two hundred years old and a plain brick mansion of the last-century style. It can scarcely be said to have a street, though the cottages are built in rows scattered around a space undefinable, partaking, as it does, of the nature of a square or a triangle and a lane. There are pleasant bits of lawn under the oaks or the elms which grow anywhere about the place and spread their mossy boughs over road, side-path, tiled or thatched house and barn, making a refreshing and snug woodland retreat. I saw no inn or tavern in the place; perhaps a population of not more than two hundred souls, if as many, does not need any, though a charter of the reign of Henry III. allowed it the privilege on payment of an annual fee to the lord of the manor. This same charter, according to an abstract I find in one of the local papers, compelled the tenants not only to pay rent, but also to perform sundry other duties. Thus on every alternate day between Midsummer and Michaelmas they were obliged to assist the lord on his estate, receiving as their reward one sheep, eight loaves of bread, a cheese and fourpence in money. During the harvest-time they had to bring into the manor-fields all the members of their family except their wives, and, as the place belonged to the monks of Coventry, they had to trudge at stated periods to that city, each tenant taking with him four hens, one cock and five eggs as an offering to the Fathers. There is now no mill in the parish, but in the reign of the Conqueror there were four such conveniences. Dissenters are unknown, nor has the board school invaded the land.

Farm-laborers are supposed to have risen in influence and in comfort during the past few years. They have the franchise and some of them read the weekly newspaper of the district as well as their Bibles; indeed, many of them can discuss Mr. Gladstone as intelligently as they can discuss Nebuchadnezzar; which is not saying much, only they have a lively appreciation of the fact that, as the Babylonish king once placed a good man in the den of lions, so the great Liberal chieftain has a weakness for doing the same thing—metaphorically, of course—with his political opponents. Large numbers of the younger men have gone to the cities and the colonies, and throughout the agricultural Midlands there has been on the whole a decrease in the population. But, notwithstanding all that has been said and done, Hodge is badly enough off. He still thinks himself lucky if he gets a piece of bacon once or twice a week, and beef—or "butcher's meat," as he calls it—as many times a month. However, though poor, he is not miserable.

Turning into Fell Mill lane at Honington—the same way by which I started for my day's jaunt—I walked for some distance with one of his kind who was slowly wending his way home after his toil. A pious, God-fearing man I found him to be after a few minutes' conversation, a little inclined to grumble, but not more so than the average Englishman. He was turning the meridian of life—a life which had been spent within a radius of a few miles, five at the outside, from where he lived. Once he had been to Stratford, nine miles off, but that was many years ago, when he was a young man and unmarried. He had heard of France, Russia and America: they were somewhere in this world, but where he did not know, for, as he put it, his "schooling" was neglected when he was a boy. As he passed from under the care of the ancient dame who taught the children of the village their letters and figures when he was about nine years old, it was little wonder. At that tender age he was promoted to the duty of minding the geese or the sheep in the meadow-lane, and was occasionally allowed to lead the first horse at the plough, so that books were beyond him and the longest thing he had ever learned was the General Confession, which he could repeat—as he did repeat it twice every Sunday of his life —without mistake, provided the parson had a clear voice. "As to my duty toward my neighbor," he said, a sad smile moving awkwardly over his tanned and thick-skinned face, "I never could manage that. My daughter Pollie can, though; she's a fine girl and knows more than her father." Nevertheless, he had brought up a family of seven to fear God and honor the queen, and to brighten his declining years he had the satisfaction of a prospect of getting his son into the police-force and of receiving for his own ten hours' work the sum of one shilling and eightpence. To help his meagre income he was able once in a while to snare a rabbit—perhaps some nobler game, of which he said nothing, being a prudent as well as a good man—and to find some mushrooms in the meadows. His wife made wine out of elderberries and sloes, and in the winter his boys went hedging for sparrows, and frequently got enough to make a decent-sized pie or pudding. On the whole, to quote his own words, he had much to be thankful for and many a man was worse off than he. The farmers, for instance, had a hard time of it, for it was cheaper to import wheat than to grow it. I gave him double his day's wages, and, grasping his hard, rough hand, bade him godspeed and "Good-eve." My path lay across the fields, but before I passed through the gate I watched him plodding along the road toward Barcheston. A true child of God, with more peace in his heart than even kings possess!

Country-people are not all like this man in this respect; possibly there are none who snarl and quarrel with one another as much as they. The women particularly give a liberty to their tongues and use language not unworthy of the traditional Billingsgate. One does not wonder that the ducking-stool was freely used. Some seem to have no control over their violent tempers, and a termagant running on day after day becomes irritating sooner or later. Poor wretches! who can tell the miseries of their past? Now religion and law have bettered them, but the ages bequeathed to them a burden almost beyond the possibility of removing. Village life six hundred years ago has been described by masters of social history, and it was a widely-different thing from village life of to-day. Then murders, suicides, robberies and crimes of all sorts were rife, and the people who slept at night in the clothes worn in the day and lived in dirt were morally wretched and depraved. There was law: criminals were hanged and torn to pieces by horses. "It is impossible for us," says a writer describing a Norfolk village in 1285, "to realize the hideous ferocity of such a state of society as this. The women were as bad as the men—furious beldames, dangerous as wild beasts, without pity; without shame, without remorse, and finding life so cheerless, so hopeless, so very, very dark and miserable, that when there was nothing to be gained by killing any one else they killed themselves."

Thank God all this has changed! but these same people of whom I speak, who let their passions run away with them, are their descendants, for there has been little migration in the remote country districts. Rough times and rough punishments! The stocks are still near the church gate at Tredington. Yonder son of the soil, now nearly out of my sight, with many defects and many weaknesses, is a new creation—nature brings lilies out of swamps and dunghills, and grace makes saints out of men—and in the transformation of which he is a type we may see the power of a pure Christianity. The old mediævalism could not help such as he; only a religion which brought Christ directly to him and gave to his perishing soul the sustaining knowledge of God's love could make him happy and hopeful. There is no cross by the wayside at which he may kneel and repeat an "Ave," but as he turns his face toward the setting sun he will rejoice in the thought of the many mansions where he shall find a home when the tribulation of this life is overpast.

The rights of footpaths are very jealously guarded. Some of these meadow-ways—such as the one I am now treading—are older than the neighboring roads; probably they are the tracks by which centuries ago the people found their way through the wilderness from settlement to settlement and from farm to farm. For any man, though he were lord of the manor, or even king of the realm, to attempt to close them from the public would be, as the old Greeks would have said, to catch the wind with a net or to write upon the surface of the sea. I have been told of a squire who tried it, and, instead of turning the people out of the paths in which their fathers had walked, by some mysterious operation or other his head was turned halfway round. When he was able to look straight behind him, he saw the evil of which he had been guilty, and, either from increased knowledge or from increased awkwardness, he repented, and the legend says he was immediately as though nothing had happened. The lesson is apparent, but possibly everybody does not know that caring for roads and paths was once regarded as a religious duty. The author of *The Sick Man's Salve*, a thoroughgoing English reformer, and chaplain to Archbishop Cranmer, enumerates, among the many virtues which justified him in thinking his "sick man" had made a Christian and godly end, that he had given freely to the repairing of highways. In one age people, when ill, vowed if they recovered to give their weight in wax to be consumed in tapers before the shrine of their patron-saint; in another, they promised to give so much stone to the roads and so much wood to the foot-bridges of the parish. Too often in such cases, it is to be feared, the old adage was verified:

> "The devil was sick:
> The devil a monk would be;
> The devil was well:
> The devil a monk was he."

Anti-climaxes and oddities are frequent and help to brighten the daily round. The other day I saw a really comical situation. A woman was standing in a cottage doorway with a boy sitting on the ground a little distance off; he was playing and she was singing the hymn, "Hark! hark, my soul! angelic songs are swelling."

The boy did something just as she got to the line "Angels sing on." She did not stop to finish it, but, breaking off abruptly, she caught him by the hair and gave him a rapid succession of severe cuffs. He cried and screamed at the top of his voice; she went back to her post and on with her song as though nothing had happened: "Sing us sweet fragments." The boy did indeed sing lustily and with a good courage.

There is Shipston over the brow of the hill, the setting sun just gilding the old church-tower with the roseate glory. All is still and restful—a lovely evening. No wonder men in all ages have been moved by Nature's charms, and especially by the splendor of the sunset. The crimson on the clouds and the purple of the shadows are inimitable, more wonderful than aught that the painter's brush can produce—more wonderful, because deeper and richer in hue, and, which no artist can accomplish, moving, fading, brightening, changing and presenting shades full of living glory. How the old Greeks delighted in this calm, sweet hour—in fact, in everything of nature! There was Athena, the queen of the air. She brought to man the sweet, pure winds of heaven and ruled over the gods of the flying clouds and the demons of the storm. She was beautiful and lovely, her robe the deep blue of the sky, sometimes set with the brilliant star-gems, sometimes fringed with the saffron of the sunrise, and in a moment such as this she seems to sit enthroned in her palace of magnificence, her crown a wreath of sunbeams, her face bright with the sweetness and the purity of the calm eventide light, and her hand uplifted to still the playful noise of nature, to cheer the tired world and to bless the expectant heart of man.

"ALL IS STILL AND RESTFUL."

What marvel if out of such scenes and times have emerged myths and legends—myths that have been dear through countless ages, sung in the nursery and unfolded in the college, and legends which seem so true and so real! We, rude Northern people, as they of the warm meridiana regard us, have our sunset story —not, perhaps, so exquisite and delicate as those of Greek imaginings, for God made only one such people, but, after all, not unworthy of the common Aryan ancestry.

Let me sit in the fading sunlight on this stile and recall the tradition of the noble Guy of Warwick. He, as all men know and have known from childhood, was a brave and renowned warrior, the hero of numberless battles and the darling knight of Christendom. With a fair maiden, Felice by name, the daughter of a great earl, he fell in love. She was, so runs the story, both beautiful and haughty—beautiful like some stately marble shaft of perfect mould, haughty as the great gerfalcon which spurns the earth and towers up into the noon to look the burning sun in the face. When he told his heart's secret, she bade him go to the war-fields and prove there by deeds of prowess his right to be the peer of a high born-lady. So he went far away and won for himself golden fame, and at last returned to claim as his own the lovely Felice. But ere the wedding-feast had ended, Guy's conscience was smitten with the thought that all his great achievements had been wrought to win a woman's love and not one deed had been done for God. Then he bade farewell to his weeping bride and sped away again to fight and to work for his Lord, and while he was doing doughty deeds in far-off lands she wore her widow's robe and wept for her brave knight. Years after he came back again to his own country, but he went not to his wife: he was content to see her as on deeds of mercy she daily passed the hermitage in the cliff where he took up his abode; only, once, all travel-worn and with his pilgrim's staff in his hand, he went to her house for alms, and she took him in and washed his feet and ministered to him, and asked him if in his distant journeyings he had seen her loving lord. Then many weeks went by, and he, feeling his end was near and he was about to go away for ever, sent his ring to Felice and bade her come to him. She knew the token and hastened to her long-mourned husband, but Guy could not speak; so they wept in each other's arms, and she kissed him, and he died. And fifteen weary days she lingered sore in grief, and then God's angel came and gently closed her own tired eyes; and both she and the lover of her youth were laid in the same grave—severed in life, but united in death.

Perhaps the story has lost its popularity, but others have believed it besides the people of fair Warwickshire, and many still visit the cave in the rocks near the country town where the hero died. Formerly a chantry was there, and in the chapel, where priests said daily solemn masses, was placed a statue of Sir Guy. In Chaucer's time the legend was sung, and some have thought it had its origin in that battle of Byran-byrig mentioned toward the end of my last chapter; but, for all that, though it may be mingled with facts, associated and colored with historical events and personages, it is a nature-myth. The brave knight Guy is none other than the sun, which rejoiceth as a giant to run its course, which in the early morn leaves his young and lovely bride amid the rose-clouds of the Orient, the beauty and hopefulness of youth and new-found happiness, and, rising in the sky, wanders through trackless wilds, doing mighty things, till at last, weary and worn, he draws toward home again and lays him down to rest and die. Then sweet Felice comes—the clouds, rosy, creamy, maiden-blush—and she clasps him in a last embrace ere he passes away, and still hovers over his grave until her beauty also fades into the night. Thus the weary sun dying in the bosom of the tender clouds is a figure of the parting of true husband and wife.

The twilight is coming on now, and soon the mists will creep up the meadows from the brook and the fairies begin their night revels. Cinderella belongs to hours nearer the morrow: the prince is the sun, the fairy the light, and she the dawn. The dress of ashen-gray is changed by the fairy into a robe of beautiful hues. The prince runs after her, but the beautiful maiden leaves only one trace behind, the glass slipper—the crystal dewdrops. Even the other nursery legend, beginning with "Sing a song o'sixpence," admits of similar explanation. The four-and-twenty blackbirds are the four-and-twenty hours, and the pie that holds them is the underlying earth covered with the overarching sky. When the pie is opened—that is, when day breaks—the birds begin to sing. The king is the sun, and his counting out his money is the pouring out the golden sunshine; while the queen is the moon and her transparent honey the moonlight. The maid hanging out the clothes is the rosy-fingered dawn, who, rising before the sun, hangs out the clouds across the sky.

But I hasten into the quiet town, there to rest after my long journeying, and to thank God that he has given me a day of rare delight—one to be remembered gratefully and fondly for years to come.

CHAPTER XIV.
A Merry Legend.

> "He picked the earliest Strawberries in Woods,
> The cluster'd Filberds, and the purple Grapes:
> He taught a prating Stare to speak my Name;
> And when he found a Nest of Nightingales,
> Or callow Linnets, he would show 'em me,
> And let me take 'em out."

SUFFER a merry and homely legend illustrating some phases of life in these secluded country regions.

Shadrack Abednego Pruce was an orphan—that is to say, his father and his mother were both dead. They died before Shadrack Abednego became an orphan,—and when they were buried, Shadrack Abednego planted a yew tree and a rose-bush on their grave, and said, "I am an orphan." He sat down on the grave and cried for nearly three minutes, and said, "I am an orphan." He walked up and down the churchyard, reading the inscriptions on the tombstones, peeping into the church, watching the rooks in the elm trees and muttering over and over again, "I am an orphan." He thought that meant something, and the words seemed to comfort his bereaved heart. Then he sat swinging on the gate that led into the meadow at the back of the church, and then he wept and thought, and "I am an orphan" came to his lips, and the rusty hinges creaked back, "Orphan! orphan!" Then he went home to dinner.

This was just a week after the funeral of Shadrack's mother, and ten days after that of his father. In the house the pictures and the looking-glasses were still toward the wall, for old Susannah—she was Shadrack's aunt on his mother's side, and now his sole protector—was somewhat superstitious and did not wish to see in the mirror the face of her lately-deceased sister.

"Not that I believe in such things," she said to the neighbors, "but there's no telling what might happen."

"That's true, Aunt Susie," was the reply from everybody; "it's always best to be on the safe side."

So every picture, portrait and looking-glass in the house had its safe side turned to the public, and even the silver tea-pot on the cupboard had a cloth thrown over it, so that the dead should not be tempted to come again.

The effect of this was that poor Shadrack Abednego had not been able to comb his hair properly for more than a week, and, as he had very long and very red hair, he did not look quite so neat as he should have done. Once he went out to the well and sought to see himself in its clear waters, but his aunt followed him and expressed her horror at his audacity so vigorously that Shadrack thought it best not to hurt her feelings again. She even cried for nearly an hour at the bare thought that as likely as not before many days dear Shadrack would be lying beside his father and his mother. Then she looked at the sturdy, rugged urchin, and she dried her eyes with the corner of her gingham apron and offered to comb Shadrack's hair herself. But Shadrack was now sixteen years old and five feet seven inches high, and he boldly declared no woman—or man, either, for that matter—should comb his hair; upon which defiant rejection of her kind offer, Aunt Susannah dropped off into hysterics, and for twenty minutes her next-door neighbor, who ran to her assistance when she heard her scream, thought it was doubtful if she would escape with her life. Hysterics, however, do not kill, and after copious doses of brandy and repeated applications of burning feathers to her nose and of cold water to the back of her neck she gradually recovered. Then the kind-hearted neighbor suggested that Shadrack should be severely punished, but Aunt Susannah said, " Poor boy! he is an orphan ;" and she went back to her task of peeling potatoes for dinner.

So on the day that Shadrack Abednego planted the bushes on his parents' grave his hair was, as the saying is, all sixes and sevens, his face had tear-tracks down his cheeks, his necktie was upside down, and he looked exactly what he called himself and everybody else called him—an orphan. Thus he sat down with Aunt Susannah at the table. He was both sad and hungry, and he ate away at the roast goose and boiled potatoes, and afterward at the apple-dumplings, with all the delight and zest imaginable. As the half-grown girl who did the rough work about the house said, " Live folks must eat, and as long as Master Shadrack wanted a good dinner he should have it." She had ideas of her own about Master Shadrack, but, having once had her ears pinched for observing to Aunt Susannah that he was becoming a fine young man, she kept them to herself. Aunt Susannah wanted no nonsense over Shadrack Abednego. Least of all did she want anybody to fall in love with him. That had been the trouble with his mother—a girl that was worth her weight in gold till she got married, and then trouble began. No; Shadrack should grow up like the great oak on the village green—grand in himself, noble in his solitude. But, for all that, the half-grown girl had her eye on Shadrack, and she longed for nothing so much as to comb out his radiant locks and wash his grief- and dirt-stained face and kiss his bright red lips.

Shadrack ate his dinner; then he drank half a mug of ale; then he sat back and looked fondly and contentedly into Aunt Susannah's admiring face.

"A nice goose, Aunt Susie," said he.

"The best in the yard," she replied; "the very one your dear father thought so much of."

Poor Shadrack began to cry, and found it not so easy as it had been before dinner.

"Don't cry, my orphan nevy—don't cry," said Aunt Susannah, sympathetically; "people must die, and so must geese, but don't ee cry."

"No, I won't," muttered Shadrack; "but just to think how fond father was of this goose, how it would run after him and eat out of his hand, and now we have ate the goose!"

"There's enough left for another dinner, Shaddy dear. So don't ee cry, but go out and see if the men are all right in the yard, and if the bay mare's colt is in the meadow. These are all your things now."

"Yes, aunty, I am an orphan;" and Shadrack Abednego went out to see if old Solomon, the unofficial but very officious overseer, was getting on well with the men and the things of the farm.

Old Solomon was a childless widower. His better

half had been dead nearly sixteen years, and never but once in all that time had his heart been moved by emotions of love. Unfortunately, it had been so effectually moved that it quivered yet. He had worked on the farm from boyhood. When a stunted lad of thirteen, he had driven the horses at plough and helped hold the sheep at the shearing. He had grown up an able and a trusted laborer, had served as wagoner and as shepherd, and now at the age of sixty he had without formal appointment dropped into the general management of the whole farm. Good wages and a free cottage, to say nothing of the possession of authority, made him a man of some importance—so much so that, next to the parson and Shadrack's father, he was regarded as the great man of the parish. And from his exalted position old Solomon looked down upon one of his womanly acquaintances—one whom he had known from her cradle, one whom he had admired from her girlhood, and one whom he had loved from the day he laid his wife beneath the sod. This acquaintance was none other than Miss Susannah, Shadrack's aunt, and now his mistress. Not that he had ever told his love; it was his heart's delight and his heart's secret.

"Does she take it very hard?" asked old Sol when, on the afternoon of which we are speaking, Shadrack stood beside him watching the cows coming up for milking.

"Who?" asked Shadrack.

"Miss Susannah," replied old Sol.

"Rather," was the laconic reply.

"Poor soul!" said old Sol; "poor soul! And hasn't she turned the looking-glass round yet?"

"No."

"Nor given the cat skim-milk instead of cream?"

"No; she says the cat's heart needs comforting as much as anybody's."

"Kind-hearted creature! Isn't she a beauty?" The first part of this observation applied to Miss Susannah; the latter, to a remarkably fat cow passing at that moment.

Shadrack thought both remarks applied to his aunt.

"I say, Sol," he put in, "none of that!"

"What?" in a tone of surprise.

"Oh, you know well enough. I say none of that; we have trouble enough."

"I know it," said old Solomon; "but she would fetch a high price any time. I know a man who would give anything for such a beast."

"Gently," said Shadrack; "gently, old man. I tell thee I will hear none of that."

"No, no!" continued Solomon, still thinking of the cow; "no, no! She's too rare a breed to part with. There's not such another brute in this parish, nor the next. So Mr. Philips said t'other day."

"If you were not an old man, I'd pitch thee into yonder water;" and Shadrack went off in great anger.

"Impatient as his father," said the old man to himself as he turned down toward the barn.

Into the house went Shadrack Abednego, and as soon as he found Aunt Susannah he began:

"Aunt Susie, old Solomon has called you a beast!"

"Ugh, the wretch!" and the words hissed through her teeth.

"Yes, and he says you are a brute."

"The scoundrel! he shall go! He shall leave the premises this very night! To think that your own mother's sister should be called a brute and a beast!" Aunt Susannah was too angry to cry.

"But that isn't all of it," continued Shadrack: "he declares you are too rare a breed to part with, and that skinny Philips said so."

"The villain! the tramp! the outcast! the disgrace of his sex! I'll prosecute him! I'll have him sent to the assizes! I'll—" and poor Aunt Susannah's rage stopped her words as well as her tears. Her face was white; her hands trembled; her teeth were tightly set. There was silence; then she said, "Tell me all about it, Shaddy dear."

"That's all," replied Shadrack—"though, to be sure, he did say you were a beauty."

"Oh!" The tide began to turn, for her gray eyes, red hair, sharp nose and chin, high cheek-bones and angular figure made Aunt Susannah anything but a beauty.

"And he also called you a kind-hearted creature."

"Now, are you sure of that?" very much mollified.

"Yes, certain."

"He's not such a bad fellow, after all," said she, musingly, as though speaking to herself.

"What! not when he called you a brute and a beast?"

"Well, Shaddy, you know that's the way of some men, especially of such as have to do much with cattle. In your dear father's eye a cow was the pink of perfection. He used to call your mother 'Cowey,' and whenever he saw anything that pleased him he would say, 'As fine as old Bess;' that was the name of one of the

Durhams. Oh no, there's nothing at all in the words 'brute' and 'beast,' when you consider where they come from."

"Well," exclaimed Shadrack, with the slightest possible contempt in his voice—"well, aunty, you are, as he said himself, a poor soul!"

"Humph! he's quite tender-hearted," in the softest of tones. "Now go, Shaddy dear, and take a look around. See if you can find some bait for fishing, for you must try for a trout to-morrow."

Shadrack stood thinking for a moment. He said nothing and went out. But he thought, "What's come over aunty now? She's getting a better woman every day. To see how quickly she forgave the old scoundrel! That comes of learning the parson's texts every Sunday. It takes all the spirit out of her, but it makes her good, fit to go to heaven, that's certain." He took his spade and went down to the willow trees by the pond to dig for grubs and worms.

This was the burden of Aunt Susannah's soliloquy: "He says I am a kind-hearted creature! Well, well! That's what I call thoughtful and manly. Oh, I remember when he was a spry young man and used to swing me under the apple tree. That's thirty-five years ago, now, I'll be bound. We have both changed since then. I would like to peep into the looking-glass, but that will never do. Only he's a good strong man yet—stronger than many a younger one. And folks said he was kind to his first wife and cried when he buried her. A faithful servant he's been. I always thought a deal of him. To think of the dear fellow calling me a brute and a beast! That's just like a boy calling his sweetheart 'ducky' and 'goosey,' only from a man 'brute' and 'beast' mean more. Well, well!" and Aunt Susannah began to wonder if the legend so ran that the mirrors should have their faces turned to the wall after the corpse left the house. "I thought it was fourteen days after the funeral," she said to herself, "but I may be mistaken." The more she thought of it, the more certain she was of her mistake. Then she remembered that when Rebecca Short died they put everything to rights the same day that she was buried. But when two died within a few days of each other? That was a problem, and Aunt Susannah began to get bewildered. "He said I was tender-hearted; no, kind-hearted: that was his word. I don't think two deaths would make any difference, and Shaddy's hair does want combing. I think I'll venture it. I do wish I had somebody to advise me what to do." She looked at the pictures and the mirrors, so dismally displaced. She thought out every thought she had. She sighed till she suddenly remembered that sighs were dangerous and cut so many hours off one's life, and then she stopped. Up and down the room she walked, out of the window she looked; then she deliberately took the cover off the silver tea-pot. She seemed startled at her daring, but nothing happened, so she turned first the picture of the old duke around, then that of his late Majesty, then that of a famous prize greyhound, and so on till all the pictures were in their proper position. She dusted each of them off, thinking rather more of old Solomon than of the risk she was running. Once the half-grown girl peeped in and exclaimed,

"Laws, missis! be'st thee not afraid?"

"Go and scrub out the pantry, you impertinent thing!" and Betsey departed.

Nothing happened. Twenty minutes passed; still no vision on any of the glittering surfaces. Then, with an air of desperate firmness, she turned around one of the mirrors. The first thing she saw in it was her own face, and she nearly fainted. She looked again. Her heart began to cease its fluttering. "He said I was pretty—a beauty. The glass shows I am passable. Humph! passable! So Ezekiel said; every man has passed me by. Still, many a high-born lady has red hair, so that's nothing; and gray eyes: they are nothing. After all, it's handsome is that handsome does. To think that old Solomon called me beautiful! What would Mary that's dead and buried say if she heard it? I'll knit him a pair of blue worsted stockings for winter, the good man!" and she continued admiring her charms, smoothing her hair and eyebrows, adjusting her dress and meditating upon the thoughtful and discerning kindness of old Solomon.

Into the room walked Shadrack Abednego. His aunt was in too great an ecstasy to hear the sound of his footsteps. He watched her for an instant, then he exclaimed,

"Aunt Susie, what have you done? What have you done? Don't you know I am an orphan?"

"Oh, Shadrack, how you frightened me!" cried Aunt Susannah, pale with fear and trembling with excitement. "You shouldn't come in so quiet as that. It's terrible to be startled so."

"But why have you turned things around?" asked Shadrack.

"I was thinking of you, Shaddy dear. You do need washing up and combing so badly."

"Dear, kind aunty!" said Shadrack, with undisguised admiration. "You are always thinking of me. Just to think of your turning the glass for my sake! Loving mother-aunt, let me kiss you."

Aunt Susannah blushed—not at the kiss, but at the abuse of praise. She held her peace.

Thus in the evening of the day our story begins this was the emotional state of the hearts belonging to the four individuals we have introduced: Shadrack loved his aunt for her devotion; old Solomon felt tender toward Aunt Susannah because of her recent grief and his own inspiration; Aunt Susannah admired herself more than ever, thought Shadrack was a good boy, and looked more kindly on old Solomon because he had discovered her charms; Betsey, the half-grown girl, was simply and completely in love with Shadrack.

When the shades of night overspread the land and crickets on the hearth and owls in the field kept watch, Shadrack and Solomon slept in peace. Aunt Susannah dreamed of the seven fat kine of Egypt and thought she was drowning in the Nile or the Red Sea, she was not sure which, when old Solomon—perhaps it was the Sphinx; she could not say: therefore it was most likely Solomon—jumped in and saved her; whereupon the king of some place married her and she became a paragon of loveliness. Poor Betsey tossed about in her trundle-bed for hours. She was happy and troubled. When first she got into the garret, she snuffed out the candle: that was a clear sign of matrimony. Then she lighted it again and stuck a pin through the wick, repeating some mystic lines about piercing Shadrack's heart and his coming to her in spirit. She watched the candle burn below the pin; it did not drop out, therefore he would be sure to appear. To be doubly sure, she set her shoes under the bed in the form of a T, and, placing one stocking under the pillow and hanging the other over the foot of the bed, she knelt down to say her prayers. These were short and simple—"just the heads, you know," Betsey used to say; for, poor girl! by bedtime she was tired out. However, hours passed this night before she could get to sleep. She lay there thinking and building castles in the air, hoping it might be her lot to be a Cinderella and marry the prince Shadrack Abednego. When she felt her foot, though, she was pretty sure, if it were a very, very small slipper, she would never get it on; so she let Cinderella go and thought of herself as a female Dick Whittington, only Shadrack was her London and she had no cat. Any way, she got Shadrack—that is to say, in her fancy—and she was married in fine style and had a half-grown girl to wash the dishes and mind the baby. Then she dropped asleep, but no Shadrack came; not even a dream of Shadrack crossed her mind. She slept till the gray dawn appeared, and then she got up disappointed and less hopeful, but comforting herself with the thought, "Poor fellow! he's an orphan—he's an orphan. And an orphan is an exception to all rules."

Now, it came to pass some few days after this that the village parson called upon Aunt Susannah and Shadrack Abednego to condole with them upon their bereavement. He had been expected, so Shadrack's hair had been cut; and when the parson arrived, the orphan looked a bright and presentable youth. His new mourning-suit fitted him neatly and greatly enhanced his appearance. His aunt was also looking her very best.

The clergyman was good and kind, as all clergymen are. He brought them his warmest sympathy, which they had looked for; he brought them something else, which they had not looked for.

This something else was a young girl of sixteen summers—his own daughter, Myrtle Muriel, a blithe, winsome maiden with long dark hair, brown eyes, rosy cheeks and pearly teeth. She was a fairy such as Shadrack had never seen before. He thought her wonderful, and blushed bright scarlet every time she spoke to him, and glowed with excitement every time she looked at him. His aunt listened attentively to the kind parson, and at the same time watched her nephew and thought of the noble oak on the village green. Myrtle was at one moment running over a list of French adjectives, the next composing a letter in her mind to her dear friend and schoolmate Valentine Louise Teeson, then watching the poultry in the yard, and thus running through things congruous and things incongruous, and thinking no more of Shadrack than she did of the mummy in the Shortstown museum. She asked Shadrack if he thought the brook had as many fish in it as in days gone by, and it was as much as he could do to gulp down his heart in order to tell her that possibly there were less. Her sweet voice seemed to fascinate him. He never felt so happy before in his life. He even thought it was a good thing to be an orphan, so as to bring the parson and his daughter to the house.

When they left, Shadrack was another being. He watched her pretty figure down the lane till she was out of sight. That night he asked Betsey to tell him the words of a certain incantation to be uttered over a cup of cowslip wine, which she, taking this to be a sign that her love-charms were working upon him and that ere long he would be hers, did with pleasure. The object, of course, was to enable him by a dream to foresee the joy that awaited him. Carefully did he go through the prescribed formula and drink the enchanted wine; then he lay down to sleep, and in his sleep the vision of glory came. He thought that he was standing before the altar at the hour of daybreak. The surpliced priest was there; the red sunlight fell upon the company and made the church strangely beautiful and strangely weird. The great edifice was still and empty; only here in the chancel were the friends and neighbors of the bridal-pair. By his side was the lovely Myrtle, crowned with the orange-wreath and robed in satin-cream. Her face was more than beautiful, it was more than earthly. He looked into her eyes, and there he saw himself and love. He touched her hand, and affection like an electric current ran from heart to heart. The vows were made, the solemn words were spoken, and then he and his bride turned away, and the radiance of the early morn followed them down the nave out into the great world of sunshine. Oh how dazzling! oh how bewildering! Shadrack watched himself and Myrtle till it seemed that they had vanished in the later meridian splendor.

"Oh, it was beautiful," said Shadrack to Betsey in the morning as he met her at the dairy door.

Betsey colored and said,

"Did 'ee see her?"

"Yes; she was lovely, a bonny bride—something like Queen Esther, you know, and ten thousand times sweeter than any other maiden I have seen."

"What did she wear?" asked Betsey.

"I am not sure—I saw only her eyes—but I think she wore a garland of daisies and a pink-colored dress."

"What eyes had she?" inquired Betsey.

"That, again, I don't remember. They were beautiful—full of love; not dreamy, but bright; a sort of— But there! I can't say. But she was splendid, that's certain. To see her in the sunlight you'd have thought her a what-d'ye-call-it come down from heaven. Oh, Betsey, if I could have gone with her! I thought, when I saw her fade into the sunbeams, that she disappeared as a lark vanishes in the bright sky. I don't know, but—"

Just at that moment Aunt Susannah, who kept a strict watch over the half-grown girl and ever associated Shadrack and the lone, lorn oak together, appeared on the scene.

"Bet, you good-for-nothing girl," she cried, "back to your work! and you, Shad, be off! Wasting time like this first thing in the morning! I'll give the both of you a trouncing!" and into the dairy Betsey went, saying to herself "I'm the bride, that's certain; I'm the bride." And Shadrack went down to the orchard and exclaimed, "What a bride she was! Oh what a bride!"

Time passed by and the autumn came, and one day,

when the leaves were falling fast, old Solomon made up his mind that he would tell his love to Aunt Susannah. He fancied that for some months past she had treated him in an unusually civil manner. She had inquired about his health and had given him some roasted Jerusalem artichokes—a mark of special favor, for Jerusalem artichokes were her delight. Therefore it was that one afternoon when going his rounds through the neighboring wood he became sentimental. The trees stripped of their foliage, the wind whistling through the bare branches, the soddened ground and swollen streamlets and the dying sunlight, brought into his tender heart that sweet melancholia which inspires and encourages love. He had been in full possession of that sublime emotion for years; but when he saw the naked boughs, and especially the white trunks, of the birch trees, he felt the emotion was getting too great for him. His heart was too small for it. Something must be done, or the emotion in his breast would burst forth in volcanic earthquakes and eruptions.

"Oh, Susannah," he exclaimed as he sat down on the stile—"oh, Susannah, I must have thee!—Lord, thy will be done, but oh, give me Susannah! She is the best hand I know of to make onion-gruel; and onion-gruel of a cold winter night is not so bad. I used to take it when I was a boy, thickened with oatmeal and seasoned with sage and thyme chopped up small. The old woman used to say it was good for chills and cramps, and in bad weather I had one or other 'most every night, the gruel was so good. Howsoever, Susannah is tiptop at that. She knows how to work and make a man comfortable, and that's everything. She's got money, too, and that's more than everything. She's not proud, so that marrying a poor man would be no come-down to her. Not that I am so poor, after all. I have three hundred pounds in the three per cents., sixty pounds in the bank, two suits of Sunday clothes and a good houseful of furniture. I'll ax her—yes, this very night I'll ax her. She can say only one thing or t'other; and if I don't ax her she'll say neither. So I'll go home and dress up in my Sunday best and face Susannah this blessed night. God knows I am a pretty good sort of fellow, and all I want now is Susannah;" and old Solomon got off the stile and hurried home as fast as he could, so that he might see the object of his affections as soon as possible. Into his Sunday habiliments he carefully deposited himself— that is to say, he dressed himself for the occasion. Then he ate a good supper, for, as experience teaches, sweethearting upon an empty stomach is not what it might be. He also drank a quart of real home-brewed—a virtuous proceeding characteristic of our fathers and strongly helpful to sentimentalism. Into his buttonhole he stuck a scarlet geranium-flower, and in his coat-pocket he carried a bunch of lavender. The moon was coming up when he started for the farm, about half a mile away. A clear sky seemed a propitious omen, and the recollection that Aunt Susannah had smiled at him a fortnight since was further cause for encouragement.

Neither Shadrack nor Betsey thought anything of Solomon's asking to see Aunt Susannah alone, for he often consulted her upon matters connected with the farm. Even his Sunday-like appearance did not surprise them, seeing that a fair was then going on in a neighboring town and he might have been there for the afternoon.

So they went out of the room, leaving Solomon and Susannah together.

"Miss Susannah," he began, "I believe I am an old fool."

"Lawk a daisy, Solomon! you are not the only one."

"Well, I am the biggest one, any way."

"I don't know that," replied Susannah, after a thoughtful pause; "I don't know that. There's no man around here knows a horse better than you do, and, as to a manager, you couldn't be better."

"Perhaps not. But do you know, Susannah—I mean Miss Susannah—I think a sight of you?"

"And I'm sure you are not a fool for that," said she, slightly blushing.

"But I think you are a seraph or a sylph, and that's going a long way."

"But there's nothing foolish about it," she replied, softly and coyly. "Only, what is a sylph?"

"It's a sort of cypher, I believe; I saw it in the newspaper the other day. You go on adding up and adding up a person's good qualities, and that is called sylphering or cyphering."

"Oh yes, I see, but I didn't know that my good qualities would make up a sum."

"There's not an angel in heaven to compare with you, and, for that matter, nor in the earth beneath, nor in the water under the earth."

"You don't mean that?" and Aunt Susannah thought her heart beat faster than ever before.

"Don't I?" exclaimed the enraptured Solomon. "Don't I? I tell thee I am a man, and I know what a woman is. There's not another such. Why, you know old Matilda Cumstock?"

Susannah nodded assent and turned up her nose slightly.

"Well, she thinks she is the skim-milk of perfection."

"The upstart!" muttered Susannah.

"She can spin."

"So can I."

"She can milk a cow."

"So can I."

"She can knit."

"So can I."

"She can read the Bible from beginning to end."

"So can I."

"There's nothing she can't do."

"She can't beat me," said Susannah, firmly and defiantly.

"No, and therefore I say you are ahead of her. Lord! you are ahead of all the Cumstocks in the world. Your Jerusalem artichokes are not to be equalled anywhere. If ever woman was born to make a man happy, you are the one."

"You are the first one that ever told me so," said the delighted Susannah; and she applied her pocket-handkerchief to her eyes and her bottle of smelling-salts to her nose, not being quite sure whether it would be more becoming and grateful to cry or to faint.

"Ah! there are few men outside of heaven," continued Solomon, "who know the fine points of female character and beauty as well as I do. I have not lived for sixty years with my eyes in my head and not learned something."

"I know it," replied Susannah; and tear number one hung like a dewdrop upon her left eyelashes and glittered in the candlelight. Solomon thought he had never seen anything so lovely.

There was silence. Shadrack and Betsey were in the kitchen together devising charms and telling ghost-stories. The room was chilly; Solomon laid a fresh log on the dying embers. Then he returned to his chair and accidentally pushed it a yard nearer to Susannah. Tear number one trickled down her cheek, and tear number two started from her right eye. She had resolved not to faint.

There was silence for five minutes. Solomon and Susannah were both thinking. The candle needed snuffing. Solomon snuffed it, and somehow or other, before he had again taken his seat, his chair got within a foot of that of Susannah.

"I tell thee, Miss Susannah," he said, with a profound sigh—"I tell thee it is nice in old age to have somebody to lean upon, somebody to comfort you. I am not an old man, nor are you an old woman—"

"Only forty-nine," put in Susannah.

"Forty-nine's nothing. You look as fresh as a wench of twenty. Still, it is nice to have one near to you to make you happy and protect your rights. As my old woman used to say to me, 'Solomon, you are the boy to make a wife contented;' and so I was, and am yet. I never swore at a woman in my life, and couldn't; nobody else would that called himself a man. As the parson says, 'Swearing lips are a' something—I forget the word —'to the Lord.' But don't you think, Miss Susannah, it is pretty to see the ivy twined around the oak, the vine climbing on the wall and the sweet peas and kidney-beans growing up the poles?"

"It's a beautiful symbol of affection, Solomon. It's as beautiful as a rainbow resting on a cloud."

"That's what I say. Miss Susannah"—his chair was close to her now—"you have learning; you know what's what. Now, let my shoulder be the cloud and your little head the rainbow;" and he slipped his arm along the back of Susannah's chair, and in another moment the red tresses were lying in blissful repose against his stalwart side.

There was silence. The log on the fire hissed and blazed. Solomon looked into the fire; Susannah looked down the years.

"Do you know," said Solomon at last, "that I love you—love you with all my heart?"

"You don't mean it," replied Susannah; "you men say such things without thinking about it."

"Did ever any man say that to you before?"

"No—at least, not that I remember."

"You would have remembered if one had; so you ought not to say I don't tell the truth." This with a slightly-injured accent.

"I didn't mean it, Solomon." This very penitently. "I only said it to try you. I know you love me; I knew you loved me from the day you called me a brute and a beast."

"I never called you that."

"Shadrack said you did."

"I'll make him prove it."

"Never mind; it was all right. I gave you credit for being a kind-hearted man."

"Well, I never said it; I'll swear to that. I couldn't do such a thing."

"Only figuratively, as the parson says; and I took it figuratively, and thought more of you ever since."

"Do you think enough of me to take me for better or for worse?"

"Oh, Solomon!" this softly and happily.

"I have loved you, Susannah, for sixteen years. Will you have me?"

"I must think about it."

"No, no! don't think about it. Take me without thinking. Oh, Susannah, if you don't marry me, I shall die!"

"You'll do that, any way; you're sixty now, and you'll not live another twenty years." She spoke sympathetically and dolefully.

"I shall not live twenty days if you say 'No.' Be kind, Susannah, and don't let me go before my time."

"I don't want you to die."

"You are the only one that can save my life."

"Then I suppose I must save it. It would only be a charity to keep a good man in the world."

Solomon kissed Susannah, and Susannah kissed Solomon. There was silence, there was sweetness, there was sublimity.

"Solomon dear, you had better go home."

"Yes, Susannah. Good-night. Shall Christmas be the wedding-day?"

"If you are good. Now go, but please don't tell anybody."

"No, no! Bye-bye!"

And as Solomon's footsteps died away in the distance

Aunt Susannah said to herself, "He said I was a beauty, and now I am to be his wife. Dear me! how my head aches! I have never been through such a time in my life. He's a good, a dear good, man. Now, I wonder what Shadrack and Betsey are at? I had forgot all about them. But he's a dear good man;" and away she went to the kitchen.

This was what Shadrack and Betsey were doing: first of all, both were trying to discover what time had in store for them; secondly, both were seeking for fuel to feed the fire burning in each of their hearts; and thirdly, each was striving to comfort the other. In the first of these objects Betsey had the advantage, for she knew all the omens and charms then and thereabouts believed in; in the second Shadrack was the better equipped, for he was poetically inclined and had the ideal of the beautiful Myrtle in his mind; in the third each had equal powers, for each knew the joys of love and the griefs of unrequited affection. For one thing, they had never been left alone so long before, and therefore they had a fair chance to procure the best of their desires. Betsey gave Shadrack the remains of a huge apple-pudding, and while he was eating it she told him a story of a haunted house that made his blood run cold and his skin get "goose-fleshed." He ate the pudding and listened. It seemed some beautiful girl broke her heart over a faithless swain and then took to walking in the night-time. Betsey said she was sure she would do the same if any chap were false to her. How any "chap" could be we know not, for, though Betsey was but a half-grown girl and a kitchen-maid to boot, she had all the making of a good-looking—and, indeed, a handsome

—woman about her. Shadrack thought that next to Myrtle she was perfection, but he further thought that between the two girls was a difference as great as that between the rose and the dandelion. If any man deserted her, he said he would drown him; to which Betsey replied rather pointedly that the one she had selected would never break his word. Shadrack nodded assent, and said he was glad to hear it. Then he told her over again, as he had done many a time before, that he loved a sweet girl, but he never gave the name; so Betsey was sure it was she.

"I don't know whether she loves me," he said.

"I am sure she does," exclaimed Betsey.

"Why?"

"Because she can't help herself."

Shadrack was tickled at the delicate flattery. Then they got the leaves out of the tea-pot and put them in a saucer of water; and when Betsey saw the forms they assumed, she was more confident than ever in her own and Shadrack's good fortune.

"The one you want," she said, "you will have, and the one I want I shall have."

"Are you sure of it?" asked Shadrack.

"Certain; everything says so."

"Well," said Shadrack, thoughtfully, "Providence is always kind to orphans. You're an orphan, Betsey?"

"Yes," she replied, with some pride.

"So am I, and therefore we agree on that point."

To think that they agreed even so far was joy inexpressible to poor Betsey. She only wished that Shadrack would see how much farther they could be one, but he, unconscious youth, held his peace. So they sat by the fire talking and dreaming, seeing visions in the fantastic embers and getting happier as the future seemed to dawn with glory. They were very still when Aunt Susannah came in. Shadrack was leaning over as though in deep study, and Betsey was sitting beside him smoothing his red locks and wondering why he did not speak the mystic words. His thoughts were far away—far away from the simple maiden at his side—with the Myrtle Muriel whom he had seen but once and thought he should now love for ever.

"That's what you're doing!" said his aunt, recalling him from his reverie and frightening Betsey almost into a fit. "Be off to bed, you bad, good-for-nothing Betty, and you too, Shadrack, and let me never see you do that again."

"What?" asked Shadrack.

"Never mind. Be off; that's all."

"I wonder if that is all?" said Betsey to herself as she went up the garret stairs. "I only wish it were. But never mind, old Susannah; I shall have Shadrack one of these days."

"I shall have Myrtle," said Shadrack as he got into bed; "darling Myrtle will be mine."

"The little wretch!" said Aunt Susannah to herself as she went to her room; "she's after my orphan-boy. I'll pay her up in the morning. I'll keep her on bread and water for a week: that'll cure her. And I am to have Solomon—dear, good soul! and he said I was a beauty—a beauty!"

The Christmas-tide had always been celebrated in true English and ancient form in the old farmhouse when

Shadrack's father was alive, and now that he was dead Aunt Susannah decided the custom should be kept up the same as ever. Moreover, Christmas morning was to witness the completion of her own and Solomon's hopes. The day before more than the usual preparations were made. The house was adorned with evergreens—the holly and the ivy, laurel, bay, box and rosemary, and a huge bunch of mistletoe in the middle of the kitchen. The mighty Yule-log was drawn in triumphantly and left ready to roll on the festive fire; geese, ducks and turkeys were plucked; plum-puddings and mince-pies were made; a great haunch of venison and a still greater sirloin of beef were prepared; a more than necessary quantity of bread was baked, but bread baked on Christmas Eve never gets mouldy; and Betsey saw that there was plenty of spice and crab-apples to put in the ale, and other condiments to make up the wassail-bowl. All the servants on the farm, the relations and friends, and even strangers, were invited, as in the days of yore. The wedding-cake had been made for more than a fortnight and carefully locked up in the parlor cupboard, where every day, and sometimes twice in the day, Aunt Susannah went to see if it were all right—neither stolen by the fairies nor eaten by the mice—and to think for a few minutes of the precious Solomon. Shadrack did all he could to further the almost endless arrangements. He made up his mind that old Solomon would die before long, so the wedding made but little difference. After all, it was better for Aunt Susannah to marry a man on in years, because, if matrimony disagreed with her, the end would not be so far off. Betsey said it was the very best thing that could happen, and she had foreseen its coming from the very day the cuckoo was first heard last spring and she found in Aunt Susannah's shoe a hair the actual color and shade of old Solomon's.

Christmas Eve set in cold and clear. The ground was covered with snow and glistened as the star-beams fell upon it from out the frosty sky. From the old church-tower, nearly a mile away, came the sound of the merry peals, now louder, now fainter, as the wind blew. A goodly company were assembled in the large kitchen, and on the hearth blazed brightly the great log. A cheery crowd they were, too; not a heavy-hearted one among them. They laughed and sang, now a carol, then a ballad, then a ringing chorus; some told strange stories of hobgoblins and ghosts, but they felt safe, for on this night no spirits walk the earth; then they danced; then came blind-man's-buff and puss-in-the-corner and hide-and-seek; and then dancing again. Gayly played the old fiddler, and far more gayly did Solomon and Susannah lead the jig. And every time a pause came in each drank of the foaming ale or of the reeking wassail. Many a kiss was given under the mistletoe; even Betsey got one from Shadrack, and, as she said afterward, it was better than anything else that night. Other girls were made happy in like manner, but she discovered the prognostic of her bliss in the fact that that morning she had put on her left stocking wrong side out. Nor had she changed that stocking when she dressed for the evening, so that the good luck might not go from her, and therefore she wore both a blue stocking and a white one, which somewhat extraordinary fact had been noticed and commented upon by nearly every one in the room. Betsey got the kiss, and she didn't care for anybody.

Three hours passed away, and a little before midnight and soon after a hearty supper the company began to disperse, some to sleep off the effects of the carousal, some to get ready for the morrow, and Solomon and Susannah to dream and dress for the bridal. As the clock struck twelve Shadrack and two or three of the other young men went out to the sheds to see the cattle go down on their knees, as they do at that time, following the example of those in the stable at Bethlehem, who thus did homage to the infant Redeemer. They also went to the hives to hear the bees sing their "Gloria in Excelsis."

Betsey went alone into the garden. She looked up at the bright stars and listened to the pealing bells as they so joyously heralded in the day of days. Then she went to the sage-bush and carefully plucked twelve leaves, but the shadowy form of the one who should make her a bride appeared not. She made a cross in the snow and laid thereon a sprig of holly full of red berries, but he came not. "He's an orphan," she said, in her disappointment, "and, I suppose, is beyond the reach even of Christmas-Eve charms." So she turned back, and ere long sought her little attic-bed. Poor Betsey! and she loved Shadrack better, far better, she said over and over again, than Susannah loved Solomon. But before she laid down she went to the tiny latticed window and looked out into the calm night. The bells still rang on, ringing down the changes rapidly and sweetly. She saw the garden quiet and deserted, the woods with their leafless and snow-laden branches, the cottages in the distance with their now-whitened thatch, the church on the hill far away and the light gleaming from the belfry, and now and then an owl sweeping silently across the fields and a brilliant meteor rushing amid the star-streams. And as she stood peering through the diamond panes she fell into musing —this half-grown girl with an uncultured mind, but a loving heart. Would Shadrack Abednego ever be hers? Would she, poor Cinderella II., ever be a bride? Ah! maidens poor as she had been highly blessed, even as was Mary, the virgin mother. The Christmas story came to her—the stable at the inn, the manger-cradle, the kindly Joseph, the Divine Child, the adoring shepherds. She saw it all, and almost thought she saw the heavenly host wheeling in clouds of light overhead: "'Glory to God in the highest!' That was what the parson said the angels sang this blessed night, and he said the Babe was the good God that loveth even me;" and she thought it passing strange that He who made the shining stars should look upon a poor kitchen-maid. Could he love a girl that scrubbed the floor and did odds and ends about the house? No wonder the angels sang! She could sing too. And the tears began to flow, but they were not sorrowful tears.

Again Betsey looked down into the garden. There was the cross in the snow close by the old cedar tree. How dark it looked on the white ground! There were the scattered sage-leaves, and there were foot-tracks. That was all. No! Betsey's blood began to creep; she shivered with fear. Out in the shadow of the cedar she saw a misty figure, a white cloud in human shape. The enchantment was working at last! Who could it be? It must, of course, be Shadrack; who else could be Betsey's groom? The indistinct form moved out of the dark cedar shade, and against the clear snow became more vague than ever. It stopped at the cross and picked up the holly-sprig and one of the sage-leaves. Then it moved slowly away, till at last it vanished and Betsey saw it no more. She was both frightened and satisfied. She had hoped her charm would succeed, and yet she did not altogether believe it would. Now, beyond a doubt, Shadrack would be the one. The more she pondered the matter over, the more certain it became. Had not the figure Shadrack's tall and youthlike form? Was not the hair Shadrack's hair? Nobody else could come, for he was the one she loved. So, happy and hopeful, she lay down to sleep—if possible, to dream of the good fortune which awaited her in the bright by and by.

Before the sun arose that Christmas morn came the waits with their hand-bells, and a little later village children singing carols. As their "God rest you, merry gentlemen!" filled the clear air Shadrack hastened to the kitchen that he might help give each rustic minstrel and songster the customary dole. After breakfast the usual Christmas boxes were given and accepted. Among the many which Shadrack received was a flute from old Solomon, made by himself out of the wood of an elder tree which grew far beyond the sound of cock-crowing—a great help to the melody of a musical instrument, for everybody knows that the song of the chanticleer dulls and injures the elder-wood. Shadrack looked upon the flute as a token of great affection, and

"VILLAGE CHILDREN SINGING CAROLS."

he trusted that Solomon would live for some years yet to hear him play it—an accomplishment he resolved forthwith to acquire. Nine o'clock was the time appointed for the wedding, and Shadrack, in spite of his improved feelings toward the bridegroom, was rather sorry he could not join his boy-friends in the time-honored Christmas sport of hunting owls and squirrels. Solomon came over dressed in a new suit—very fine corduroy knee-breeches, a richly-decorated silk vest, a plush velvet coat, a great beaver hat and red cardinal hose. He was straight in figure and smiling in countenance. Everybody remarked upon his youthful appearance: Mr. Solomon never looked so well before Aunt Susannah had sent off to the churchyard before she began to dress, to make sure that no grave was open—a point of vast importance. Then she arrayed herself in her gay attire, and in good time the whole party set out for the church.

Brightly shone the sun; the sacred edifice was gay with festal dress and filled with interested spectators. The ceremony went on and was concluded, as nearly all such ceremonies are, without let or hindrance. Solomon and Susannah were pronounced man and wife; they were happy and Shadrack had an uncle. He even kissed his new relative, who in his delight at getting Susannah kissed first every woman in the company, then every man, and finished with the parson. Then the books were signed and the bells began to ring, and Solomon led his bride to the family pew. Soon the morning service began, and after a short sermon everybody started for home very well satisfied that the singers had never sung better, nor the parson preached more eloquently, nor the church appeared to greater advantage, nor a bridal pair looked more interesting.

Some good-natured neighbors threw several pairs of old shoes after the newly-married couple as they passed by, and on reaching the house broken cake was sprinkled over them. Betsey managed to be the first one to steal a pin from the bride and to rub her shoulder against her, which feats were regarded by all as highly fortunate and promising. All the other pins used by Susannah were as speedily as possible thrown away. Then the happy soul sat down and tried to cry. Woe betide the bride who on her wedding-day does not shed a tear! But she could do nothing but laugh, she was so pleased and contented. They pinched her and tickled her; one fat woman stepped upon her corn, but in vain. They brought a piece of beef highly seasoned with mustard, but she ate it and not a mist of moisture appeared in her eye. Some one urged Solomon to swear at her, but he declined. The more they tried, the more she laughed. She could not even go into hysterics, though they set seven bottles of smelling-salts in a row on the table before her. At last Betsey brought in a pan of onions and began to peel them under her nose, and in a few minutes the tears came. All was well. Solomon kissed her and the company were satisfied. Doubtless, Susannah would get along all right in her new sphere of life.

The day drew joyously to its close. Before the sun went down old and young were merry as merry could be. They feasted and drank gayly and heartily. The house rang with the happy revelry. Nobody thought of cares and toil to come. This was a happy Christmas, and a wedding-day besides, and who had evil heart enough to be sad?

"I say, Shaddy," whispered Betsey to her wished-for lord as they sat for a few minutes in a distant corner of the room to rest after a violent game—"I say, Shaddy, it seems to me love is a sweet thing."

"Yes, Betsey; that boy in the gray smock over there says it's like bread and butter with sugar on the top."

"He doesn't know. It's more like sugar with the bread and butter thrown in. But just to see old Solomon and your aunt Susie in the chimney-corner beats all I ever heard of. First he kisses her, then she kisses him. Look at them now! One moment she asks him if he likes roast turkey better than boiled goose; the next he asks her if she likes her ale warm with a roasted crab bobbing in it. And he smooths her dress, and see! that's the fifth time this very night she's tied up his garter. I believe he unties it on purpose. They seem to forget that there's anybody here but themselves."

"Oh Betsey, love, you know, is always forgetful," observed Shadrack, thoughtfully.

"Do you think so? I don't."

"I couldn't say for certain, but that's the saying."

"Well, the saying is wrong. Do you think, Shadrack, you would ever forget the girl you loved?"

"Never! never!" he replied, with unusual decision and vigor.

"Have you ever really loved?" she asked, after a moment's pause.

"Oh, Betsey, I am in love now. I love a beautiful girl—the one, you know, I saw in my dream. I am dying with love."

"You won't die; nobody dies with love. They may die with eating too much, but no man ever died with love."

"Why not?"

"They don't love enough; and if they do love enough, they always succeed before love kills them."

"I love— Oh, Betsey, I love as no one else ever loved. I do believe—"

"That you are the first man who knew what love is?" interrupted Betsey. "But I noticed you ate as much roast beef and as many mince-pies as the rest; and if you were so deeply in love, you couldn't eat like that. The larger the heart gets, the less room there is for the stomach."

"I have to eat, you know. Uncle Solomon, there, has done little else but eat and drink all day. I believe we shall have to carry him to bed yet."

"He's an old fool," said Betsey, decidedly. "But have you ever told your girl you loved her?"

"No; I have had no chance, and I don't believe I could. I don't know what to say."

"That's another proof you're not in love, Think of a fellow being in love and not knowing what to say! Why, love has a tongue of its own, and a tongue that can speak too, I tell you. All you have to do—at least, all that you, Shaddy, would have to do—is to go straight to your heart's love and say to her, 'Sweetheart, may I love you?' and she would say, 'Love me? Ay, till death!'"

"I never could say that," replied Shadrack; "I should drop before the words were out of my mouth."

"Well, don't say anything, then; actions speak louder

than words sometimes. Sit down beside her and look into her face. You could do that? All right. Then take her by the hand, then put your arm around her neck, then kiss her, and she will understand the rest."

"But suppose she shouldn't?" said the doubtful Shadrack.

"But she will—oh, I know she will! Every girl knows what that means. Just try it and see."

"I will, Betsey. I'll take the first chance, though I've never had one yet."

"I suppose you keep putting it off and saying, 'Next time! next time!' There's no time like the present."

"That's true. But see! Tom Hodges is looking for me. I must run."

"Tom Hodges is always in the way," said Betsey to herself after Shadrack had left her; "another minute, and Shaddy would have been mine. Oh dear! a heartful of love is a heavy burden. But the figure was Shaddy's; that's as clear as cream. And hasn't my right eye itched all day—a sure sign that I should see my love? And who could my love be but Shadrack? If old Solomon got the aunt, why shouldn't I get the nephew—more so, seeing he's an orphan? It's all right; only I do wish Tom Hodges hadn't come at all. Shadrack nearly got it out—nearly told me I was the one he loved with all his heart. This is a merry Christmas for me! But now for the dishes; I suppose I must go and help wash them. Oh, Shaddy, for your sake! for your sake!" and she left the room.

Over this day we drop the curtain—drop it amid the flourish of trumpets and the scraping of violins; and again we move on to a bright day a year and a half farther down time's stream, when June birds were singing and June flowers were blooming.

Beyond the fact of everybody and everything being so many months older, there was little change in the home where Solomon and Susannah now held united sway, and Shadrack awaited the time when he would become lord and master. There was peace. Solomon and Susannah were happy; no disturbance had come near them. Their love flowed on in the same even course. Betsey had not yet heard the words that should rejoice her heart. She wondered, but still believed. In the mean time, she had developed into a comely damsel, and had received many compliments from the young men of the neighborhood, but she kept faithful to Shadrack. Every charm she tried, whether successful or not, convinced her that he was destined for her. Why he held his peace she could not understand. She had again and again tried to help him, but he did not seem to grasp the idea. So, looking upon his silence as an infirmity of orphanage, she quietly and assuredly waited the time.

As to Shadrack, never but once had he seen the idol of his heart, Myrtle Muriel. That young lady had been away, and had only just returned to the parish. Rumors of her growing beauty had reached Shadrack and helped to strengthen his unswerving loyalty. He sought to see her, but for some time in vain, till one day he met her unexpectedly, and once and for all.

In an afternoon in June when the sun was shining brightly and the wind scarcely moved the fresh green leaves Shadrack was wandering alone in the woods. As

he walked along the little path, now listening to the
blackbird's song, now admiring the white May-bloom,
now peering into the thicket or the bush where busy
songsters were building their nests, and now watching
the tiny streamlet as it dashed down the hill, he thought
and dreamed. Quite a philosopher had he become
since the day when Cupid's arrow rather than Betsey's
pin pierced his heart. Imagination had perforce to take
the place of reality; and when imagination is thus
obliged to work, it responds heartily and happily. So
now Shadrack walked on picturing to himself the
glories of Myrtle Muriel. One moment he arrayed her
in sylph-like drapery white as the peach-blossom; the
next she was as though dipped in liquid gold—a sort of
theatrical and bronze-tint appearance; then she was radiant in rainbow hues, and then pure and white again.
He rather liked to think of her with her hair hanging
in long wavy tresses, her eyes bright and brimful of
mischief and her sweet voice prattling merry nonsense.
And to-day the old picture came up again, and the old
dream went on the same as before, from the day she
consented to be his bride till the early morn when the
sun-glory fell upon them both. When he reached this
stage in his castle-building, he began to whistle and
move along more briskly. He felt already a joyous victory and fancied the laurel-wreath rested on his brow.
As he continued to walk he suddenly came to a little
knoll from the summit of which was to be had a fine
view of both plain and woodland. He knew the spot
well, but this time his heart began to leap; for there,
seated on this knoll, was none other than the dream of
his life, the beautiful Myrtle. She was alone, sketching.

Shadrack stood still, at first scarcely knowing what to do. Yet so much had he thought of her, so often had he gone over imaginary interviews with her, that he felt brave enough for anything that might happen. He paused for a few seconds, and then advanced. She looked up, but evidently recognized him, or, at least, instinctively discerned him to be one from whom she had nothing to fear. She even went so far as to return his not ungraceful bow; and when he said, "Good-afternoon, miss," she replied, "Good-afternoon, sir." What a wonderful voice! How sweetly its accents lingered in the summer air!

"This is a beautiful country, miss," observed Shadrack, both proud of his native parish and by this time able to appreciate such things.

"Yes," she replied, with almost equal enthusiasm; "I think that road yonder running under the avenue of elms by the old barn is lovely. I am trying to sketch it."

"May I look at your picture?" asked Shadrack, with respectful deference.

"Certainly," said she, "but it is not what it might be. No artist could reproduce that green lane; it is better than anything I saw in Italy, and simply beyond copying. But I have done my best."

"And your best," said he, with unfeigned admiration, "is pure perfection. The sketch is prettier than the thing itself. That hedge is well done, and nothing could be better than the cow looking over the gate. I remember one evening when it was almost dark my aunt Susannah— You must know her, Miss Myrtle, for I am Shadrack Abednego Pruce, her nephew."

Myrtle nodded assent.

"Well, she was walking along that very lane when suddenly she saw what she thought was a ghost sitting on that gate. Away she ran as fast as her feet could carry her; but when I got up to the place—I was behind, you know—I saw it was nothing but a cow, just as you have it in your picture. How I laughed at her when I got home! She would say, 'Any way, it had a long face,' and I would say, 'So has the cow, auntie;' and she said no more. Now, when she says that a certain unmentionable individual has horns or hoofs or a tail, I always reply 'So has the cow;' and I do believe she prays every night that I may not be punished for my profanity by having to spend some time with that nameless gentleman. 'Should you,' she observes, 'you would never forget it;' and I don't suppose I ever should. But you have hit it splendidly. I never saw anything so good."

"I remember your aunt Susannah," said Myrtle, pleased at Shadrack's praise. "You lost your father and mother, did you not?"

"Yes; I am an orphan."

"I know—of course you must be if your parents are dead—and pretty lonely you must be."

"Oh no," replied Shadrack; "I am a lone orphan, as Betsey says, but I am not lonely. You see, I have plenty to do and my health is good. I am always well and can always eat, day or night, and never get tired."

"Ah! you are a big, strong young man."

Shadrack felt that he had grown another ten inches at once.

"I am nearly six feet high and shall soon be eighteen

years old," said he, "and there's not a man a surer shot than I am. I have killed a snipe on the wing—a thing few sportsmen can boast of. Oh, but it was fun! May I sit down on the grass and tell you about it? Thank you. There isn't much to tell, when I think of it. It was down in the low meadow there; you can see the very spot from where you are sitting. I and Uncle Solomon were about with our guns looking for anything that might turn up. I had learned so much as to shoot a rabbit running, but I had never shot a snipe flying. 'Very few men ever have,' said Uncle Solomon.—'What if I should?' asked I.—'I'll give you my best gun,' he replied. The words were scarcely out of his mouth when up sprang a snipe. In an instant I fired, and the bird fell. He rubbed his eyes and cried, 'My best gun! my best gun! But, Shaddy, old fellow, lend it me the rest of my days, and you shall have it when I am gone.' How I teased him! No, I must have it there and then. I saw the tears in his eyes, so I promised to lend him the gun if he would stuff the bird for me. He did so, and it's now in a glass case in our parlor. I have heard it said that I shall never shoot another snipe like that; the chance comes only once in a lifetime."

"How's that?" asked Myrtle, very much interested in the boyish story.

"The bird flies so zigzag. Some say it's like a girl: you see her here, and the next moment she's there."

"That's true," said Myrtle, smiling.

"No, it isn't true," replied Shadrack, positively; "I don't believe it. I don't believe half the things they say about girls. Solomon says there's only one first-rate girl in the country, and that's Aunt Susie, but I know there's at least another."

"That May-bloom over there is beautiful, isn't it?" said Myrtle, pointing to a hedge white with blossoms.

"Yes; but there, again! the greatest beauty in the world is to be found in a girl's eyes."

"Don't believe it, Mr. Shadrack. Girls' eyes are deceitful, sometimes, at least. They are pretty and changeable as April skies. The man who trusts them makes a mistake."

"No, no!" interposed Shadrack; "the eye is the window of the heart, and there is nothing in a good girl's heart but what is of heaven."

"You are a young admirer of the sex. But then all girls are not good."

"Perhaps not. I never saw one, though, that wasn't good. My mother was good, so is Aunt Susannah, so is Betsey, so are you, and—"

"But you don't know me," said Myrtle.

"Not know you!" said the enthusiastic youth. "Do you think I don't know every tree in this wood? Well, I know you better than I know them. I have dreamed and thought of you for two full years, and, though I have seen you but once, I have lived as though I saw you all the time."

Myrtle blushed—rather with delight than with displeasure. She got up and said with a half smile,

"You read romances, fair sir; young gentlemen all do. But I must go; so good-day. Many thanks for your company. No, thank you; I'll carry the book myself. There, now! Good-bye."

"But, Miss Myrtle," said Shadrack, desperately—"Miss Myrtle, this is the only chance I may have of seeing you, and—"

"Were you looking for a silly girl when you found me?" she asked, laughingly.

"No; only I have been wanting to see you for so long, and this is the first time. May I not tell you all? I am only a country youth, but by and by I shall be next man to your father in the parish. I have red hair—I know it—and am too big and gawky, but I have a good heart, and you know—"

"There, now! not another word, my noble youth. You are a valiant knight to woo the first maiden you meet in the merry greenwood! Prithee walk a little farther off. So runs the language of the books, but you know them better than I. Nay, hold thy peace. Thou wilt swear by the waving poplar trees that thou dost love me. I see it in thine eye; I feel it in thy voice. Oh how the little darts fall upon my heart like the sharp hailstones in an August day! Say not a word, my baron so bluff and bold, but walk on faster, lest the even shades fall upon us ere we reach the open road. Let me laugh, O my good Shadrack, let me laugh! for, though thy hair be red, yet doubtless it ariseth from the scorching of the furnace. Thy namesake, you remember, went through fire; you, I suppose, would go through fire and water for your ladylove?"

"You have said for me, Miss Myrtle, much that I could not have said," replied the slightly-crestfallen Shadrack. "I never could have told you that I loved you, but 'tis true all the same. I am only a plain yeoman, or that's all I shall be, but I speak truth when I say you tell the truth. It was bold of me to look up to a parson's daughter—to one who is the queenliest of all maidens; but I have not sinned."

"There's no harm done, friend Shadrack," she replied, more seriously—"no harm done; and if I thought the same of you, no doubt we should agree. However, you are kind to think of me as you do—too kind, I fear. Only don't speak of such things again. Now, this is my way," pointing down the road which they had now reached, "and that is yours; here we part, and there's no harm done."

"Let me walk with you a little way," said Shadrack. .

"No, not a step. You have said enough already."

"I haven't said anything—at least, not all."

"I know all the rest; so good-bye;" and she tripped lightly away.

Shadrack stood watching her as she went up the road, so pretty, so light-hearted. He sighed and shook his head. "It's strange," said he to himself, "but still I love her. I'll have her yet. She's young and giddy, but never mind. There! she's gone. There's no one else like her;" and he turned round and went home.

A few nights later was Midsummer Eve, when the country-people light bonfires and maidens watch in the church porch for their lovers. How the latter managed when, say, half a dozen sought the sombre portal for the same purpose, we are not told; but there is no doubt the believing damsel was oftentimes rewarded, for did not the young men know the custom, and did not they too watch and wait?

It would have been unnatural for Betsey to have

missed so good an opportunity of confirming her hopes and dreams. The fact that Shadrack was an orphan seemed to run counter to all her charms. Nothing worked exactly as it should, and she began to doubt whether it was he whom she saw on Christmas Eve long ago. However, her love was strong as ever, and she still clung to the belief that destiny had decreed in her favor. If he would only speak! That was the trouble. He was in love, as any novice might see. Everything he did—his absent manner, his dreamy words, his evident desire for sympathy—showed that he was deeply wounded. One might almost fancy one saw the blood trickling from his broken heart, each drop sufficient to satisfy the most ardent maidenly longing. But why did he not tell his love? Why should he seek to hide it? Shadrack was an orphan: that was all.

So an hour before midnight Betsey started off for the old church. The people of the farm were feasting in the kitchen or around the huge bonfire, and therefore she got away unnoticed. Up the hill she hasted, almost breathless with excitement, anxious to read fate and afraid lest fate should speak. The moon was just rising as she entered the churchyard. There was no sign of living creature, not even an owl or a night-hawk. The graves lay, as graves generally do, silent and suggestive —so suggestive that Betsey's nerves began to give way when she looked at them. But it was near twelve o'clock, and now was the golden opportunity. Into the deep porch she went. It felt chilly and dismal. She shivered with fear, and did not help herself much when she thought that instead of a lover she might catch her death. Still, she was a brave girl, and withal a good girl; so she repeated the Creed and said the Lord's Prayer, and then she knew no evil could possibly befall her.

"Strange, though," said she to herself, "that nearly every time I have failed. Last year I took a clean garment and wetted it and turned it wrong side out and set it on the back of a chair to dry, but no sweetheart came to turn it right again. I lay on my back and stopped my ears with laurel-leaves, but he did not appear. I put beneath my pillow a coal which I found under a plantain-root, but that night I dreamt nothing. I have gathered a rose, walking backward to the bush, and I have kept it in clean paper till Christmas without looking at it, and then I stuck it in my bosom, but no lover came to pluck it out. I don't know what I haven't tried. Are all orphans like Shadrack?" and then the great bell in the tower struck the first note of midnight.

Betsey trembled and muttered the words of incantation. The last note died away, and she saw nothing. Then she heard a footstep on the gravel-walk, and if she could she would have screamed. The footsteps came nearer the porch, but she stood motionless, unable to move hand or foot, unable even to think. Another instant, and Shadrack stood before her.

"Oh, Betsey, Betsey!" cried he. "Quick! come with me." She neither moved nor spoke. "I saw you come in. Don't be frightened; it is I myself, in my own flesh and blood. Come, come!" Her face was ashy pale; the moonlight was beginning to fall upon her. Shadrack took her by the arm: "Oh, Betsey, do wake up! A dreadful thing has happened. Myrtle is dead—lying out here in the churchyard dead and stiff. I came up just now, and I saw the white form on the ground. Oh, come and see what can be done." He half dragged her out of the porch.

"Shaddy," Betsey gasped, "I am bewildered."

"But she is dead," said Shadrack, still pulling Betsey along.

"Who?" asked she.

"Myrtle. See! here she lies." He pointed to a figure lying on the green sward. "It is Myrtle," said he, with hushed breath. "I have lifted her hand that lies across her face; she is dead. What can we do?"

"Stay by her, Shaddy, while I run to the vicarage for help."

Betsey was all right now; the evident anguish of Shadrack brought back her senses. She was off at once.

"Poor Myrtle!" said Shadrack. "My Myrtle, now thou canst never be mine. Gone for ever!" He stood there in the moonlight looking down upon the lifeless body. This was the end of the dreaming, and the glory was not the early bridal and the meridian splendor, but midnight sorrow and a grave.

In a few minutes Betsey returned with a number of people—among them, the clergyman. He stooped down and lifted his daughter's hand, and cried, "My Myrtle! My love!" but she was dead. They took her up and carried her to the house. "It was her heart," one whispered to another; "her heart troubled her." Shadrack told them how he had found her. What took her to the churchyard at that time of night? It could not be that she might keep the village custom? No one could tell; no one ever would know. Only when Shadrack and Betsey were about to leave for home the clergyman took him by the hand and said,

"She told me all about it, and she laughed, but she wasn't angry. She didn't know you; but when I told her about you, she said she was sorry. That was all. Good-night;" and he went back to weep by Myrtle's bed.

Betsey was not so smitten with grief as to forget that Shadrack had appeared to her at the midnight hour. She was sorry that a catastrophe had happened, but she was satisfied that the youth by her side was now her own. Not that she suspected for one moment Shadrack's feeling toward Myrtle. He had spoken of love in the abstract, and never in the concrete. It was therefore with honest regret that she said as they were walking home,

"It's a sad thing, Shaddy."

"Yes, it's dreadful," replied he, mournfully.

"Everybody who loved her will be broken up," she observed, gravely.

"Broken up completely, Betsey."

"Such a beautiful girl! Did you see how her long hair lay upon the grass?"

"Yes."

The two walked on for some time without speaking.

"I am very sorry, Shaddy," said she, at length.

"You are a kind-hearted body."

They were home now.

Ere long Myrtle was laid in the ground, and Shadrack more than ever realized that his dream was gone. Every Sunday morning while the summer lasted he lay a garland of flowers upon her grave. Betsey helped to gather and arrange this weekly offering. But time works both changes and cures. Shadrack did not forget Myrtle, but he was young and could not grieve for ever. People wondered he was sad so long. Some said the sudden fright had unsettled his mind. Old Solomon said he would be all right when the partridge-shooting came in, and Aunt Susannah believed that when the blenheims ripened he would be the same cheery soul as of yore. Betsey had almost lost heart. She had no confidante, and she was obliged to hide her thoughts, but more than ever did she wish something would come true.

The day came at last.

"Betsey," said Shadrack one October evening as they were looking for nuts—"Betsey, do you remember the dream I had long ago of the wedding—of my wedding, you know?"

"I remember it very well."

"It can never be now, Betsey."

"No? Why not?"

"I haven't any one to love."

"No one to love!" exclaimed Betsey, astonished. "No one to love! Where am *I*?"

"Well, I might love you, but I never thought of you. Forgive me, Betsey, but I never thought of you."

"I don't wish you to think of me," said she, in a penitent tone.

"No, Betsey, I won't—at least, not unless you wish me to."

"I don't wish you to, Shaddy: I am not good enough for you." She stood in the golden autumn sunset, her blue eyes deep with shaded emotion, her cheeks brightly red. "I am a nobody—only an orphan; not one for you to love."

"I can't help loving you a little," he replied. "You are so kind to me, and you do look beautiful in the sunlight—almost like the maiden in my dream."

Betsey smiled.

"You must not look at me, Shadrack," she said, "but seek to find the dream come true in a better girl than I. So think not of me."

"I won't; only, the more I look at you, Betsey, the more I see you as the bride of my dream. Your eyes, your figure and your hair are hers. And now the light falls on you— Nay, stand still and let me see you in the glory. Yes, Betsey, you are the very one; only, it is in the evening and not in the morning light that I behold you."

"You are fancying this;" and she stooped to pluck a blue flower. "Please don't try to love me. If there's nobody else in the world, don't think of me. I am only Betsey."

"But you are a queen," said he, enthusiastically.

"No; I am an orphan."

"So am I. And I say you are a queen. Who can be more beautiful than you at this moment? Who can stand beside you now?"

"Let us go," said Betsey. "Aunt Susannah will wonder that we are not in before this."

But Shadrack was being driven along in a current that grew swifter every moment.

"No, Betsey," he said; "you say I must not think of you, but now I know I cannot help it. You say I must not love you, but for me not to love you is impossible.

I must love you, I will love you. Do not turn aside. I am Shadrack; don't you think you could love me?"

"I might try, but who would love a youth so tall as you?"

"Never mind; I only want you to love me."

"I do, Shaddy. I have loved you for long."

And Shadrack kissed her.

Betsey's triumph-day had come. The sun went down; and when she stood before Aunt Susannah in the kitchen, demure and silent, that worthy asked,

"What kept you so long in the orchard? Dreaming, I suppose."

"Yes, Aunt Susie, dreaming," she replied.

That night Betsey slept in peace.

In the visions of the darkness Shadrack saw Myrtle standing beside him, and he heard her say, "Betsey is the bride;" then, smiling, she vanished from his sight.

"I knew it," said Aunt Susannah to her loving spouse when the news came out; "I knew it. That minx was after Shadrack Abednego from the first."

"She's a likely wench," observed Solomon.

"I have nothing against her, only that she's going to have Shadrack," said Susannah.

"Somebody must have had him, and why not Betsey?"

"That's so," she replied, thoughtfully.

"That's so," he returned.

And it was so.

From the triumph-day to the wedding-day was not long; and when the bells rang out the bridal peal, the whole parish said Shadrack had the best of girls and Betsey had the best of men. Everybody, for a wonder, was pleased, if not satisfied. The envy common at such times was softened down, and no word or look reached the happy couple but of congratulation and good wishes. This was as it should be. At the same time, it may be doubted if a groom or a bride is not all the happier for knowing that he or she is looked upon with some little envy. Who wants a husband no other woman would have? Who wants a wife no other man would seek? There was not a maiden present who did not wish she was Betsey; there was not a man who did not wish he was Shadrack. However, it was a good-natured feeling, and soon passed away—a sort of soft April mist that disappeared in the sunshine.

One scene more, and we must leave our wedded orphans. In the dull November, when the leaves had all fallen, and bleak winds and chilly rains swept across the fields and made home more attractive than ever, a happy company were assembled in the old farmhouse. Solomon and Susannah, Shadrack and Betsey, and a few of the neighbors were sitting around the great open fireplace in the light of the blazing logs. They were laughing and joking as is the manner of free-hearted country-folk. Village gossip formed the staple of conversation. When it lagged, some one called out to Betsey for a ghost-story. Strange how people love such stories, and stranger still that civilization cannot destroy the fascination!

"No," said Betsey; "I cannot tell one to-day. Mine are all old. Perhaps Shaddy will."

"Now, Shad!" cried the company; and after a minute's thought he began.

"My story is true; mine own eyes saw that which I

shall tell. You remember the parson's daughter, Miss Myrtle Muriel, the one I found in the churchyard on Midsummer Eve? Well, early in the morning of my wedding-day, when I was running over in my mind the days gone by and the days to come, suddenly I saw before me none other than the same Myrtle. She was robed in white and her hair was in long tresses. I was not frightened—scarcely startled—for I was thinking of her at that moment. She spoke to me and said, 'The bridal-day, good sir! I bless you and your bride.' I could not speak; I simply bowed. 'Love shall crown your life,' she went on—'love shall crown your life.' Still I looked, and I saw her fade away, and, though it was a spirit, yet was I glad. We stood before the altar—Betsey and I—and as the parson read the words that made us one for ever I saw beyond him on the higher step the figure of poor Myrtle. The sunbeams fell upon her and bathed her in more than earthly glory. She looked upon me with her soft, sweet eyes and seemed to breathe a benediction upon us. Oh, I saw her so plainly! I fancied once she spoke, but what she said I could not tell. Then, when all was done, I saw a thin white mist before the altar; the sun shone brighter, and it had gone. That was all, and it is true."

"What did it mean?" asked Aunt Susannah.

"Yes, Shaddy dear," put in Betsey; "what did it mean?"

"Nothing more than this that you can understand—a blessing from the dead, a prophecy that love shall indeed crown our life."

"And so it shall, dear Shadrack," cried the devoted Betsey.

Shadrack kissed his bride, and the company pledged their health in sparkling ale.

"No longer an orphan, Shaddy," whispered Betsey.

"No; a good wife is a second mother," replied Shadrack.

The rain fell fast, the wind blew fierce, the fire blazed brighter than ever; and then, with loved ones beside them, Shadrack and Betsey sat hand in hand looking into the leaping flames and beyond them down the years—the years that should be to them as a vineyard of ripened grapes, as a garden of sweet roses.

CHAPTER XV.

Last Glimpses.

"Than orange and myrtle more fragrant to me
Is the sweet-brier rose and the hawthorn tree
In the land of my nativity."

THEY who would see Nature in her prettiest and gentlest moods must go to England. There, in a climate in which extremes of heat and cold are practically unknown, she displays her charms and unfolds her graces in a rich and unique manner. Association also increases the beauty of the picture, and history becomes attractive and delightful. You look with pleasure upon wooded hills, red-brown wheat-fields, green meadows, sparkling streamlets, lawns soft and velvety as an Oriental carpet, fruit-laden orchards and innumerable flower-gardens; you also look with no less pleasure upon churches, cathedrals and abbeys gray and sacred with age, upon castles and towers set in the cloudland of romance and chivalry, and upon old manor-houses with their twisted chimneys and timbered gables and legends of men and women who had their day long, long ago and now dwell amidst the mists and the shadows.

What more delightful place is there than Hampton Court Palace, the noble foundation of Cardinal Wolsey and the home for many generations of the sovereigns of England? Not only are the grounds exquisitely and

Hampton Court Palace.

beautifully laid out and furnished and the house grand with long galleries and spacious chambers on the walls of which art displays its highest—and perhaps its lowest—powers, but everything reminds one of the days of yore. In the garden, amid the same yew and holly trees which now grow there, Henry VIII. strolled with Anne Boleyn and other of his lady-loves. Queen Elizabeth traversed the same walks, played upon the same green lawn and listened to the songs of gay singers under the same elms of royal splendor. In the long bower Mary of England held converse with her ladies or with her own sad spirit. It requires no effort, indeed, to see again the men whose memories haunt the place, and dull must he be who cannot catch a glimpse of Wolsey's red robe and of Henry's stout figure as they move along the garden-paths or through the ancient gateways.

Inside, the same wondrous past lives again. There is the chamber of William III. with its paintings in which masses of nudity are set forth in delicate figuring and soft coloring. There are also the beautiful and frail women of the court of Charles II., but not one of them is as attractive as Miss Pitt among the " Hampton Court Beauties." She looks pure, sweet and lovely, reminding one of the old lines:

> "Her cheeks like ripened lilies steeped in wine,
>   Or fair pomegranate-kernels washed in milk,
>   Or snow-white threads in nets of crimson silk,
>   Or gorgeous clouds upon the sun's decline."

The old state bedsteads, the clocks, weather-glasses and mirrors, the carvings and the pictures are replete with interest, but beyond them think of the regal life, the court intrigues and plans, the galaxy of learning, wit and beauty, with which these walls were once familiar—of great banquets in the noble tapestried hall, and of princes, statesmen and bishops who walked hither and thither in the corridors and the rooms. Two centuries of England's history are there, but, alas! vanity of vanities, Death casts the trail of his black robe over all.

A day at Hampton Court will unfold more than anything else the delightful and mysterious attractiveness of England; the beauty of nature and the charm of history unite in a picture the memory of which will cling for life. Among the legends is that of the Haunted Gallery. This is now used by the repairers of the arras, but it was not long since said to be frequented by Catherine Howard. That unfortunate queen early one morning escaped from the chamber in which she was confined before being sent to the Tower, and ran along this gallery to seek the king, who had just entered the chapel leading out of it. At the door of the chapel she was seized by the guards and carried back, her ruthless husband, notwithstanding her piercing screams, which were heard almost all over the palace, continuing his devotions unmoved. The poor woman perished at the Tower, but many times since then, it is said, a female figure draped in white has been seen in this gallery coming toward the door of the royal pew, and as she reaches it has been observed to hurry back with disordered garments and a ghastly look of despair, uttering at the same time the most unearthly shrieks till she passes through the door at the end of the gallery.

The character of Henry VIII. does not improve upon acquaintance. He may have been a great statesman and an ardent lover, but he made a bad husband. Possibly it would have been for his good had he gone through the processes practised in his day to correct unfaithful and cruel spouses. One of these customs still survives in some parts of the country—in Denbighshire, for instance. Once a year the villagers meet and bring before them any who have made themselves notorious as drunkards, slanderers or wife-beaters. If the offender is found guilty, his right arm is fastened up to the bough of a tree, and gallons of cold water are poured down his sleeves amidst the jeers and the merriment of the crowd. That, however, would have been too gentle for the heartless lord of Anne Boleyn and Catherine Howard. Their memory also clings with his to Hampton Court Palace.

A like unscrupulous monster was Dudley, earl of Leicester. I mention him because the visitor to the Heart of Merrie England will undoubtedly go to Kenilworth. The story of poor Amy Robsart is known to all, nor is there any doubt that she fell a victim to ambition. The tempting bait of Elizabeth's hand was too much for the unprincipled Leicester; he did not hesitate to consign the gentle wife to the cruelties of foul men. In a secluded house near Oxford, Lady Dudley was secretly imprisoned; there she was ill-treated, neglected and subjected to attempts at poisoning. Gentler means failing, rougher were employed. One night the deed was done:

> "And ere the dawn of day appeared
> In Cumnor Hall, so lone and drear,
> Full many a piercing scream was heard,
> And many a cry of mortal fear."

The wicked earl did not become the consort of the queen, but in 1575 he gave to her at Kenilworth an entertainment of rare magnificence and luxury. For seventeen days the feast was kept up; the cost was enormous. Besides the queen and the ladies of her court, there were thirty-one barons and four hundred servants. Ten oxen were slaughtered every morning, and the consumption of wine is said to have been sixteen hogsheads, and of beer forty hogsheads, daily. "The clock-bell rang not a note all the while Her Highness was there; the clock stood also still withal; the hands of both the tables stood firm and fast, *always pointing at two o'clock*"—the hour of banquet! There were gorgeous spectacles, masks, farces, feats of skill, allegories, mythologies, and all that could amuse or while away the time. The queen was received by a sibyl "comely clad in a pall of white silk," who addressed her in becoming terms. Amid the shouts of the attendants, the royal company having reached the tilt-yard, was heard the rough speech of the porter demanding the cause of the din and uproar, "but upon seeing the queen, as if he had been instantly stricken, he falls down upon his knees, humbly begs pardon for his ignorance, yields up his club and keys, and proclaims open gates and free passage to all." Elizabeth loved that sort of thing, though she doubtless saw through it and inwardly laughed at the extravagant flattery. One day a savage dressed in moss and ivy discoursed before her with Echo in her praise. Another day, as she was returning from the chase, Triton, rising from the lake, prays her, in the name of Neptune, to deliver the enchanted lady pursued by ruthless Sir Bruce. " Presently the lady appears, surrounded by nymphs, followed close by Proteus, who is borne by an enormous dolphin. Concealed in the dolphin, a band of musicians, with a chorus of ocean-deities, sing the praise of the powerful, beautiful, chaste queen of England." There were rougher sports. Thirteen bears were set fighting with dogs—a pastime much enjoyed by the queen and described by an eye-witness as "a matter of goodly relief." Wrestlers from Coventry, Italian tumblers and rope-dancers and rural clowns played their part. There was a mock-wedding full of gross humor, in which the homely joys of the simple country-folk were made ridiculous; yet the same eye-witness just quoted says, " By my troth, 'twas a lively pastime! I believe it would have moved a man to a right merry mood though it had been told him that his wife lay dying." Did Leicester in the midst of that revelry, when his hopes were so near fruition, give a thought to the gentle wife of his youth?

Kenilworth never but then saw such magnificence. As one wanders about the splendid ruins, halls and yards seem to live again, lords and ladies gayly dressed in scarlet satin, sable cloaks, rich laces, costly jewels, rare embroidery, rustling silk and sparkling gold move hither and thither with that free, boundless life of the old times. The heavy tramp of the retainer echoes along the stone corridors; the soft songs of courtiers float on the summer air and suggest the romance and the voluptuous sweetness of an age of poetry and imagination. It is but for a moment, and as a dream the picture of life and of chivalry, of lordly splendor and of vast ambitions, vanishes away, and the eye rests upon ivy-clad walls, grass-covered courts, crumbling towers, vacant chambers and broken windows—the sad desolation of departed grandeur and the painful reminder of the transitoriness of human life. The irony is sharpened when the merry tattle of picnickers breaks in upon the silence; the incongruity of sandwiches and ginger ale is apparent. Better to see the great pile in the still night when the clear moonbeams fall upon the thick ivy and the dark walls, stealing here and there through loophole or window, and the owls sweep noiselessly around the turrets or over the swampy bed of the old lake. Then the weird mystery of bygone days steals into the heart, legends and traditions come to mind, and throughout life memory retains not only a wondrous and romantic scene, but also the thoughts and the visions created thereby.

The ruins of Kenilworth are on a high, rocky site commanding a wide view of the country around. From the top of the Strong Tower may be seen one of those extensive landscapes, quiet and lovely, full of picturesque beauty and rural charm, for which England is remarkable. Stand there in an early summer morning when the purple haze lies low on the horizon and the warm light brings out the freshness of woods and fields, the silvery sheen of brook and river, and the spires and towers of village churches, and Nature will give the soul a satisfaction that shall be as full as it is sweet and as real as it is undying.

Wandering through the country districts with which this book has had to do, one speedily discovers the darling love of the English people—viz., the garden. Everywhere flowers abound—in the windows, around the door, among the orchard trees and in the strips and plots of ground at the back of the house, by the side of the walk leading from the road or the street and along the edges of the vegetable-patch. Here and there are old-fashioned gardens with their winding walks, quaintly-shaped flower-beds and curiously-cut hedges and box trees. There are sure to be roses—roses white and red, roses ruby and cream—in the cottager's garden tended by the housewife, and in the squire's by the ladies of the family. In the early morn, when the dewwet buds are scarcely unfolded, delicate hands prune and tend them, pluck off dead leaves, cut some of the choicest flowers to adorn the breakfast-table and tie up straying branches. No wonder the frozen Norwegians on the first sight of roses dared not touch what they conceived were trees budding with fire; the brilliant splendor of the bush obtains the highest admiration and surprise. The poets of all ages have sung its royal glories, the gem of earth and the diadem of flowers, and have loved to crown it with praise and to liken beautiful maidens to it; the lines of Herrick are peculiarly true of English girls who live much in the open air, breathing the fragrance of the morning and delighting in such pastimes as archery, tennis, hunting and gardening:

> "One asked me where the roses grow;
> I bade him not go seek,
> But forthwith bade my Julia show
> A bud in either cheek."

The heavy work naturally falls to the gardener, who is, as a rule, a man of independent and pronounced character. We may picture him as a sunburnt, bright-eyed elderly individual, brimful of opinions on all sorts of subjects, experienced in the management of trees, shrubs, flowers and vegetables, and knowing well the idiosyncrasies of every member of the family. He has grown up on the place since boyhood, and loves every nook and corner, every laurel, bay or holly bush, as though all were his own. Honesty and integrity go to show that his full beard is not the indication of subtilty and guile, as some used to think. The schoolmen said that Adam was created a handsome young man without a beard; his face was afterward degraded with hair like the beasts' for his disobedience; Eve, being less guilty, was permitted to retain her smooth face. This was highly complimentary to woman, and shows that at times the monks could say something in her favor; but our gardener is by no means like an individual undergoing punishment. He is talkative, as are most people in the country. What is known as English reserve belongs more to the upper than to the lower classes. The latter are obstrusively garrulous, and press their opinions and their counsel upon the stranger with temerity, and even with rudeness. Only ask a question, and you open the sluice of a millpond. The gardener will tell you all about his work, and as he speaks his eyes will sparkle with pride and delight. He knows nothing about the busy, stifling city. God first placed man in a garden; England is the garden of Europe, and the finest garden of all is that over which he has charge. His love for nature is common to all around him.

If one sought to sum up the leading characteristics of the English country-people, one might find it in the legendary lore of Robin Hood. That mighty hero of the merry greenwood has for centuries been their ideal and their favorite. He has been made the expression of their own aspirations and prejudices. The higher classes have made King Arthur, the prince of honor, chivalry and gentleness, their pattern and illustration; the lower cling to the son of the yeoman. Robin, we are told, robbed only the rich; the poor he befriended and helped. He was the Socialist of his day, adjusting differences, equalizing wealth and carrying out that dream of the centuries, that vision of perennial freshness and strength, in which every man is the peer of his brother and all have enough for their needs. The English are not revolutionists, but Robin expressed their thought. Ever and anon they have broken out into sturdy rebellion and sought to free themselves from social bondage. Servitude is irksome; never was it more so than it is to-day. Like true men, they are ready to do their duty in that state of life in which it has pleased God to place them, but also like true men they seek to enter into higher states of life which God has as truly placed before them. They do not understand contentment to mean inaction, subjection or retrogression. Right or wrong, they wait for the arrow-shaft that shall speed through the Sherwood Forest of modern civilization and force the rich to help the poor and make the way easy for every man to rise who will. Even as Robin loved the freedom of the woodlands, so do they love to cast aside the restraints of an artificial life and to revel in the liberty which God has ordained for man.

Another characteristic comes out in Robin Hood. He is displayed in the ballads as a religious man: he heard three masses every day and was remarkable for his devotion to the Blessed Virgin; but, notwithstanding this manifest piety, he fought vigorously against the clergy. He would beat and bind every bishop or abbot that came within his reach. He would allure a church dignitary into the distant parts of his forest-home, and after robbing him tie him to a tree and make him sing Mass for the good of Robin's own soul. Some friars were made to kneel down and pray for the robbers, and were then bound on their horses, with their heads to the tail, and sent away. This curious intermingling of reverence for religion and of irreverence for the ministers of religion still largely prevails. The people who are most devout in the discharge of their spiritual duties are oftentimes as determined in their opposition to the clergy. There are exceptions, but they arise from the clergyman having qualities which bring him closer to the people than is ordinarily the case—a gentle, sympathizing spirit, an earnest zeal or great preaching-gifts. In a word, the English people dread a priesthood. Their race is the only one which has a religion without one, nor is there any hope that the effort of the nineteenth century to provide them with one will succeed. The masses are touched by the hand of a John Wycliffe and a John Wesley, by the preaching of Lollard, Reformer and Puritan. When such as they speak, then the loud response follows, and in the village-folk we see again the bold archer who loved religion and hated those who called themselves its priests.

In Robin Hood's devotion to woman is expressed another English ideal. The days have long since gone by when preachers used to recommend husbands to punish, and even to chastise, their wives that they might be healed of their sins and made obedient. Even the custom of selling a wife at auction has passed away. She was led by a halter to the market-place and set up for the highest bidder. Such sales were considered legal, and were common as late as 1797; indeed, instances much later have been cited. Once in a while the newspapers tell of brutes who err against their wives and for whom the whipping-post is not too severe, but the masses realize that Robin was right and that woman was made to be loved and honored. They do not yet understand women receiving honors at the university and managing large enterprises with ability and success, nor do they like to think of female physicians or of female lawyers; but when they become accustomed to these things, they will take them as matters of course. Any way, they are struggling on to show in deeds the thought of their heart.

The people love athletic sports and feats of skill, and in these their popular hero is made to excel. He was a mighty wrestler and an unequalled bowman. The ruder sports of earlier days are not common, but every town of any size has its cricket club and its bowling-green. Every one is interested in them, and the best player at quoits, the fleetest runner and the ablest rider receive an honor like unto that which former ages yielded to the winner in the tournament and to the victor in the fight. The universities encourage boat-racing as well as scholarship, and the Houses of Parliament adjourn over the Derby races.

One would have to search very closely to find anything approaching the spirit which Addison describes as existing between Sir Roger de Coverley and his dependants. Landlords and tenants are still friendly with each other, but the commercial rather than the moral element binds them together. So with masters and servants, mistresses and maids. The old pictures of social felicity in which the lord of the house had an intimate interest in every member of his family—from the heir himself to the boy who waited on the cook or kept the birds from the strawberry-plot or cherry tree— and received in return a loyalty and an obedience both personal and lifelong, have long since passed away. There are, indeed, some who still believe that man was made to plough and till the land, and that they who cannot do that are appointed by Providence to make wagons, ploughs, spades, mattocks, chairs and tables, to dig graves and grow vegetables, to look after foxes, ferrets and pheasants, to rear chickens, canary-birds and children, and to tend sheep and oxen, pigs and hounds; but this opinion of the whole duty of man is not general. The growth of a plebeian plutocracy and the spread of nineteenth-century Socialism, assisted by the press, the railway and the telegraph, have effected great and lasting changes. In the outlying districts there is still a warm loyalty on the part of the villagers to the squire whose family has held the manor from time immemorial, but his sense of responsibility and of duty toward them is much stronger and more unselfish than is their attachment to him. He will lower his tenants' rents, give liberally to improvements, put himself out of the way to further their interests, without increasing their affection or their devotion. They will scarcely think of the ties that bound their forefathers to his— of the days when his ancestors struggled for theirs on the field of battle or in the social or political arena, and theirs served his by following to the war or tilling the land. Hodge is as good as his master, or is fast becoming so. He reads more than the Bible and hears speak more men than the parson. Even the maid in the kitchen resents the old maternal interest which her mistress may show in her. She does so much work for so much wages, and beyond the bare contract she asks for and desires no more. The difference between her and her lady is not so much of blood, nor even of beauty or scholarship, but of money. For better wages or an easier place she will leave at a month's notice. The gentry and the clergy rebel against this spirit; but when the humblest child of the soil can without fear or favor leave the village and go to the ends of the earth, there by industry and perseverance to make a new home, perhaps to win a larger estate and a greater fortune than those of rural magnates in the old land, remonstrance goes for naught. Whether the new state of affairs will be better than the old, whether people will be happier when the present age has done its work, or whether in the old semi-feudalism there were not important elements of social economy which we are unwisely losing sight of, are questions into which we may not enter.

The freedom of speech is one of the illustrations of the irresistible progress of the times. Theoretically, speech has been free in England for ages. If a man could find anybody to listen to him, the law allowed him to say what he chose, so long as he abstained from gross blasphemy or from treason. But in the country districts practice differed from the theory; magistrates gave a wide interpretation to the terms defining forbidden subjects. If a man spoke in favor of striking the Athanasian Creed out of the Prayer-Book, it was blasphemy; if of repealing an obnoxious law or of revising the constitution, it was treason. In 1866, at the village on the Stour spoken of in these pages, there was in the employ of a butcher a young man who, thinking he had a mission to his townspeople and being filled with Birmingham politics, rolled into the High street a barrel and from its upper end sought to express his views to the small company who cared to hear them. What he lacked in continuity of thought he made up in vigor of utterance. Among other things, he was troubled about lay rectors, clerical magistrates, German princes, long hours of work, expensive funerals and the limited franchise. These were strange and startling topics in a quiet, sleepy place like Shipston and among a people who religiously applied to everything in Church and State the latter part of the Gloria Patri. They did not know what to make of them, but they listened respectfully. A week later, when the rural radical again posed upon his barrel-head, he was taken therefrom by the order of the rector, who not only threatened him with severe penalties should he persist in making "seditious" speeches, but also insisted upon his employer forthwith discharging him. The poor fellow soon found every face set against him, his character gone, his future darkened, and he was obliged to seek refuge in the great town from whence he obtained his ideas of men and manners. Everywhere he was spoken against. The good folks who measured cloth and sold sugar, the tradespeople and the gentry, avowed him to be an idle, dangerous wretch, and even the old men who weeded garden-walks and swept the streets, and the old women who went out washing and took snuff, shook their heads and said he would bring ruin upon himself. This was twenty years since. In the mean time, the great agricultural strike has taken place; Joseph Arch went through this same district and taught the farm-laborer that it was no sin for him to wish his week's wages increased from ten shillings to twenty, and to look forward to the day when his class should have a vote and be represented in Parliament. Agitation became the order of the day. Addresses of extreme violence are made and no one thinks them out of order, and what is stranger still is that things are said not only of the government, but also of the queen, which suggest rankest disloyalty and not so long since would have cost a man his head. Speech is now free, and neither clergyman nor magistrate seeks to suppress it. I would not imply that dissatisfaction has increased. The people are firmly attached to the Crown, and not only are the probabilities of the kingdom changing into a republic becoming less, but the world looks upon the anomaly of a nation both democratical and monarchical and intensely loyal to both ideals.

The greatest of all questions in England is that of population. This is more apparent in the towns than in the country. Take Liverpool, for instance. An hour's walk through the streets of that great shipping-port, so massive in its buildings and so cosmopolitan in its appearance, will bring to sight more pauperism and vice than will be revealed by years of residence in an American city. The number of barefooted children and of ragged men and women is appalling. How they keep body and soul together is a mystery. Boys sell fairly-printed copies of standard works, such as *Pickwick Papers*, for a penny each; girls hawk matches at a farthing a box. Everywhere the eye beholds objects of woe, hungry wretches, dissolute rogues and abandoned beggars. Such poor souls, the refuse and residuum of high civilization, are not desirable as emigrants—they take vice with them wherever they go—nor does emigration decrease population. Nature is a curious dame and counteracts with renewed energy the efforts to reduce the numbers. It is a sad thought that these worthless classes grow far more rapidly than do they who make up the brain and the muscle of a nation. What can be done with them? Whatever vice may be elsewhere, here it is gross, heavy and bold. Drunkenness abounds, depravity is rampant. To disguise the fact is impossible. The only hope seems to be in bringing the power of the gospel to bear upon the masses. That may at least make the people fit to bear the burden of life and to do their duty in distant lands where there is room for them to live and to work. Much is being done in this direction; more remains to be done.

The last paragraph is as a cloud upon the fair, sunny picture of England which we have sought to present, but from Hampton Court Palace to the slums of London and from Kenilworth to the smoke of Birmingham the distance is not great. That the cloud will pass away none can doubt. It does not even now retain the attention so long as do the brilliant features of English life. There are glories far greater than the shadows.

I have already spoken of the perennial youth of England. Some things grow slowly and live long; they are young when their neighbors are old. The primrose and the oak both have their day; generations of the former pass away before the acorn has developed into a sapling. Age is a relative thing, and the fly whose life lasts ten minutes becomes old in the time which it takes the eagle to wing its way from one mountain-top to another or the tortoise to drag itself a few yards along the shore-sand. There are as yet no signs of declining power or of decaying vitality in England. Institutions are created, reformed, abolished, as the times demand. Her old men bear the weight of empire with a vigor and a strength unequalled; her young men are as hopeful as though millenniums were yet in store for their country. Nobody thinks of decay in England; nobody there thinks of the fading of splendor or the weakening of force. The people set to work to deal with legislative questions with all the enthusiasm of a nation just beginning to shape its constitution. They are not trying to patch up a weatherbeaten, worn-out thing, sticking a bit of straw on the roof to keep the rain out till the old house falls down; they do not think about houses the work and shelter of a generation: they deal with rocks moss-grown and heavy, the formation of ages, and they quarry, shape and build, mould the massive stone into that which neither wind can overthrow nor rain wash away, set it against ocean's wave and war's artillery, and thus work, not for an age, but for all time.

The religion of England is another glory. I need not speak of its nature; all men know the vitality and the purity of the Christianity which has long reigned there. It is Protestant, and Protestant it will remain till the end of time. In the great moral and spiritual reforms of the age the Church is doing her part, wrestling with the ignorance, irreligion and shame of the masses in the great cities, striving to stay the deadly flood of intemperance which at one time threatened to destroy all things and is still mighty for evil, and seeking in every way to better the lot of the people and to guide them to an inheritance beyond the flood of time and of change. Moreover, the best of England's sons are going forth to bear the tidings of a redeeming Lord to the ends of the earth. Nations that have long sat in darkness are beginning to see the great light; the cross is uplifted in the cities of China and in the forest-wilds of Africa; martyr-blood has watered the seed of truth sown; the same hymns and the same prayers which are offered up to the Almighty amid the ancient glories of a Westminster are sung and said in tens of thousands of humbler temples scattered on distant shores. And though other nations are doing good work for Christ, yet it seems given to men of Anglo-Saxon race to lead the way and to be the first in the army of spiritual conquest and occupation. It was through the people of Canaan that all the nations of the earth were blessed; it is through us to-day that those blessings are increased. The glory and the life of England's future will be long and great even as she is faithful to her trust and true to her God.

Nor must the colonies be forgotten. England has fringed the sea with her settlements and developed nations in distant parts of the earth. Take the map of the world and see how the red lines of her realm rest in every quarter of the globe, on every continent and in every sea. Venice built a city on the flood; England has created an empire on the mighty main. Think of vast Australia, and the beautiful islands of New Zealand; of golden India, and the rich Africa of the South; of myriad isles which dot the tide-stirred waters; and of wide, ocean-bounded and vigorous Canada. These communities have all the same language, institutions, beliefs and books. They are peopled by the descendants of the men who ages back ploughed the plains and subdued the mountains of Great Britain. The manners and the customs which prevail in England prevail in these other lands. As children of the one mother they are bound by the indissoluble ties of race. What may be their future political connection I cannot say; only this I know—that there are stronger bonds of union than mere legislative acts. Each may be independent so far as parliaments are concerned, and yet be one in religion, sentiment, literature, tongue, habits, history and aim. These were found to hold the Greek colonies of three thousand years ago loyal to their mother-land; they will be found to be the strength of a nobler empire than scholars can devise or statesmen create. A whiff of opinion can sever mere political ties; no revolution, be it ever so violent or wide-reaching, can possibly change the language taught by the fathers. It was once a prevailing idea that the Christian Church could not be held together unless every member of it believed the same doctrines and obeyed the same supreme jurisdiction; we have lived to see that Christianity suffers nothing from having burst asunder the bands of cast-iron organization. This very century, which is by some so severely condemned for its denominationalism, has been equalled by no age in its devotion to Christ and to the propagation of the faith. Possibly the like truth may be reached in the social life. At any rate, even in the streets of London or in the meadows of Warwickshire the thoughts go out to the greater Englands beyond the seas. There is the vision of this vast continent —its happy homes, its wide farmlands, its vast cities, busy towns and flourishing villages, its comparative freedom from the pauperism of the Old World, its schools and colleges, its advantages of success to all who are sober, industrious and plodding,—a picture of peace and plenty, of joy and hope. England is as a sacred shrine around which men of her race are building the walls of a noble minster. Nations that shall love her shall be her strength and her glory. Nations that shall speak her tongue shall sing the praises of her past, delight themselves in her history and show in their own life the beauty and the power of inherited virtues and transmitted graces. Shakespeare shall live beside the St. Lawrence, the Hudson and the Murray, as well as on the Avon and the Thames; the same Scriptures shall be read in the valleys of the great mountains of the West as in the glens and on the plains of God-fearing Britain. Transplanting does not injure the Anglo-Saxon. The dahlia is a native of tropical America; there it rears its yellow disk and its dull scarlet rays to the sun: in our Northern gardens it has developed into a flower of brighter hue and deeper color. Change of clime has done much for it, and even here its cuttings are found to flourish best in a soil different from that in which grows the parent-plant. So the Anglo-Saxon has not suffered by passing from his European home to America or to

Australia. He has taken with him the spirit, the courage and the devotion of his race; he has developed them till he has given to the land of his adoption a greater lustre and a stronger life than belong to the land of his birth; he has made ancient virtues grow as lovely and as true as ever, whether in homes beneath the burning suns of the South or on the borders of the eternal icebound North.

I lay down my pen and turn my thoughts away from the social problems, the physical beauties, the delightful associations and the pleasant memories of the old country. The work is done, the story is told; if the reader is not satisfied, be sure the fault lies in the author, and not in the subject. One picture only remains—not that of the reader casting aside as a thing of little value a book written both to please and to instruct—which he may do or not at his pleasure—but that of a summer eventide beside the flowing Stour. The willows deepen the shadows on the water; the nightingale sings the song of love in the apple trees close by; from far away comes the murmuring melody of pealing bells, and the setting sun sends the streams of golden light through the elms, over the fields and past the hoary church-tower. There are rowers on the river, and the soft winds bear hither and thither the aroma of gardens and orchards and the chorus of young men and young maidens. Quiet, gentle, joyful peace! The great world is far away, and as the twilight comes on and the glow of the west fades into night-shadows the strange sweetness of rural life makes itself felt, and the soul passes into the mystical borderland between earth and heaven, far away from turmoil and from tumult into the restfulness of the garden of delights. The days gone by and the days to come mingle with the day that now is: time seems to have died and misery and sin to have gone for ever; and in the glory of the dying eventide I pluck a folded daisy from the grass and I lay it beside a pure red rose, emblem of homely virtues and lovely graces twined together in eternal oneness, even as Nature and History have made one beautiful realm, and a gentle spirit by my side whispers,

"Truth and love, restfulness and peace—the Heart of Merrie England!"

THE END.

www.ingramcontent.com/pod-product-compliance
Lightning Source LLC
Chambersburg PA
CBHW020535300426
44111CB00008B/678